# Stylistics
# and Social Cognition

PALA

POETICS AND LINGUISTICS ASSOCIATION

4

# Stylistics
# and Social Cognition

Edited by

Lesley Jeffries, Dan McIntyre
and Derek Bousfield

Amsterdam - New York, NY 2007

Cover design: Aart Jan Bergshoeff

The paper on which this book is printed meets the requirements of
"ISO 9706: 1994, Information and documentation - Paper for documents -
Requirements for permanence".

ISBN: 978-90-420-2312-3
Editions Rodopi B.V., Amsterdam - New York, NY 2007
Printed in The Netherlands

Printed by Printforce, the Netherlands

# Contents

# Introduction

## Lesley Jeffries

### 1 Social cognition – an answer to which problem?

This volume of articles comprises papers from the 25th annual conference of the Poetics and Linguistics Association (PALA), which was held at the University of Huddersfield, England, in July 2005. The theme of the conference was 'Stylistics and Social Cognition', and as usual at a PALA conference, this theme was interpreted very widely by the participants, as the reader of this book will no doubt conclude.

Most of those involved in stylistics (and indeed in all branches of literary studies) would not focus these days on author intention to the exclusion of reader's meaning. There was, nevertheless, an 'authorial' intention behind the choice of theme for the conference, which this introduction will attempt to convey by reproducing the issues that I raised at the open panel discussion, held as part of the conference. At the heart of this intention, there was something of a reaction against the cognitive developments in stylistics, which might be seen as being in danger of privileging the individual interpretation of literature over something more social. My concern was to consider whether there was a more collective approach that could be taken to the meaning of text, and whether recent insights from cognitive stylistics could work with this idea of collectivity to define something we might call 'commonality' of meaning in texts.

My contribution to the 'Social Cognition forum', then, was to ask – and only partly answer – a series of questions:

- What is the place of textual analysis in stylistics?

In order to address this question, we first need to establish what text analysis is. It clearly involves the consideration of the material of texts, whether spoken or written, linguistic or non-linguistic (but semiotic). This 'consideration', it seems to me, will depend upon models and frames of reference that are recognised or have been developed beyond the bounds of stylistics, for example, in general linguistics or psychology. It is important not to fall into the trap of creating tools to fit our theories. Also, we should not put ourselves into the position of taking textual meaning to be transparent, which may be one potential danger of distancing ourselves from textual analysis.

- What is the unique contribution that stylistics can make to our consideration of reader-meaning?

I have a concern that what linguists have to offer could be lost in the move toward psychological theories of meaning. Through stylistics and such textual analytic practices as are found in other sub-fields of linguistics such as Critical Discourse Analysis, we have insights into the structure of meaning in texts that is unparalleled. We can show what a text is unlikely to mean, as well as demonstrating its potential range of meaning. I sometimes wonder why we don't celebrate these advances a little more and persuade psychologists and others to become more subtle in their understanding of texts, just as we learn from their theories and methods. Of course, there are some stylisticians and text analysts who do just this, and two prominent members of PALA, Cathy Emmott and Gerard Steen, may be mentioned in this connection.

As an example of how we *can* say something about textual meaning, independently of context, I have referred to a poem that I analysed at various times. Called 'Silent Game' (de Galleani), the poem is clearly not about three elephants tap-dancing but about two people painting, and it is also about some kind of difficulty in their relationship. All readers seem to agree at least on these basic insights into the text's meaning. What conclusions they draw beyond this, about whether the problem is temporary or long-term and what kind of relationship exists between the two painters is hard to say from the text, and those who draw very clear   conclusions about such things may not be drawing only on the text, but on their own experiences and knowledge of the world. One of the projects for stylistics, it seems to me, is to elaborate the methods by which we can trace both the common meanings of a poem (and other texts) and also the range of possible further interpretative processes that readers engage upon when reading them. One can imagine a situation where the openness of the genre of poetry in respect of individual interpretation may be contrasted with the lack of such a range in the case of more functional texts, such as letters from a lawyer or bank manager. Whilst such insights in general terms may have been commented upon repeatedly in literary studies, stylistics has the potential to describe such differences in detail and with more accuracy than ever before.

- How can linguists (as opposed to psychologists) test cognitive theories of meaning?

On this topic, I would like to cite Cathy Emmott (see, for example, Emmott 1997) as exemplary in her crusade to get psychologists taking as much notice of us as we take of them. But there are other things we can do on our own too – and these are the methods which will avoid a danger I see of cognitive theories of style being interesting but ultimately vacuous. There is a danger that if we divorce our comments from texts (both base texts and derived texts) and forget to tie our insights into textual features, we will be able to say less about meaning than we can at present. Theory at the expense of analysis is not the aim of stylistics.

What I propose as one of the strategies to take us forward is that we should use what we know best: text. If we accept that all texts throw a kind of 'shadow' which includes their interpretation by immediate and intended readers as well as their interpretation by readers increasingly distant in space and/or time, we could despair of ever really understanding the 'meaning' of a text. On the other hand, we could hypothesise that any text produced in response to a 'base text' (e.g. an 'intervention' in a text - see Pope 1995) will form part of that 'shadow', and this in turn will allow us to begin to map the (overlapping) meaning-potential of texts, whilst acknowledging that this job is never finished.

- Is individual reader-meaning more or less important than communal meaning?

The idea of a text's 'shadow' is taken from terminology employed by criminologists and others to describe the great many unreported and unsolved crimes lying behind the ones we know about. How it relates to textual meaning is that it seems to me that there is a very deep shadow close to the text, representing the communal meaning that most readers would agree on, and a lighter and lighter shadow as you get further away from this consensus, including accidental meanings that relate to the individual circumstances of readers and changing meanings that are anachronistic to the text's context of production but happen to resonate with later historical audiences.

As an example of this, I investigated the publicity material used at one time for courses in the Humanities and Music at the University of Huddersfield (reported in Jeffries 2002). Whilst I knew that the 'authors' of the text, which was mainly a photograph of a number of artefacts, had intended to put across certain 'meanings', students often misconstrued these. For instance, a soft toy in the shape of a kangaroo was used by the authors to represent the kind of comforter that students leaving home for the first time might bring to their hall of residence. A teddy bear would have been more prototypical, but the kangaroo happened to be to hand when the photo shoot was being set up. The respondents, who were first year students, and thus in the intended reader group of this text saw the kangaroo as emblematic of travelling, possibly because they were already more sophisticated than the authors had predicted and had either travelled on a gap year or knew friends who had done so.

If required to answer my own question, I would answer that yes, I think communal meaning is *far* more important than individual meaning, even if it is only communal for a small sub-set of people who share some kind of understanding or experience. This is not to say that individual processes of understanding aren't interesting, but they are trying to get at what happens when readers access the text's meaning in some part of its shadow. The darker the shadow, the more the reader shares the meaning with others.

- What do *readers* think meaning is?

I think it is worth remembering that readers believe in a text's meaning – and quite often they also believe in authorial meaning too. That includes us. Evidence for this comes from the projects I have already mentioned – the analysis of a poem and that of a publicity folder – both of which were used as the base text for a number of responses by students and other readers. In each case, the major thematic choices for all respondents were to put the text (the poem or the photographic image) into thematic (usually subject) position in their sentences, though the producers (i.e. authors) also turned up as themes in some cases. The reader her/himself was very rarely put into thematic position. These mini projects found readers becoming self-conscious because they knew the 'kind' of thing a text meant, but knew they hadn't quite 'got it'. They also sometimes claimed to know what the authors meant (*"I think it's meant to mean"*), but criticised them on the grounds that their texts didn't work properly!

- Does it make any sense to say that we can get the meaning of a text right? Or wrong?

Yes and no. As the metaphor of the text's shadow implies, I think we can establish certain things about textual meaning, and sometimes we can also establish a consensus about its meaning, but there are some reader-effects that we can't pin down, because they will be specific to experience, outlook etc. Take, for example, ideological embeddings and naturalisation. I think we can clearly trace some such views in texts. This doesn't mean we can attribute them to conscious author-meaning, nor does it mean that we can predict reader reactions to them (e.g. acceptance or rejection of the ideologies) – but that doesn't mean they're not there. A similar point can be made with regard to more traditional stylistic concepts such as foregrounding, which can be shown to exist by argument and exemplification, but whose effect may range from aesthetically-pleasing to mundane, depending on the reader and/or the actual example.

I think that we can also establish textual meaning quite a long way into the shadow, including, for example, the range of correct but approximate meanings that readers might draw legitimately from a text without necessarily understanding all the possible implications of some of the references for example. We can also show misdirected meaning, where the authors might intend one thing, but the execution is poor and results in a consensus which works for the text, but possibly inappropriately as far as the author is concerned. We have seen this working already in the example of the kangaroo (above), and in the same text there were other similar cases, where a traffic cone in one instance was taken to indicate the skill of driving by a number of respondents, and a policeman's helmet was thought to refer to the study of Law. In both of these cases, the original authors were referring to the stereotypical 'high jinks' activities of students of an earlier generation (1960s and 1970s) which was clearly not prioritised in the understanding of students in the early 21$^{st}$ century.

I also think that we can find examples where a reader simply gets it wrong. This may say something about the reader's knowledge and understanding, and it may be part of the very outer shadow, where the meanings are not only quite faint, but also far from each other – like the fielders on the boundary in a cricket match.

- Was Humpty Dumpty right? And if not, how can we formulate an answer to the question of what texts mean?

The nursery rhyme character Humpty Dumpty is sometimes credited with having been the forerunner of much post-modern critical theory when he claimed (as a character in Lewis Carroll's *Through the Looking Glass*) that words (or texts in our terms) can mean anything we want them to mean. And this absolute faith in the slipperiness of meaning has now been with us for over a hundred years. It grows out of some of early linguistics of course (including the notion that language is basically arbitrary) but despite the attractions of the various 'movements' that have been based on the slipperiness of meaning, it seems to me that there is more to the 'core' – both of the language system and the semiotic context in which it operates – than many such theories acknowledge.

Indeed, it is one of the ironies of the challenges to textual meaning by 'artists' (e.g. the existentialists, the L-A-N-G-U-A-G-E poets, feminists and so on) that they cannot escape entirely the existing codification of language – that the social agreement on how we communicate may not be 'god-given' in some absolute way (i.e. language is indeed arbitrary) but that does not mean it is always and absolutely fluctuating in reference, structure and effect. In fact, the interpretation of texts which challenge the code relies for its success on an understanding of the very rules that are being broken.

- Does it help to think in terms of a text's 'shadow and how can we study this?

Yes – I think it is useful to use the metaphor of the shadow, if only to remind ourselves that the world depends on a lot of commonality of meanings to function, and needs further commonality in order not to break down altogether. I would suggest a couple of practical measures that we linguists can take here. One is to trust our tools – whilst developing them of course. Let's not throw them away and start again with only a pale imitation of others' tools. The other measure is to use the shadow to collect texts that are produced in reaction to texts – then to submit them to *the same kind* of analysis that we would use on primary texts.

This could result in a number of possible activities. It could mean protocol analysis of the kind undertaken in Alderson and Short (1989) and Short and van Peer (1989). It could mean interventions of the kind introduced most clearly by Pope (1995). But it could also just mean straightforward question-asking with readers being required to write simple answers to 'what is this text about'. All three of these techniques (and others) produce usable texts which are then open to all of the usual analytical techniques, and these can demonstrate the ideologies, relative priorities and viewpoint of the readers in relation to the base text.

## 2 Social cognition in practice

This volume contains fifteen articles written in response to the questions that were implicit in the conference title (Stylistics and Social Cognition). Some of them come close to the kinds of issues I have raised above. Others take a completely different view of what is meant by common meaning. All of them raise interesting questions about the nature of textual meaning.

The first four articles (1-4) draw on or develop theories about how readers access meanings from text, and in particular from metaphors. West's chapter is a re-valuation of the contribution of I. A. Richards to our understanding of metaphor. Cronquist develops the theory of understanding from a cognitive perspective, emphasising the need for analysts to take whole texts as their basis. Huang takes relevance theory and salience and Porto Requejo takes text world theory as the theoretical basis for understanding the contribution of metaphor to textual meaning.

The next five chapters (5-9) are concerned with the kinds of ideological meanings that can be retrieved from texts by readers, and their potential hegemonic effect, which in itself is part of the 'shadow' of these texts. Davies (M.) explores the construction of opposites in a news text to demonstrate the textual creation of commonly held views of political activists. Davies (D.) takes the 'real home' magazine feature as the basis of an investigation of ideologies about the home. Tryshchenko uses fictional examples to illuminate a potentially wider use of metaphorical address forms and their common meanings. Lambrou and Stewart each consider the gendering of story-telling, in the Greek-Cypriot community in Lambrou's case, and in eighteenth-century novels in Stewart's case.

The following three chapters (10-12) investigate aspects of poetry in relation to interpretative processes, which we could conclude are deemed to be common to readers. Lilja considers the role of the sub-genre of free verse in the construction of meaning with reference to Eliot's 'Ash-Wednesday' and its reception in Sweden, Bonačić compares the effects of deviation in English and Croatian using a poem by Cummings and Munat draws meaning from what is *not* in the text in American love poetry.

The final three chapters (13-15) concern the empirical study of texts, using the term 'empirical' here to refer to the precise measurement and quantitative study of linguistic features, reader's attitudes etc. Albers uses shortened forms of narrative plots to test readers' assessment of their potential for bestseller status. Shepherd *et al.* report on research which matches certain kinds of lexical patterning with social class and background and Zyngier considers students' approaches to the empirical study of literature. In each case, the commonality of meaning, illustrated in clear statistical comparisons, can be said to be at the heart of this research.

## References

Alderson, J. Charles. and Short, Mick. 1989. 'Reading Literature' in Short, M. (ed.) *Reading, Analysing and Teaching Literature.* London: Longman: 72-119.

de Galleani J. 1989. 'Silent Game' in Blackman, Roy and Laskey, Michael (eds). *Smiths Knoll* 3.

Emmott, Catherine. 1997. *Narrative Comprehension.* Oxford: Oxford University Press.

Jeffries, Lesley. 2000. 'Don't throw out the baby with the bathwater: in defence of theoretical eclecticism in stylistics' in *PALA Occasional Papers* 12.

Jeffries, Lesley. 2002. 'Meaning Negotiated: An Investigation into Reader and Author Meaning' in Csábi, Szilvia. and Zerkowitz, Judit. (eds.). *Textual Secrets: The Message of the Medium.* Budapest: Eötvös Loránd University: 247-61.

Pope, Rob. 1995. *Textual Intervention: Critical and Creative Strategies for Literary Studies.* London: Routledge.

Short, Mick and van Peer, Willie. 1989. 'Accident! Stylisticians Evaluate: Aims and Methods of Stylistic Analysis', in Short, M.

(ed.) *Reading, Analysing and Teaching Literature*. London: Longman: 22-71.

# I. A. Richards' Theory of Metaphor: Between Protocognitivism and Poststructuralism

## David West

### Abstract

This paper returns to an early contribution to the cognitive theory of metaphor: that of I. A. Richards. Richards' theory, outlined in the 1930s as part of his philosophy of rhetoric, saw metaphor as language's 'omnipresent principle' and 'the essence of thinking'. As such, the theory anticipated two of the three central claims of cognitive metaphor theory. Interestingly, though, the third claim - that metaphor is motivated - is absent from Richards' theory, and this because Richards was something of a poststructuralist, in the sense that he accepted Saussure's basic proposition that language is arbitrary and therefore relative. This paper, then, investigates what Richards means when he writes that metaphor is language's 'omnipresent principle' and 'the essence of thinking', and investigates also the basis of Richards' claim that metaphor is, in essence, unmotivated and therefore infinite. In doing so, I point to ways in which Richards' theory not only anticipates cognitive metaphor theory, but also poses important challenges to it, in particular in its argument that metaphor is not so much a manifestation of our experience of the world as the principle by which we construct that world.

Keywords: metaphor, I. A. Richards, cognitivism, poststructuralism, linguistics, psychology

## 1 Introduction

In the chapter on conceptual metaphor in his recent introduction to cognitive poetics, Peter Stockwell (2002: 106) writes that 'traditional literary criticism has differentiated *tenor* (the familiar element) and *vehicle* (the new element which is described in terms of the old familiar element)' in its analysis of metaphor. For example, he continues, in the statement 'Juliet is the sun', 'Juliet' is the vehicle and 'the sun' is the tenor (106). The two terms *vehicle* and *tenor* (and a third mentioned by Stockwell, *ground*, which refers to the common properties between the two) were first introduced by I. A. Richards in the 1930s to describe the different constituents of metaphor, but Richards' name is strangely absent from Stockwell's account. More seriously, Stockwell confuses Richards' terms, for, according to Richards himself (1938: 152), *vehicle* stands for 'what is transferred' and *tenor* to 'what it is transferred to'. 'Juliet' in the above statement would therefore be the tenor, and 'the sun' would be the vehicle; or, in the cognitive-metaphor lexicon, 'Juliet' would belong to the target domain (Richards' *tenor*) and 'the sun' to the source domain (Richards' *vehicle*). Thus, to talk, as Stockwell does (2002: 107), of 'the target vehicle' is to add further confusion.

Perhaps most seriously of all, though, is the implicit identification of Richards with 'traditional literary criticism', and the further implication that Richards' theory of metaphor is a theory which is representative of the view on metaphor of 'traditional literary criticism'. If we accept Stockwell's general description of cognitive poetics (11) - that it 'is all about reading literature, and it represents nothing less than the democratisation of literary study, and a new science of literature and reading' - then Richards can be seen as an early precursor of cognitive poetics. For Richards' entire intellectual career (from the early 1920s until his death in 1979) was oriented towards discovering, as he and C. K. Ogden put it in *The Meaning of Meaning* (1923: 40), 'what happens to (or in the mind of) an Interpreter', and he was particularly interested in our 'mental goings-on' when we read literature. In fact, he even designed and carried out an experiment to investigate this (the first such experiment, as far as I know), the results of which were published in 1929 as *Practical Criticism*. His work, too, represents 'the democratisation of literary study', for, far from sharing the elitism of his contemporaries (of Eliot and Leavis, for example), Richards saw literature as something arising from and connected to our ordinary human experiences. 'The world of poetry', he wrote in *Principles of Literary Criticism* (1924: 70-1), 'is made up of experiences of exactly the same kinds as those that come to us in other ways'.

In his central concern with interpretation, and with relating our literary experiences to our ordinary human experiences, Richards established nothing less than a new science of literature and reading, a new science founded upon the twin disciplines of psychology and linguistics. Indeed, his work in literature only really makes sense within the context of his work in psychology and linguistics. Richards' lowly contemporary status (symptomatically, the title which

the *London Review of Books* gave to a – largely positive – review of
the 10-volume *Collected Works* in 2002 was 'Terry Eagleton exhumes
I.A. Richards' (Eagleton 2002)), I would argue, is due to the fact that
his work in literature is seen in splendid isolation. Like the early
anthropologist Malinowski, whose work Richards and Ogden did
much to introduce to the English-speaking world (they included an
essay by Malinowski as an appendix in the first edition of *The
Meaning of Meaning*), Richards was 'a field-worker … on the
peculiarly difficult borderlands of linguistics and psychology'
(Richards & Ogden 1923: 7), and he used our interactions with
literature, which he saw as a peculiar form of language (*emotive*
language), to explore those 'difficult borderlands' and to come to an
understanding of 'what happens to (or in the mind of) an Interpreter'.

Moreover, the fact that Richards himself used Aristotle to represent a
theory of metaphor which his own would overturn would suggest that
the alignment of Richards with the view on metaphor of 'traditional
literary criticism' is highly problematical. Indeed, two of what I take
to be the three defining principles of cognitive metaphor theory - that
metaphor is a property of all language, not just of literature; and that
metaphor is primarily a matter of thought, of how we conceptualise
the world, rather than of language - were articulated by Richards in
the two texts in which he outlined his theory of metaphor, *The
Philosophy of Rhetoric* (1936) and *Interpretation in Teaching* (1938).
The third defining principle - that metaphor is not random but
motivated (i.e. by our bodily cognition or experience of the world) -
is, it is true, absent from Richards' work. But absent in interesting and
challenging ways. For, in denying that there exists anything outside of
metaphor which could limit what can act as vehicle and what as tenor,
Richards is more a poststructuralist than a protocognitivist. And this in
two senses.

First, in the simple sense that Richards post-dated Saussure; that he
read Saussure closely, though not entirely uncritically (*The Meaning
of Meaning* is perhaps best read as a long rejoinder to Saussure's
*Course in General Linguistics* (1916)); and that he accepted the basic
tenet of Saussure's theory - namely, that language, being arbitrary, has
at its core the principle of relativity (i.e. an element cannot exist in and
of itself, but only in relation to all the other elements within the same
linguistic structure). In *The Philosophy of Rhetoric*, for example,

Richards (1936: 6) writes of the 'universal relativity or, better, interdependence of meanings'. Second, in not seeing metaphor as being - in the final instance - reducible or traceable to something outside itself (for example, to our fundamental, extra-linguistic bodily experience or cognition of the world), Richards anticipated in important respects Derrida's central claim that *Il n'y a pas de hors-texte* ('there is nothing outside the text', or 'there is no outside-of-text'). For Richards, text relates to another text (which he calls *context*) in the same way that metaphor relates to another metaphor.

Written in the latter half of the 1930s, *The Philosophy of Rhetoric* and *Interpretation in Teaching* can be seen as the culmination of Richards' work up until then - and certainly as the two texts which mark the end of his most productive and significant period, a period which began with *The Meaning of Meaning* (1923) and *Principles of Literary Criticism* (1924), and continued with *Practical Criticism* (1929) and *Coleridge on Imagination* (1934). Indeed, his work on metaphor is the logical culmination of the work carried out in these prior texts in psychology, linguistics and literary theory; and dealing with metaphor allowed Richards to bring together many of his central concerns - with meaning and interpretation, with mental processes in reading literature, with the nature of communication. To investigate Richards' theory of metaphor therefore provides a useful way to investigate his work as a whole. Moreover, his work on metaphor - being neither entirely cognitivist nor poststructuralist, but nevertheless bearing the traces of both - provides an opportunity to think through again some of the central issues with which contemporary metaphor theorists are engaged. At the very least, it should serve to remind us that cognitive metaphor theory is not entirely new, and that there are important antecedents which can still make a contribution; and that it is important to yield to Derrida's imperative: 'do not judge until you have read' (quoted in Reynolds & Roffe 2004: 1).

## 2 The philosophy of rhetoric

The theory of metaphor which Richards outlines in *The Philosophy of Rhetoric* and *Interpretation in Teaching* is, precisely, an *outline*. The theory does not receive sustained treatment and is certainly not entirely coherent or consistent. Rather, it emerges from Richards' primary aim in those two texts, which is to 'revive an old subject', that 'old subject' being rhetoric (Richards 1936: 1). For Richards, rhetoric has lost its initial focus - the focus given to it by Aristotle, it should be stressed - and has become instead a discipline which sees the central problem of language as being 'merely one of disposing the given and unquestioned powers of words to the best advantage' (5). However, according to Richards, rhetoric has a far more important role to play: it 'can become a study that will minister successfully to important needs' (1). Rhetoric, Richards urges, should be 'a study of misunderstanding and its remedies', and it should help us 'to calculate the extent and degree of our hourly losses in communication' (1). In short, it should become '*the* Art' of discourse (3), by which Richards means 'a philosophic discipline aiming at a mastery of the fundamental laws of the use of language' (3), 'a philosophic enquiry into how words work in discourse' (4). Moreover, 'with enough improvement in Rhetoric', Richards argues, 'we may in time learn so much about words that they will tell us how our minds work' (92), since 'Thought' is 'accessible largely through Language' (8).

Rhetoric, then, far from dealing with the superficialities of how to use words 'to the best advantage', will concern itself with interpretation, communication and misunderstanding; with language and thought, and the relations between them. As such, Richards' philosophy of rhetoric aims to explore the question of who we are as human beings, and the nature of our relationship with the world. The 'problems' that the philosophy will deal with, he says, 'are those upon which, wittingly or unwittingly, we spend our whole waking life' (13). It is within this context that Richards' claims that 'the theory of interpretation is obviously a branch of biology' (7), and that interpretation 'is rooted in our biological continuity one with another' (1938: 93), make sense, for to study interpretation - what occurs in the mind when dealing with language - is to study what makes us distinctively human, what distinguishes us as a species. As Richards and Ogden wrote in *The Meaning of Meaning* (1923: 68), an account of the process of interpretation is 'the beginning of wisdom'.

To account for 'how words work in discourse', and therefore to begin the journey towards wisdom, Richards sees the importance of rejecting what he calls Proper Meaning Superstition, by which he means (1936: 6-7) 'the common belief ... that a word has a meaning of its own (ideally, only one) independent of and controlling its use and the purpose for which it should be uttered', or 'the view that words just have their meanings and that what a discourse does is to be explained as a composition of these meanings' (5). 'In themselves [meanings] are nothing', Richards insists (6). Rather, they are 'figments, abstractions, unreal things that we invent' (6). Words do not have 'fixed proper meanings', but 'change their meanings' as 'they pass from context to context' (6). Thus, meaning is not fixed or stable, but characterised by 'shift' (47) or 'movement' (32). Richards regards 'all discourse', therefore, 'as over-determined, as having multiplicity of meaning' (26), and encourages us to 'expect ambiguity to the widest extent and of the subtlest kinds nearly everywhere' (27). Richards does exclude 'the technicalities of science' (26) from his general argument that language is characterised by 'systematic ambiguity or transference patterns' (48) (hence that 'nearly everywhere'), arguing - rather dubiously - that scientific language is stable and transparent because the conditions or contexts in which the words of science are used and which govern their meanings 'are so constant that we can disregard them' (6). However, language in its archetypal state - and Richards sees poetry as representing language at its most archetypal - is language in which 'the whole meaning of the sentence shifts, and with it any meanings we may try to ascribe to the individual words' (32).

Ambiguity and transference are, then, for Richards, 'an inevitable consequence of the powers of language' and 'the indispensable means of most of our most important utterances' (27). It is futile, therefore, to rail against them; to do so would be to rail against language itself, for language works through ambiguity and transference. Rather, we should embrace the 'systematic ambiguity or transference patterns of language' and understand how they arise. Since they come about because words 'change their meanings' as 'they pass from context to context', it is through taking account of context that their depths can be fathomed. To take account of context, Richards elaborates a 'context theorem of meaning', a theorem which, first articulated in *The Meaning of Meaning*, is at the heart of his philosophy of rhetoric, and therefore of his theory of metaphor.

### 3 The context theorem of meaning
The theorem is modelled quite explicitly upon the theory of the conditioned reflex which Pavlov elaborated as a result of his stimulus-response experiments (Pavlov 1927). Pavlov's theory has two main

elements. The first is that we do not respond to a stimulus in isolation. In Pavlov's experiments with dogs, for example, one stimulus (the smell of food) is combined synchronically with another stimulus (the ringing of a bell). The second element of the theory is related to the first: after a certain period of being exposed to these two stimuli in combination (this element is diachronic), the dog transfers its response to the first stimulus to its response to the second stimulus; in other words, the dog becomes conditioned to respond appropriately (by salivating in anticipation of food) when only the second stimulus is present. Thus, according to Pavlov's theory, one stimulus combines with another synchronically, and the way in which we respond to these stimuli in combination conditions how we respond to the same or similar stimuli in the future.

Richards' theorem comprises a synchronic and a diachronic element, too. '[W]e are things peculiarly responsive to other things', Richards remarks (1936: 19), by which he means that 'we [n]ever respond to a stimulus in a way which is not influenced by the other things that happened to us when more or less similar stimuli struck us in the past' (20). 'Effects from more or less similar happenings in the past', in other words, 'come in to give our response its character, and this as far as it went would be "meaning"' (20). Richards denies 'that we have any sensations', if by 'sensation' is meant 'something that was just *so*, on its own, a datum' (20). On the contrary, what we have are 'perceptions, responses whose character comes to them from the past as well as the present occasion' (20). Thus, 'our principal terms', Richards argues, and the term *metaphor* belongs very much to that category, 'incessantly change their meanings with the sentences they go into and the contexts they derive from' (47). According to Richards' context theorem of meaning, then, terms, or words in general, have no inherent meaning, but derive their meaning from two different types of context: the context of the text which 'they go into', and the context - or 'contexts', we should stress - of the texts in which they have been used in the past.

'[A] word's context', Richards writes (1938: 6), referring to the first - synchronic - type of context, 'is *the words which surround it in the utterance*, and the other *contemporaneous* signs which govern its interpretation'. In other words, a word combines with the other words in an utterance, and it is from this combination that each word derives its meaning. Taken out of one context and used in another, a word's meaning would shift; conversely, the replacement of any single word in an utterance would change the meaning of the utterance as a whole, and the meanings of each individual word. For example, in the statement *Achilles is a lion*, the meaning of the word *lion* is different to the meaning of the same word in the statement *A lion is dangerous* (in the first, *lion* combines with *Achilles* metaphorically; in the second, *lion* combines with *dangerous* to produce a statement which we interpret literally). Similarly, if *lion* were to be replaced in the statement by *man*, then the meanings of the other words (particularly of the word *Achilles*) and of the statement as a whole would change (we would no longer interpret the statement metaphorically, of course).

This sense of context corresponds to Saussure's syntagmatic kind of comparison. Saussure's paradigmatic kind, which works to bestow discourse its meaning *in absentia*, also has a correspondence in Richards' context theorem of meaning, and can be glimpsed in his reference to 'the other *contemporaneous* signs which govern [the utterance's] interpretation'. '[A]ny part of a discourse', Richards argues (1936: 6), 'does what it does only because the other parts of the surrounding, *uttered or unuttered*, discourse and its conditions are what they are' (my emphasis), and he stresses the importance of considering the influence not only 'of words actually present in the passage', but also those 'which are not actually being uttered and are only in the background' (39). This 'unuttered' discourse is absent from the uttered syntagmatic chain, but nonetheless supports the chain *in absentia*. This is the principle, for example, by which 'expressive, symbolic, or simulative words' – what we now call phonaesthemes – work, the fact that they seem 'peculiarly appropriate, or fitting, to the meanings we use them for' (39) arising not from any property which they themselves hold but from their belonging to a network of 'other words sharing the morpheme which support them in the background of the mind' (42). Thus, for example, we think that the word *flash* is peculiarly fitting when used to describe something connected with moving light, but this is not because the *fl-* morpheme means, intrinsically, 'moving light'. Rather, it is because the word shares the same morpheme with other words – *flare, flame, flicker, flimmer* – with a similar meaning. 'As the movement of my hand uses nearly the whole skeletal system of the muscles and is supported by them', writes Richards in a particularly graceful analogy, 'so a phrase may take its powers from an immense system of supporting uses of other words in other contexts' (44).

The synchronic element in Richards' context theorem of meaning – with its emphasis upon 'uttered' and 'unuttered' discourse – corresponds closely to Saussure's syntagmatic and paradigmatic kinds of combination. Richards then adds a diachronic element, something which is absent from Saussure's theory. (Saussure, interestingly, projects the diachronic onto *la langue*, language itself, and empties *la parole*, the actual utterance, of any diachronic element, a move perhaps resulting from Saussure's determination to separate linguistics from psychology, and his unfamiliarity with Pavlovian psychology). 'A word, like any other sign', Richards writes (1938: 6), referring to the second - diachronic - type of context, 'gets whatever meaning it has through belonging to a recurrent group of events, which may be called its context'. 'Thus', Richards continues, 'a word's context, *in this sense*, is a certain recurrent pattern of *past* groups of events, and to say that its meaning depends upon its context would be to point to the process by which it has acquired its meaning' (6). Put simply, what Richards is arguing is that the way in which we respond to, or interpret, a word in the present is conditioned by the history of our responses to the same word in various contexts in the past. A word's meaning in the present, therefore, is an amalgam, or combination, of the meanings that the word has accrued in the synchronic contexts in which it has previously appeared. The past contexts in which the word has appeared fall away and are absent from the context in which the word currently finds itself, but these past contexts combine *in absentia* with the word to bestow upon it its meaning. To return to the earlier example, our response to the word *lion* in *Achilles is a lion* is built up from, and determined by, the contexts in which that word has appeared in the past.

Context, therefore, 'is a name for a whole cluster of events that recur together' (Richards 1936: 23), the recurrence being the diachronic element, and the togetherness being the synchronic element. However, not all the events in the cluster recur together. Rather, 'one item – typically a word – takes over the duties of parts which can then be omitted from the recurrence', that 'abridgement of the context' being what Richards terms 'delegated efficacy' (23). In other words, and

Richards' theorem is somewhat vague here, 'what the sign or word –
the item with these delegated powers – means is the missing parts of
the context' (23). Thus, to articulate what Richards is saying in the
terms of the Pavlovian model from which his context theorem of
meaning is derived, when two stimuli occur together – say, the smell
of food and the ringing of a bell – both are present in, and contribute
to, the synchronic context. However, once the two stimuli have
occurred together in the past, one stimulus – say, the smell of food –
can be omitted from any recurrence, with the other stimulus – say, the
ringing of a bell – then taking over the duties of the stimulus that is
omitted through its 'delegated efficacy'. What the stimulus with the
'delegated efficacy' means is therefore what is missing from the
recurrence, i.e. the stimulus with which it combined in the past.
Precisely what aspects of the 'missing' stimulus are transferred to the
synchronic context depends upon the nature of that synchronic
context.

## 4 The principle of metaphor

According to the context theorem of meaning, then, meaning is 'the
delegated efficacy of signs by which they bring together into new
unities the abstracts, or aspects, which are the missing parts of their
various contexts' (62). A sign, or a word, then, 'is normally a
substitute for (or means) not one discrete past impression but a
combination of general aspects' (62). By this, Richards means that a
word emerges from one context with a 'delegated efficacy' to mean
the 'missing parts' of that context, and it transfers those 'missing
parts' – or 'abstracts' – to the new context in which it used. Through
combining with the other words in the new context and the 'missing
parts' of those words, the word creates 'new unities' or meanings.
This, Richards says, 'is itself a summary account of the principle of
metaphor', since, 'when we use a metaphor we have two thoughts of
different things active together and supported by a single word, or
phrase, whose meaning is a resultant of their interaction' (62). Both
language and metaphor work, then, according to the principle of
*combination.* On the one hand, a word's meaning is created from its
combination with two different types of context (synchronic and
diachronic). And, on the other, metaphor combines two different
thoughts to produce a new meaning - it is these two different thoughts
that Richards terms *vehicle* (i.e. 'what is transferred') and *tenor* (i.e.
'what it is transferred to'). Thus, in the same way that language is

comprised of elements which only have meaning in relation to each other, so metaphor consists of 'two halves' which, together, form a 'whole double unit' (64). One part of the metaphorical copula without the other would break the metaphor completely. In the same way that words combine to create a new meaning, one that is more than the sum of the individual words themselves, so the interaction of the two halves of a metaphor results in a new meaning, one which is more than simply an amalgam of the two halves. As Richards stresses, 'the co-presence of the vehicle and tenor results in a meaning ... which is not attainable without their interaction' (67).

For Richards, therefore, metaphor is not 'a grace or ornament or *added* power of language', as Aristotle implied, but 'the omnipresent principle of all its free action', its 'constitutive form' (60). The omnipresence of metaphor in language can be observed in the fact that 'we cannot get through three sentences of ordinary fluid discourse without it' (61), a fact illustrated by Richards' careful choice of words, of course. However, Richards' theory goes deeper than that. Metaphor is language's 'omnipresent *principle*', and it is so because language works according to the same 'principle' as metaphor; that is, the working of language is analogous to the working of metaphor.

The fact that metaphor is language's 'omnipresent principle' - that metaphor is ubiquitous, and that language operates in the same way as metaphor - would suggest that metaphor is more than merely linguistic, that its roots lie deeper than language. And that is indeed the case. 'My point', Richards writes, 'is *not* that language is full of metaphors' (Richards 1938: 73). Rather, 'it is that thought is itself metaphoric - not merely that it expresses itself in linguistic metaphors' (73). Metaphor, then, is not merely an expression or manifestation of thought, but is, in actual fact, 'the essence of thinking' (73). For Richards, metaphor is the principle which makes thought possible. 'Thinking is radically metaphoric', Richards argues, and it is so because 'linkage by analogy is its constituent law or principle, its causal nexus' (73). 'Linkage by analogy', then, which is synonymous with metaphor, is the 'causal nexus' of thinking, the principle which brings thinking into existence, 'since meaning only arises through the causal *contexts* by which a sign stands for (takes the place of) an instance of a sort' (73). While language, then, operates through 'causal contexts', thought is founded upon the principle of 'an instance of a sort'. 'To think of anything', Richards continues, 'is to take it *as* of a sort (as a such and such) and that "as" brings in (openly or in disguise) the analogy, the parallel, the metaphoric grapple or ground or grasp or draw by which alone the mind takes hold' (73). Therefore, 'all thought is sorting, and we can think of nothing without taking it as of a sort' (37). Rather, to think of something is necessarily to compare or link it to the other things within the sort to which, according to the mind's sorting processes, it belongs, and in opposition to the sorts to which it does not belong. Without that process of sorting - of comparing or linking one thing to another - thought is simply not possible; the mind cannot take hold.

For example, 'cats and dogs are instances' of the sort 'animal life' because 'we range them together as examples of a class, naming their common property' through the process of 'paralleling' (83). In other words, we find a common property or common properties between cats and dogs (say, the fact that they are both quadrupeds), and on that basis assign them to the same sort or class or category. However, the principle of comparison operates not only through similarity and commonality but also through difference and distinction. 'The classes, kinds or sorts by which we handle the things we think of are', Richards points out, 'the parallels, analogies, recurrent togethernesses, contexts, or equivalent others with which we separate what we are taking from what we are not taking' (74). Thus, our grouping of cats and dogs within the same class is founded upon their perceived similarities (what we are taking is the fact that both have four legs, and this enables us to group the two together); but our recognition of the existence of cats *and* dogs is founded upon their perceived dissimilarities (what we are not taking is the fact that they have different behavioural patterns, for example, and this enables us to distinguish cats from dogs). Similarly, of course, one sort or class or category is distinguished from another – indeed, a sort can only exist in relation to other sorts against which it distinguishes itself. For example, we can only have the sort 'animal life' because other sorts, such as 'human life', exist.

## 5 The infinitude of metaphor

Since Richards sees metaphor as being language's 'omnipresent principle' and 'the essence of thinking', he conceives of metaphor as being all-pervading, as being (to change the metaphor) a container (a prison-house?) from which 'there is no escape' (72). However much we attempt to escape the container that metaphor builds for or around us by reaching for non-metaphorical or literal language, or by thinking in a non-metaphorical or literal manner, 'we only substitute another metaphor - recognised as such or not - for the one we are eluding' (72). Behind every metaphor, then, lies not something non-metaphorical or literal, but another metaphor, another vehicle-tenor copula. 'The processes of metaphor in language, the exchanges between the meanings of words which we study in explicit verbal metaphors', Richards argues, 'are superimposed upon a perceived world which is itself a product of earlier or unwitting metaphor' (Richards 1936: 73). Nothing is outside metaphor, then, since both thought and language work according to the metaphorical principle. This goes to the heart of who we are and of the nature of our relationship with the world. 'Our world is a projected world', Richards continues, 'shot through with characters lent to it from our own life' (73). The world, therefore, has no existence in and of itself, but is the result of our perception of or our projection onto it; the world originates within the human mind. 'The fabrics of all our various worlds are the fabrics of our meanings' (12), Richards argues, since the world is not 'a solid matter of fact', but rather 'a fabric of conventions' (28). It is metaphor which enables us to weave the fabric of our world.

Thus, for Richards, metaphor does not reflect a world which exists outside it, but actually constitutes that world. Without an external point of reference, there is no limitation to metaphor; there is no restriction on the metaphors that we can produce, and therefore no world-fabric that we cannot weave. Richards, it is true, does suggest at one point that 'we can find no word or description for any of the intellectual operations which … is not seen to have been taken, by metaphor, from a general description of some physical happening' (60), which anticipates the cognitive-metaphor view that we tend to understand the intellectual (or abstract) through the physical (or concrete). However, the overwhelming argument that Richards makes (1938: 87) is that, if 'a special enough setting' is supplied, then 'anything may be linked with anything'. This view of the infinitude of metaphor is, I would argue, a result of Richards' immersion in Pavlovian psychology, a psychology which, as we have seen, is founded upon the principle of connection: one stimulus is connected to another stimulus. 'The mind is a connecting organ, it works only by connecting', he argues at one point, which means that 'it can connect any two things *in an indefinitely large number of different ways*' (Richards 1936: 84; my italics). It is this process of connecting which is metaphor, of course. What Richards is arguing here is that metaphor can take any form; in other words, any two things - any vehicle and tenor - can be connected, since there is nothing extra-metaphorical which limits what can be connected with what. The only limitation that can be imposed derives from the mind, and the mind, being in essence 'a connecting organ', can connect any one thing with another.

This is the reason that Richards rejects Aristotle's central claim (and, indeed, of the claim of most metaphor theorists up until that point) that the relation between the two different elements of the metaphorical copula is a relation of resemblance or identification - Aristotle claimed that an ability to create metaphor implies 'an eye for resemblances'. 'By introducing these technicalities, "tenor" and "vehicle"', Richards writes (1938: 169), 'I have made this quasi-identification of two different things (of several pairs of different things it is really) less plausible'. Metaphor, for Richards, is not about using one thing instead of another thing which it resembles. Rather, 'fundamentally it is a borrowing between and intercourse of *thoughts*, a transaction between contexts' (Richards 1936: 63). The movement is not simply from one domain (a source) to another domain (a target). Instead, it is bidirectional: a 'borrowing between', an 'intercourse', a 'transaction'. Hence Richards' choice of *vehicle* and *tenor* (they are metaphors, of course) as the names of the two different elements of the metaphorical copula, for they do not imply a relation in which one has primacy over the other. For Richards, the two elements are held in balance, with both playing an equal role in the construction of the metaphorical whole, and therefore of the fabric of our world. 'At one end the tenor is at the forefront and the vehicle is in the background; at the other the vehicle is in front and the tenor behind', Richards argues (1938: 152), while 'in the middle case, tenor and vehicle are equally prominent; neither is subordinated to the other'.

## 6 Concluding remarks

Richards uses the term *metaphor* in two senses. In the first, 'narrower' sense, *metaphor* refers to a primarily linguistic phenomenon in which 'we cross sorts to make new occasional sorts' (1938: 75). In this 'restricted sense' of metaphor, which is similar to how metaphor is commonly conceived, 'there is a cross-grouping and a resultant tension between the particular similarity employed and more stable habitual classifications, which would be absent [from this new cross-grouping]' (84). Thus, for example, *lion* is an instance of the sort 'animal life', while *Achilles* is an instance of the sort human life. In the statement *Achilles is a lion*, therefore, we are crossing sorts (the human and the animal) to create a new, ephemeral sort (a combination of the human and the animal). There is a tension precisely because it is a metaphor, precisely because 'the particular similarity employed' (both a lion and Achilles are courageous, for example) is in conflict with 'more stable habitual classifications' (we normally range lions and humans into different sorts or groupings because the former are quadrupeds and the latter are bipeds, for example). What is absent from the metaphor are those features from the human world and the animal world which we omit in the process of transference - for example, we do not transfer all of a lion's qualities onto Achilles, and nor do we transfer all of Achilles' qualities onto a lion (we do not conceive of Achilles as being a quadruped, and nor of a lion as being a biped, for example).

This 'restricted' sense of metaphor - in which metaphor works by combining into one sort two things which normally belong to two different sorts - is then transferred to metaphor in the 'fully extended sense'. In this 'fully extended sense', *metaphor* refers to the principle by which both language and thought work. According to Richards, it is only when we take metaphor to refer to 'all modes of thinking', to 'the mode of operation of all language (and all signs)', to the fundamental 'sorting operation' with which all human beings are constantly engaged, that a study of metaphor 'become[s] really fruitful' (75). For Richards, then, according to the 'fully extended sense', metaphor is 'the essence of thinking', 'the omnipresent principle of language', the means by which 'the individual life and its world grow together' (1936: 73). And it is for this reason that Richards accords metaphor the central role in his philosophy of rhetoric - metaphor is not only a constituent of thought and language, but actually the principle by which thought and language operate. Thus, to study rhetoric - to study modes of interpretation, of understanding and misunderstanding - is to study language and thought; and to study language and thought is to study metaphor, which is cast as the principle by which language and thought operate. It is also the reason that Richards accords metaphor the central role in human life, equating as he does 'a command of metaphor' with 'a command of life'. Indeed, Richards' central claim that 'the mind is a connecting organ' is a claim for the mind to be seen as, in essence, metaphoric, since 'connecting', like 'borrowing between', 'intercourse' and 'transaction', is a term which describes the principle of metaphor. Thus, metaphor, for Richards, is not only a manifestation or a byproduct of human life, but actually the principle by which we as a species live. Thus, it is no exaggeration to say that Richards' theory of metaphor posits as its central principle the notion of *homo metaphoricus*.

In his recent introduction to cognitive metaphor theory, Zoltan Kövecses (2002) writes: 'what is new' about the theory is that it is 'comprehensive, generalized, and empirically tested'. Cognitive metaphor theory may be new in that sense. Richards' theory is certainly not 'comprehensive, generalized, and empirically tested'. Indeed, it only emerges from a more general philosophy of rhetoric, although the theory is the central element of that philosophy. As such, Richards' presentation of his metaphor theory is piecemeal, fragmentary, and often opaque. What I have attempted to do here is to piece the fragments together to produce a theory for Richards which bears at least a degree of cohesiveness and comprehensibility.

Nonetheless, in his emphasis upon the omnipresence of metaphor and on the fact that metaphor is more a matter of thought than of language, Richards anticipated two of the key principles of cognitive metaphor theory. Richards' theory also goes deeper than cognitive metaphor theory in the sense that it sees metaphor not only as a fundamental constituent of language but actually as the omnipresent principle by which language operates; and not only as a device by which we think about or conceive the world but the actual principle which enables thinking to take place. It is because he sees metaphor as being intrinsic to both language and thought, and therefore intrinsic, too, to what we are as human beings, that Richards does not anticipate the third principle of cognitive metaphor theory - namely, that metaphor is motivated. For, Richards sees no distinction between metaphor and the world from which metaphor derives. For Richards, indeed, metaphor constitutes the world rather than being motivated by our experience of it. It is in this sense that Richards' theory is not only an anticipation of cognitive metaphor theory but also a challenge to it, and a challenge which is motivated by Richards' poststructuralism.

## References

Eagleton, Terry. 2002. 'Review of *I. A. Richards' Selected Works 1919-1938* ed. John Constable (London: Routledge, 2001)' in *London Review of Books* 24(8): 13-5.

Kövecses, Zoltan. 2002. *Metaphor: A Practical Introduction*. Oxford: Oxford University Press.

Pavlov, I. P. 1927. *Conditioned Reflexes: An Investigation of the Physiological Activity of the Cerebral Cortex* (tr. G.V. Anrep). Oxford: Oxford University Press.

Reynolds, Jack, and Jonathan Roffe. 2004. 'An Invitation to Philosophy' in Reynolds, Jack, and Jonathan Roffe (eds.) *Understanding Derrida*. London: Continuum: 1-4.

Richards, I. A., and C. K. Ogden. 1923. *The Meaning of Meaning: A Study of the Influence of Language upon Thought and of the Science of Symbolism* in *I. A. Richards' Selected Works 1919-1938*, Vol. II (ed. John Constable). London: Routledge, 2001.

Richards, I. A. 1924. *Principles of Literary Criticism* in *I. A. Richards' Selected Works 1919-1938*, Vol. III (ed. John Constable). London: Routledge, 2001.

Richards, I. A. 1929. *Practical Criticism: A Study of Literary Judgement* in *I. A. Richards' Selected Works 1919-1938*, Vol. IV (ed. John Constable). London: Routledge, 2001.

Richards, I. A. 1934. *Coleridge on Imagination* in *I. A. Richards' Selected Works 1919-1938*, Vol. VI (ed. John Constable). London: Routledge, 2001.

Richards, I. A. 1936. *The Philosophy of Rhetoric* in *I. A. Richards' Selected Works 1919-1938*, Vol. VII (ed. John Constable). London: Routledge, 2001.

Richards, I. A. 1938. *Interpretation in Teaching* in *I. A. Richards' Selected Works 1919-1938*, Vol. VIII (ed. John Constable). London: Routledge, 2001.

Saussure, Ferdinand de. [1916] 1983. *Course in General Linguistics* (tr. Roy Harris). London: Duckworth.

Stockwell, Peter. 2002. *Cognitive Poetics: An Introduction*. London:
    Routledge.

# The Socio-Psychology of 'Interpretive Communities' and a Cognitive-Semiotic Model for Analysis

## Ulf Cronquist

### Abstract

All research environments can be called 'interpretive communities' (Fish 1980), where activities are assessed according to scientific principles that are functional within that community. With *cognitive poetics* (e.g. Stockwell 2002, Semino & Culpeper 2002, Gavins & Steen 2003) a research environment has emerged that is grounded in a British tradition of stylistics. My starting point here is that this kind of cognitive poetics is an 'interpretive community' where in general stylistic methodology is used, only to be secondarily linked to terminology from cognitive science – far from the basic principles agreed upon in the community of researchers within cognitive science.

Instead I propose that a cognitive poetics should proceed from methodological principles that apply in cognitive science *per se*. That is, first, a given problem is formulated in terms of *information processing*, secondly a *cognitive architecture* is specified for studying the problem, and third, the analysis is developed in terms of *algorithmic sequencing* – in total the cognitive analysis should make as explicit as possible how the information is processed from inputs to output (Hogan 2003).

As an example and to discuss my points about poetics, stylistics, cognitive architecture and more, I provide an analysis of Wallace Stevens' poem 'Theory.'

Key words: interpretive communities, cognitive poetics/semiotics, blending theory, narrative *diegesis*, Wallace Stevens

## 1 Introduction

> Certainty is given to the simple-minded. To know what one thinks under all circumstances, to have definite and final opinions, is a matter of doubt to the ethical intellect. It is matter for doubt. (Hejinian 2000: 20)

All knowledge is socially constructed and specific knowledge sometimes lives a life of its own within certain circles of researchers. There is a defined socio-psychology concerning specialist knowledge that is necessary: without the continued dialogue among researchers, a forum for giving and taking critique, there would be no scientific development at all. In teaching literature there is also a defined socio-psychology as the focus is to teach students how to read and interpret literary texts. When Stanley Fish (1980) discussed 'interpretive communities' he said something important about intersubjective scientific agreement. But, Fish's argument in itself is weak since it provides no ontology – perhaps merely a reflection on terms of agreement that goes for any 'wine and cheese party' where it is socio-psychologically comfortable to agree. I want to take the notion of 'interpretive community' seriously here and make some remarks about intersubjectivity, shared meaning and ontology from a cognitive perspective. My starting point is that both in reader-response theories and cognitively linguistic approaches to literature we are usually presented with the individual researcher's introspective distinctions, often too fine-grained and too focused on local relationships of words and sentences to describe the real reading process[1]. Instead I argue that a cognitive approach to literature and interpretation must proceed from a detailed analysis of the entire literary text (a piece of art seen in its entirety), and that such an analysis should aim at describing the shared intersubjectivity in the minds of the producer of the text and its recipients.

A poem, like any piece of art, attracts our attention specifically – as a poem – since it attracts our attention as a non-generic artifact. But the cognizing mind also processes words on printed page as natural language, words, and clusters of words, as natural shapes or forms. In a *cognitive poetics*, this relation between aesthetic presentation and natural linguistic processing should be in focus: a cognitive approach to literature 'naturalizes' the culture specificity of the poem. To avoid reductionism, I propose that a text should be studied as a global configuration as regards its linguistic organization, its semantics, its composition – and where *interpretation* follows as anchored in the description of the global configuration and is linked to aesthetic evaluation in the appropriate genre the text is presented.

In other words I propose a cognitive-semiotic analysis that begins by assuming that literary, textual, analysis should be performed through the categories of description and interpretive evaluation, proceeding from a careful consideration of the text as a *whole*, which is often not the case in traditional stylistics. As Brandt and Brandt (2005a) argue, such an analysis involves a structural stratification that is universally present in the production of literary meaning – ontologically given parts of what we experience as a literary text. It should also be stressed that while such an analytic enterprise is an effort to keep descriptive and aesthetic categories separate, the strata must also be seen as interconnected on several layers.

As regards the global configuration[2] of the text we must assume not only that the descriptive categories brought to the text are ontologically given, but that they are also valid as scientific tools for mapping out the production of meaning in reading a literary text. From a cognitive perspective this entails that the recipient processes the text as a reconstruction of the producer's intentionality and this further entails the fact that reading and writing is always a matter of shared, intersubjective, meaning.[3] From a general semiotic perspective, similarly, the scientific enterprise concerns a thorough investigation as to how we make intersubjective sense of meaningful sign relations. From a *cognitive-semiotic* perspective then a scientifically valid description – and evaluation – of the object of attention, the piece of art, the text, is what it is about: the task is to outline how we make sense of the signs that are given to us.

## 2 Cognitive Semiotics and Literary Analysis

Generally, my method of analysis proceeds from the research program in cognitive semiotics, integrating European semiotics and philosophy and American cognitive science, initiated and developed by Per Aage Brandt over the last 10-15 years at the Center for Semiotics, Aarhus University, Denmark (cf. Brandt 2004).

Per Aage Brandt defines cognitive semiotics as the study of meaning, seen as an effect of mankind's disposition for cognitive re-working of the experienced life-world, i.e. the human interpretation of sensations as information that are integrated in consciousness and memory in the form of different concepts, motives for action and the understanding of specific situations, thoughts and feelings, which appear through the force of signs and combinations of signs, concepts determined by language and symbolic abstractions of different kinds (P. Aa. Brandt 2007: 122). Further, Brandt remarks that cognitive semiotics is a discipline that combines cognitive inductive (bottom-up) reasoning with semiotic deductive (top-bottom) analysis and that the two approaches fruitfully combine in a research program where phenomenology and experimentalism meet – as in the cognitive semiotics' project (Brandt 2007: 123).

My platform for the following textual analysis of the Wallace Stevens' poem proceeds from a defined focus on the construction of signifieds, where meaning production is a question of cognitive-semiotic intersubjectivity, i.e. the exchange of signs between intentional minds. As Line Brandt puts it:

> Meaning, within cognitive semiotics, is taken to refer to the signified (signifié) side of signs occurring in communication and other expressive practices, and 'construction' is taken to be a mental endeavor engaging multiple minds, as the exchange of signs (semiosis) is essentially an intersubjective enterprise. (Brandt 2006)

## 3 Cognitive Science and Cognitive Poetics as 'Interpretive Communities'

Patrick Colm Hogan (2003) remarks that cognitive science consists of a great many interdisciplinary research areas that often seem to have little or nothing at all to do with each other. But there are some basic methodological principles that most researchers agree upon. First, a given problem is formulated in terms of *information processing*, secondly a *cognitive architecture* is specified for studying the problem, and third, the analysis is developed in terms of *algorithmic sequencing*: the cognitive analysis should make as explicit as possible how the information is processed from inputs to output(s).

Let us compare Hogan's remarks on methodology with the opening chapter of Peter Stockwell's *Cognitive Poetics. An Introduction* (2002). The first words here are that 'Cognitive poetics is all about reading' and Stockwell soon stresses that the text alone is an artifact, and that reading usually takes place in solitude. However, reading as science deals with 'the more natural process of reading when one [the text] is engaged with the other [the reader]' (Stockwell 2002: 2). Stockwell then stresses that *context* is a crucial notion for cognitive poetics: although there is nothing wrong with idiosyncratic readings, we are 'discussing literature within an institutional setting ...[belonging] to the discipline of literary studies' (Stockwell 2002: 3). That is, idiosyncratic readings will be understood when we talk with one another in some kind of institutional interpretive community.

Alternately, claims Stockwell, we can take a *purely textual approach*, where the example given is metrics[4], and the two approaches 'can even be brought together' – but now Stockwell suddenly calls the notion of *context* the 'historical approach' (Stockwell 2002: 3*)*. So far we can summarize Stockwell's definition of reading thus:

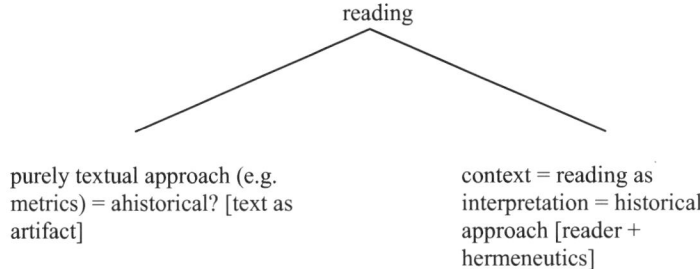

reading

purely textual approach (e.g. metrics) = ahistorical? [text as artifact]

context = reading as interpretation = historical approach [reader + hermeneutics]

But soon Stockwell confuses matters by drawing a distinction between **interpretation** as what readers do when they begin to move through the text and **reading** as the process of arriving at a sense of the text that is personally and collectively acceptable (Stockwell 2002: 8). So:

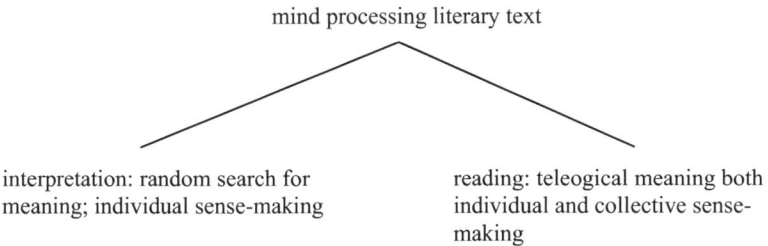

mind processing literary text

interpretation: random search for meaning; individual sense-making

reading: teleogical meaning both individual and collective sense-making

So although Stockwell underlines that 'cognitive poetics takes context seriously' (Stockwell 2002: 4), his description so far has only set up two pairs of binaries, taking no account of the *cognitive* aspects of reading that are not sorted out. The first binary concerns something that is 'purely textual' and something that is contextually 'historical.' It is not at all clear whether this purely 'textual' is supposed to be ahistorical, or if consideration should be taken e.g. as to whose metrics we are referring to and other questions as regards verse semantics and rhythm. Also, it is unclear why reading and context are mixed up by the categories of interpretation and history. As regards the second binary, the terminology is further confused when interpretation is no longer the 'historical approach' and reading, which consists of a purely textual approach and some kind of interpretation in the first binary, is now a matter of exegesis.

The attempt to first describe the text and then provide an interpretation is of course the basic model for stylistics. Stockwell also claims that, within sub-disciplines of literary studies, 'cognitive poetics is most closely connected with stylistics' (Stockwell 2002: 6). Thus terminologically speaking what Stockwell asserts is that cognitive poetics equals reading which equals description and interpretation which equals stylistics. And the fact that (some of) these processes go on in readers' minds apparently make it a cognitive approach. Stockwell's approach is, undoubtedly, as a cognitive research program far from the basic methodology that Hogan outlines.

Perhaps we can learn something here about interpretive communities and intersubjectivity. The way Stockwell describes these matters in the context of a cognitive poetics is focused on how literary scholars might *agree* about certain *interpretations* – i.e. he focuses on the social constructedness of interpretation. I cannot see this as a cognitive approach to literary studies, rather it is a socio-psychological reflection based on some sort of constructivism – and an alibi for intuitive interpretive practices that are difficult to falsify.

Instead, I would suggest that we take up Hogan's methodology for research in cognitive science as the starting point for any literary analysis that calls itself cognitive, since it proceeds by asking the question *what* the text is, *who* is speaking and *how* this is done. That is, we proceed from the fact that intersubjectivity is about the human capacity for *shared meaning* and from a cognitive perspective this entails that the recipient processes the text as a reconstruction of the producer's intentionality[5].

Methodologically this means that the description of cognitive architecture is not entirely 'innocent': the scientist works in a defined environment and in the case of literary studies we are of course more directed to the processes of understanding rather than explaining physical facts. However, the effort involved in reading literature from a cognitive point of view gives us certain advantages: when we claim something about the text we can always relate that claim to a specified cognitive architecture. In the analysis here I will use Brandt and

Brandt's (2005b) model for analyzing conceptual blends and also Brandt's (1983; 1989[6]) model for analyzing narratives. But first of all I suggest that a basic inventory of the poem be carried out in relation to the syntax and semantics.

## 4 Wallace Stevens' 'Theory' – Initial Reading

Syntactically Stevens' poem is quite straightforward. Apart from its presentational title it consists of five propositions:

1. I am what is around me.

2. Women understand this.

3. One is not a duchess/A hundred yards from a carriage

4. These, then are the portraits:/ A black vestibule; /A high bed sheltered by curtains.

5. These are merely instances.

Semantically, we enter deictic territory in the first phrasing where the six words are all closed word class. To begin with we do not know who the 'I' is and we never will. However, with propositions (2) and (3) as evidential, we can assume that 'I' is expressed as a generic pronoun – it is a statement about *a* subject. And as a pronoun it is linked to the equally generic 'One' in line 3. Therefore we can deduct that the 'I – One' is functional in terms of agency and subjectivity. Subsequently the first proposition relates to the second and third propositions as a comparison, i.e. the following lines qualify as a metaphor or an *exemplum*. 'One is not a duchess/A hundred yards from the carriage' connotes conceptually that A SUBJECT IS SOCIALLY CONSTRUCTED[7]. That is, the metaphor underlines that if you do not stay close to your defined social context you are out of it. Also, the metaphor problematizes the conceptualization of THE SUBJECT IS A CONTAINER since the subject is 'contained' by external circumstances, i.e. the subject is determined by its social situatedness – if there are no defining traits *around* the subject the 'I' cannot be, is empty as a subject[8].

Before proceeding we notice that there is a gender issue here. There is the statement here that women understand – which characterizes men as 'out of it'[9]; and this of course relates to an understanding of women as caring, interested in close relations, and men as seeking autonomy away from relations. From an ideological point of view we can of course criticize Stevens here for adhering to cultural stereotypes, but we can also sense a reference to natural survival here: the female is the first to nurture the new-born, one is not a mother 100 yards away from the infant while the father may be a father 10.000 yards away on his way to work. However, regardless of ideology – what we choose to believe in for conventional reasons – Stevens's metaphor is clear as far as a theory of the subject goes in terms of social and cognitive distribution and the importance of the subject's relations to a community for survival.

Then there are the portraits. It is evident that the two portraits of 'A black vestibule' and 'A high bed sheltered by curtains' are without human subjects, empty spaces that nonetheless are man-made, culturally specific. Something or someone might be hiding in the darkness of the vestibule; the unknown is sheltered behind curtains. Subjectivity here is textually indexical: a black vestibule is horrific if one begins to expect someone/something to suddenly appear; a high bed sheltered by curtains hides traces of unknown human or supernatural activities. There is a general gothic horror index, or a general index of uncertainty here: somebody/thing might be hiding here, a scary, exciting, delusional object of attention. But, one must also observe that these are *not* portraits in a fundamental sense since there is no likeness to a person or a person's face in this vestibule, in this bed.

And then the final statement that these are 'merely instances.' The words *merely* and *instances* are of course prominent here as the two open word-class words. '[I]nstances' denote the quality of indexicality while 'merely' is a question of negative quantity. And the 'These' pronoun in line 8 is linked to the same word in line 5: portraits without humans are the instances. But what are they instances of? The logical inference is of course that these instances refer back to the first statement in the poem about what a subject is, i.e. nothing in itself but relying on social situatedness; cultural attributes determine any subjectivity. This is the general 'Theory' of the poem put forth, as far as a first reading or general overview takes us considering the poem as a whole *gestalt*.

## 5 Cognitive Architecture: Blends

The cognitive architecture used in describing a *blend* is relatively simple to begin with: the blend emerges when one concept is *mapped* on another. For example in the metaphorical expression 'this surgeon is a butcher!' a butcher in white coat with a meat-axe is mapped on the surgeon with his white coat[10], his scalpels and the human body he is working on[11]. The Aarhus blending model presented by Brandt and Brandt (2005b; see Figure 1), provides a detailed network for mapping meaning production consisting of six spaces. First there is the *semiotic space* which indicates the actual speech act and which can be analyzed in detail as regards enunciation. Then there is the *presentation space* and the *reference space*, where, in a metaphor analogically the latter is the vehicle and the former is the tenor. Brandt and Brandt also present a *relevance-pragmatic space* that refers to the specific context that structures the meaning production. This space makes it possible to discern between a first *literal* blend and a second *emergent* blend. In the butcher-surgeon example, the first blend literally results in a representation where the two professionals' coats melt together, but where the surgeon gets a butcher's cap on his head and a meat-axe in his hand. This blend says nothing specific about the surgeon's professional behavior – since a context has to be specified through the relevance-pragmatic space, e.g. if the expression refers to an amputation or a scar[12] (see Figure 2).

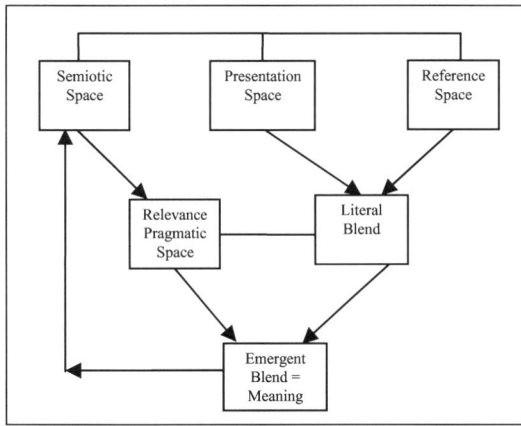

**Figure 1** The Aarhus blending model

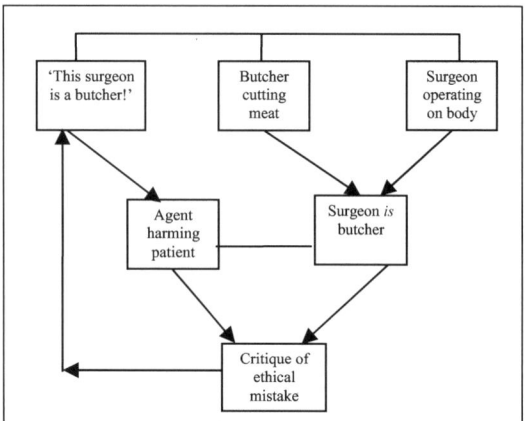

**Figure 2** 'This surgeon is a butcher!'

In Steven's 'Theory' the overriding blend that structures the poem proceeds from the first statement in the poem about subjectivity[13]. The conceptual 'I' is blended with the conceptual examples of the duchess's status, in relation to her proximity to her carriage, and the portraits, man-made but lacking in representations of man. In the first literal blend the 'I' is determined by surrounding objects – a very literal and abstract blend since the 'I' is relatively undetermined (could be any 'I') and the determining objects are equally undetermined (especially the (non-) portraits.) There is some philosophical risk-taking here, and since most thoughts – that could possibly interest us in human-philosophical terms – center around the risky relations of nature and culture, this is the overriding context that structures the emergent blend. In other words, the man/animal interface is at stake here. That is, the emergent blend is decidedly anthropological: man is defined by his extensions, *the* prehistoric event being the first use of tools some 50.000 years ago. Without tools man would have remained one among other mammals, and by extension the process involved in abstract thinking about tools is what we today call externalizing of memory or 'social constructions,' strictly human features that defines mankind (see Figure 3).

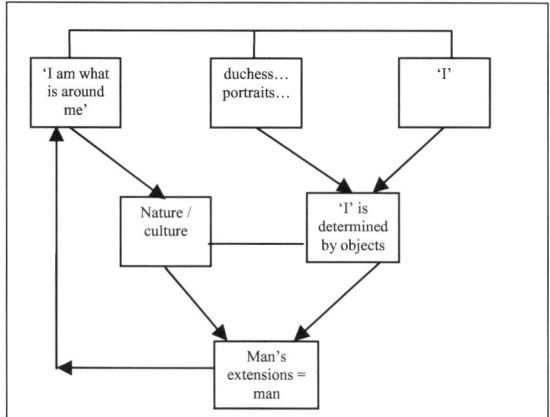

**Figure 3** 'Theory': overriding blend

While this overriding blend is structured around the first line in the poem, we can also see an intertextual relation to John Donne's *Meditation XVII* here: 'No man is an island, entire of itself.' That is, being human depends on partaking in cultural practices that involve other human beings and man-made artifacts.

On a meta-level we can see that Stevens is not writing from a social vacuum, like most writers he is a writer who reads and refers to other instances of literature and then shapes his own vision of language, literature, life. In the poem there is also a negation, a dark subject-as-abject – like a Lear on the heath stripped of all his humanity; a subject without cultural determination cut loose from other cultural objects. I refer here specifically to the strange *portraits* in the poem. By definition a portrait depicts a person or a person's face – which is negated in Steven's poem, there is a vestibule and a bed, but no persons.

The rhetorical term *prosopopoeia* is a device in which a writer communicates to the audience by speaking as another person or object, a term with the Greek roots meaning 'a face, a person, to make.' Stevens's enunciation in the poem provides just the opposite: it represents a person, 'I,' as an abstraction *without* a human face. And this is mirrored in the poem's dark vestibule and the bed sheltered by curtains where there might be faces, persons, but nothing in the text indicates such presence. Thus, the cultural specificity of the face/person is un-done, and we see a blend structured through this facelessness (see Figure 4).

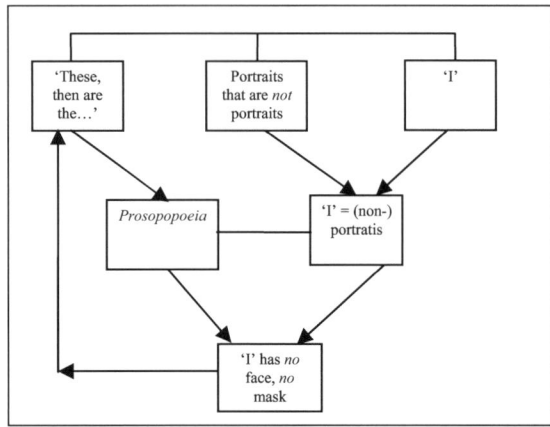

**Figure 4** 'Theory': subject as negation (abject)

Since there is an opposition in the text between the 'I' as social construction and the 'I' as a non-persona a third blend must be considered – of this opposition. Technically speaking this third blend follows logically in time and space as regards the mental processing of the poem. First there is an overriding blend in the first two stanzas, second there is the blend that concerns the subject as negation, and third a blend that concerns the whole poem, inclusive of the first two blends. As in most poems it is the final reflection that triggers a re-consideration of previous descriptions: 'These are merely instances.' From this phrasing we are led back to consider the 'I' as cultural construct *and* the 'I' as empty negation and the result in the literal blend is a Janus-faced subject. Contextually, what structures this emergent blend is the notion of subjectivity as becoming, in flux: in 'Theory' the subject oscillates between the negativity of the empty abject and the positivity of the cultural construct. We can summarize so far that Stevens' 'Theory' blends several concepts that express something about the contingency of the subject (see Figure 5).

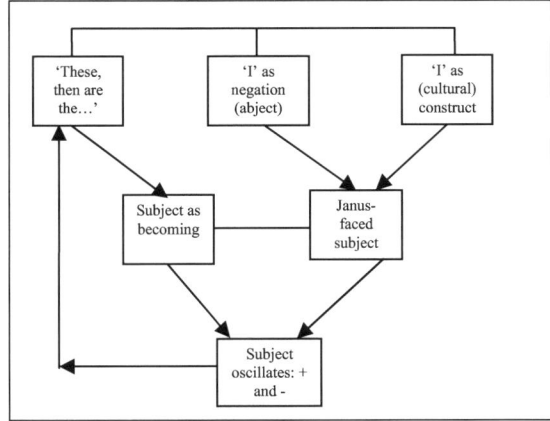

**Figure 5** 'Theory': subject-in-process

## 6 Cognitive Architecture: Diegesis

Probing further into the reality of cognitive architecture, I will now refer to Per Aage Brandt's model of *diegesis*[14], which explains how a narrative runs through a diegetic formation. As the narrative begins S1 is in a *contractual* relation with S0. This relation is then disturbed by S2, something that turns S1 away from S0 and so causes a *crisis*. In the next exchange S1 has to direct all his attention to S3, which has *catastrophic* consequences: the original narrative structure is dissolved. S4 then denotes the change in S1 and a platform for a perspectivizing, interpretive, discourse (see Figure 6).

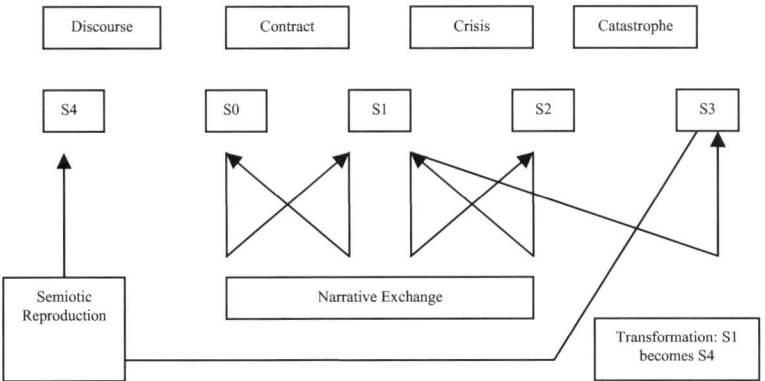

**Figure 6** Per Aage Brandt's *diegesis* model

In Stevens' 'Theory' there are two distinct narratives. First, there is the narrative structure that begins with the contract between 'I' (S1) and 'Women' (S0) where a subject is established according to the culture it is in. The crisis appears in relation to 'the portraits' (S2) – which are *not* portraits since there are, strictly speaking, no humans in them. The catastrophe then follows with these characterized as 'instances' (S3) of subjectivity: 'I' both as enunciator and category is marked by emptiness and ultimately death, since the portrait-instances are dead as representations. S1 began as an entity (defined in the contract with S0) and changes to S4, an entity that is a non-entity (see Figure 7).

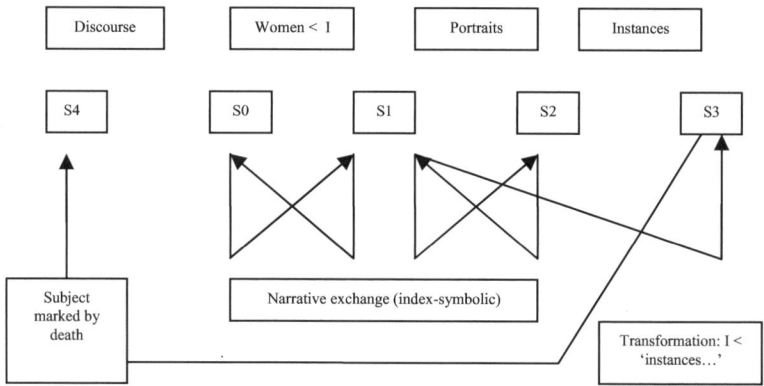

**Figure 7** 'Gender theory'

A second diegesis proceeds from 'Theory' as S1 and 'I' as S0 in a contractual and predicative relation – this is the title and the first two stanzas. The crisis, as in the first diegesis, appears with 'the portraits' (S2) that are not portraits. And the catastrophe then follows with these characterized as 'instances' (S3) of the *theory* of subjectivity, i.e. what began as a straightforward, propositional statement is now a contingent theory. S1 changes to S4, from a positive statement to a proposition marked by uncertainty (see Figure 8).

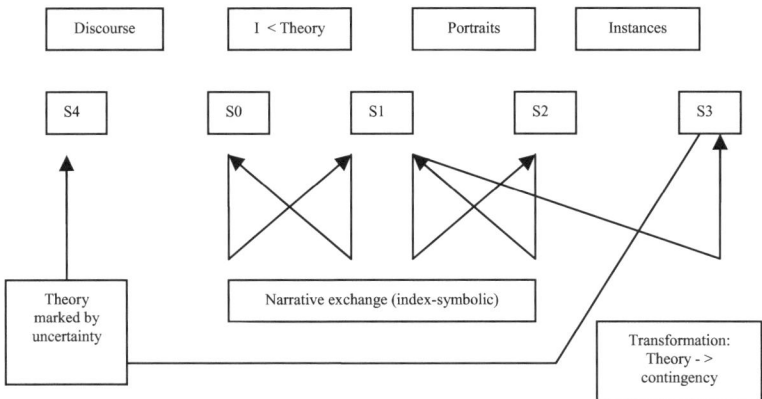

**Figure 8** 'Male subjectivity theory'

## 7 Interpretation

We have seen that both blends and narrative patterns in Stevens' poem revolve around the issue of subjectivity and what a theory of subjectivity can be. The last S1>S4 transformation give us the mark of uncertainty and on a meta-level this tells us something about the ontology of reading a text. According to Heisenberg's 'principle of uncertainty' we change an object when we study it. That is, we must *reduce* our reading to what we can observe and make as sure as possible that the descriptive categories we use are valid, though we should be careful not to mistake causality for intentionality, i.e. careful not to play dice with the poem's global configuration. Reduction *vis-à-vis* validity is of course present in describing cognitive architecture and it should be relatively easy to falsify such analyses. In the relation between causality and intentionality, however, we enter the more difficult domain that concerns interpretation *per se.*

In other words, when we interpret we have to attend to the causality of the text to make sense of its form and content. And here the principle of uncertainty tells us that one semantic frame gives us no *exact* information about the previous, or coming, semantic frame – our causal knowledge can only be probabilistic. At the same time the reader is free to decide how to interpret, provided that his or her reading is reasonably motivated by what there is in the text, what it is reasonable that the mind of the writer intended, i.e. a sense of protypicality[15] is necessary (see Figure 9).

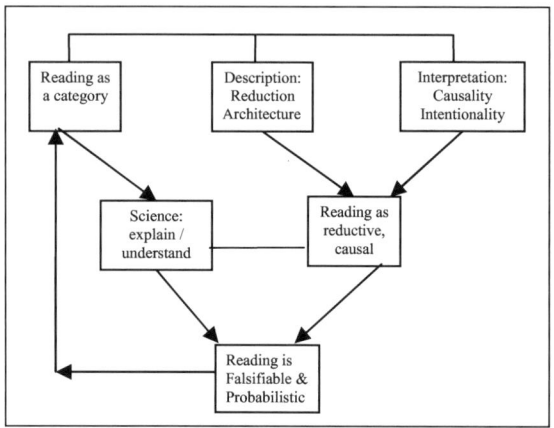

**Figure 9** Reading as a blend

As regards Stevens' 'Theory' so far we have described its basic cognitive architecture without making any conclusions as to how we interpret the poem. It is very clear that our interpretation will be disturbed by the causal uncertainty in the poem, especially in the crack between the first two stanzas and the last two stanzas. That is, while we can identify the portraits that are not portraits as cultural objects the causal relation to the rest of the poem is highly uncertain. In terms of intentionality, however, we can interpret these spaces empty of human subjects as having to do with the cultural construction of an 'I.' And, the rest as regards this incongruity, would be speculation rather than interpretation.

We can of course consider other – more local – interpretive possibilities in the text. In terms of metrics we might consider the relation between the end-rhymes: a-b-b-a-b-a-b-b, or the irregularity in beats in lines 5-6-7, or if the hammering double (spondee) beats in 'I am,' 'black vestibule' and 'high bed' have some perverse aesthetic meaning, or if the iconic enjambment in lines 3 and 4 is of particular importance. These are merely instances for a perspectivizing discourse that could deal with the heartbeats of the poem, for example in

Lacanian terms of the imaginary and the symbolic. But I leave such possibilities (and other) to scholars who are more inclined to partake in the Big Interpretation Competition, the 'modern successors to the sophists of Aristophanes thinkery' (Turner 1991: 3) who are doomed not to 'get out of the prison-house of intuition' (Hamilton 2002:3).

## 8 Concluding Remarks

I have suggested that in analyses of literary works based on reader-response theories and analyses grounded in cognitive poetics, theory is often used as an alibi for intuitive interpretations presented by the individual critic – anchored in ideas about scientific agreement in 'interpretive communities.' The model for analysis that I instead propose studies the text as a global configuration and proceeds according to the minimum requirements for a cognitive analysis, i.e. studying the text from the perspective of information-processing, specifying cognitive architecture and describing algorithmic sequencing to make explicit how information is processed from input to output.

As an example I have analyzed Wallace Stevens' poems 'Theory,' which, like most of Stevens' writing, is easy to analyze in its straightforward syntax, semantics and metaphoricity. It is also relatively simple to specify the basic cognitive processing in the poem, while with interpretations of the text we must – as always – be careful to distinguish between layers of causality and intentionality.

The literary text is always irreducible; unlike everyday linguistic discourse it invites a wealth of pragmatic-semantic frames grounded in human intentionality and imagination. But our cognitive-semiotic analysis must necessarily come to a halt here within the frame of this chapter.

## Endnotes

[1]As regards *cognitive poetics/stylistics*, most analyses in e.g. Stockwell (2002), Gavins & Steen (2003) and Semino & Culpeper (2002) deal, as in traditional stylistics, with fragments of instead of whole literary texts. My point is to question the use of the term *cognitive* here, since the cognizing mind processes texts as meaningful wholes, not as fragments that exemplify theoretical points.

[2]Meaning production, and its analysis, proceeds according to *the phenomena* that we actually perceive and the fact that we perceive *meaningful wholes* (*gestalts*). Thus, many stylistic analyses, including those made in the name of cognitive poetics, remain

on a simplified sentence level that is not compatible with the basics of human phenomenology.

[3]Language is always intentional since somebody always intends something with a speech act. Joyce's *Finnegans Wake* for example may be difficult to process, but any reading and understanding of such a work of art is built on the human-specific capacity for tuning in to the intentionality of an 'other.' The fact that we have shared meaning and intersubjectivity, in cognitive terms, distinguishes man from other animals. When we map cognitive architecture it is to the background that most of the information processing goes on, mainly, naturally, in the unconscious; generally, then, what we humans share is the same capacity for conceptual meaning production, for making sense of signs. We are thus not, in textual analysis, interested in finding out what the author was consciously thinking about when he wrote his poem to determine its aesthetic value (cf. the 'intentional fallacy').

[4]It is problematic to call metrics 'purely textual,' since there is always some cognitive rhythm and verse semantics at work in the reader's and the writer's mind.

[5]Cf. endnote 3.

[6]Brandt has written a great number of articles on *diegesis* in Danish, French and Spanish. Unfortunately, so far nothing has been published in English.

[7]I follow the convention here of writing out conceptual metaphors in small ALL CAPS, beginning in Lakoff & Johnson's *Metaphors We Live By* (1980).

[8]That is, there is a difference between the subject being a container of his subjectivity, very common in popular psychology ("Who are you really inside?" etc.) and the subject being contained by external circumstances.

[9]My allusion here, of course, to Joseph Conrad's *Heart of Darkness* – in the reverse as regards gender.

[10]The mapping between white coats is perhaps somewhat dated. In the US today, e.g., surgeons perform in green apparel. But in the case referred to, this would only enhance the 'surrealistic' effect of the virtual blend, adding contrasting colours.

[11]The theory about blending, or 'conceptual integration networks', was originally developed by Fauconnier & Turner (see e.g. Fauconnier & Turner 1998, 2000, 2004). In literary studies where cognitive perspectives have been used for textual analysis Fauconnier & Turner's model has sometimes become more popular than Lakoff & Johnson's conceptual metaphor theory. This is probably because while the model of the latter couple describes *general,* underlying, cognitive structures the model by Fauconnier & Turner offers a description of *particular* moments in language.

[12]Cf. note 6.

[13]The title is generic and abstract – mainly it suggests that the philosophy of the following eight lines is *a* theory.

[14]A motivated interpretation relies on prototypicality, which is a basic cognitive feature. That is, e.g. in the first two stanzas of Stevens' poem a motivated interpretation relates to the fact that there is a subject, there are objects and there are

distances between the subject and the objects, prototypically a matter of spatial relations.

[15]The first quote is from Mark Turner (1991: 3), the second from Craig Hamilton (2002: 3), two scholars working with cognitive approaches to literature that have declined to partake in the Big Interpretation Competition.

## References

Brandt, Line. 2006. 'Dramatization in the Semiotic Base Space: A Semiotic Approach to Fictive Interaction as a Representational Strategy in Communicative Meaning Construction' in Oakley, Todd and Anders Hougaard (eds). *Mental Spaces Approaches to Discourse and Interaction.* Amsterdam: John Benjamins.

Brandt, Line, and Per Aage Brandt. 2005a. 'Conceptual Metaphor and Imagery'. Online at: www.hum.au.dk/semiotics/ (consulted February 2006).

Brandt, Line, and Per Aage Brandt. 2005b. 'Making sense of a blend: A Cognitive-Semiotic Approach to Metaphor' in *Annual Review of Cognitive Linguistics* 3: 216-49.

Brandt, Per Aage. 1983. *Sandheden, saetningen och döden – Semiotiske aspekter af kulturanalysen.* Copenhagen: Basilisk.

Brandt, Per Aage. 1989. 'Genese og diegese – Et problem i den almene narratologi' in *Religionsvidenskabeligt tidsskrift* 14: 75-85.

Brandt, Per Aage. 2004. *Spaces, Domains and Meaning. Essays in Cognitive Semiotics.* Bern: Peter Lang.

Brandt, Per Aage. 2007. 'Kognitiv semiotic,' in Thellefsen, Torkild and Sörensen, Bent (eds). *Livstegn. Encyklopaedi semiotik.dk*: Copenhagen: Haase and Söns Forlag: 122-24.

Fauconnier, Gilles, and Mark Turner. 1998. 'Conceptual Integration Networks' in *Cognitive Science* 22(2): 133-87.

Fauconnier, Gilles, and Mark Turner. 2000. 'Conceptual Integration Networks'. Online at: http://markturner.org/cin.web/cin.html (consulted February 2006).

Fauconnier, Gilles, and Mark Turner. 2004 *The Way We Think. Conceptual Blending and the Mind's Hidden Complexities.* New York: Basic Books.

Fish, Stanley. 1980. *Is There a Text in this Class? The Authority of Interpretive Communities.* Harvard: Harvard University Press.

Gavins, Joanna, and Gerard Steen. 2003. *Cognitive Poetics in Practice*. London: Routledge.

Hamilton, Craig. 2002. 'Conceptual Integration in Christine de Pizan's *City of Ladies,*' in Semino, Elena and Culpeper, Jonathan (eds). *Cognitive Stylistics. Language and Cognition in Text Analysis*. Amsterdam: John Benjamins: 1-22.

Hejinian, Lyn. 2000. *The Language of Inquiry*. Berkeley: University of California Press.

Hogan, Patrick Colm. 2003. *Cognitive Science, Literature and the Arts: A Guide for Humanists*. New York: Routledge.

Lakoff, George, and Mark Johnson. 1980. *Metaphors We Live By*. Chicago: Chicago University Press.

Oakley, Todd, and Anders Hougaard. (eds). *Mental Spaces Approaches to Discourse and Interaction*. Amsterdam: John Benjamins.

Semino, Elena, and Jonathan Culpeper. 2002. *Cognitive Stylistics. Language and Cognition in Text Analysis*. Amsterdam: John Benjamins.

Stockwell, Peter. 2002. *Cognitive Poetics. An Introduction*. London: Routledge.

Thellefsen, Torkild, and Bent Sörensen. 2007. *Livstegn. Encyklopaedi.dk*. Copenhagen: Haase and Söns Forlag.

Turner, Mark. 1991. *Reading Minds. The Study of English in the Age of Cognitive Science*. New Jersey: Princeton University Press.

# Interpreting Cognitive Metaphor: Using Relevance Theory and an Alternative Account

## Ziwei Mimi Huang

### Abstract

This chapter aims to examine how metaphoric meanings are constructed in discourse processing, especially in a literary context. The relevance model, according to its pragmatic stand, should be able to interpret cognitive metaphor. However, some potential problems emerge when using the relevance model in metaphor studies. In order to solve these problems, I further review a salience model, which emphasizes the salient lexical meanings in the initial stage of metaphoric processing. As salience and relevance are both important aspects in interpreting metaphor in discourse context, I further propose an alternative account that reveals both of the notion of salience and relevance. This proposed account is applied to analyse a selected literary text, *Chest*, to illustrate its metaphorical use of language. It is argued in this paper that relevance and salience are both important in metaphoric processing, and an analytical account that has both pragmatic and cognitive elements is needed to reveal the development of salient and relevant metaphorical meanings in the discourse context.

Keywords: Relevance, salience, metaphor, context, *ad hoc* concept

## 1 Introduction

The study of metaphor has become an interdisciplinary subject following the development of cognitive science in recent years. Contributions have been made by different cognitive approaches, including pragmatic, psychological, stylistic, etc (e.g. Sperber & Wilson 1986, 1995; Gibbs 1994; Pilkington 2000). The phenomenon of metaphor, in the light of cognitive studies, has been examined widely and much attention has been paid to the general characteristics of language usage, such as everyday language (Lakoff 1990; Lakoff & Johnson 1980; Fauconnier & Turner 2002), rather than language in a specific context, such as literary texts.

This paper aims to examine the features of metaphorical language by balancing the features of metaphor in general language usage, and metaphor in a literary context. This paper will follow a pragmatic approach with a cognitive stance. Specifically, I will review the relevance model developed by Sperber & Wilson (1986, 1995) in Section 2.1 for its merits in analysing communication in discourse contexts. More importantly, in Section 2.2, some of the potential problems in the relevance model will be examined when it is applied to metaphor study. Then in Section 2.3, an alternative account, based on Giora's graded salience hypothesis (Giora 2003), will be proposed to work together with the relevance model to provide a better understanding of metaphoric processing. The discussion of the application of the alternative account in poetic metaphors will be carried out in Section 3.1. Then Section 3.2 will apply this account to analyse a literary text – Will Self's short story *Chest* (1994). Finally in Section 4, a summary and conclusion will be given.

## 2 The relevance model and an alternative account in metaphoric processing

The relevance model is a theory for human cognition and communication. It departs from one of Grice's central claims: that utterances automatically create expectations which guide the hearer towards the speaker's meaning (Grice 1989; see also Wilson & Sperber 2003). While the relevance model accords to the Gricean tradition that utterances invite expectations of relevance, it differs from the Gricean pragmatic account in several other aspects. One of the differences is that the relevance model challenges the Gricean maxim or convention of truthfulness in the treatment of figurative utterance (Wilson & Sperber 2003).

In the following, I will give a brief review of relevance theory, giving special attention to its account on meanings and context. The following discussion will examine whether the relevance model is sufficient to account for the way we process metaphors, both in day to day language, and in more poetic, creative ways.

### 2.1 Overview of the relevance model

The central claim of the relevance model is that human cognition and communication is achieved by seeking relevance. A detailed explanation of the relevance model has been given by Sperber & Wilson (1986), and is updated by relevance theorists (Sperber & Wilson 1995; Pilkington 2000; Carston 2002). In the updated version,

Sperber & Wilson revise the model and emphasize that there are two principles of relevance (1995: 260):

(1) Human cognition tends to be geared to the maximisation of relevance.

(2) Every act of ostensive communication communicates a presumption of its own optimal relevance.

The first principle assumes that human cognition is designed in such a way as to tend to achieve maximal relevance. It should be noted that the First Principle of Relevance indicates that relevance is a property of the inputs to cognitive processes. The property can be stimuli, which can be perceptual and external; or can be assumptions, which can be inferential or internal (Sperber & Wilson 1995: 261). The First Principle of Relevance provides the cognitive foundation for the relevance model, and suggests that the objective truth or falsity is not the particular concern for a cognitive system when it allocates its resource. The first Principle of Relevance thus reveals one of the aspects that distinguish the relevance model from Grice's maxim of quality (i.e. truth).

When talking about the two Principles of Relevance, Sperber & Wilson (1995) have emphasized that the First Principle of Relevance is about our mechanism of cognition, yet it is the Second Principle of Relevance, i.e., the communicative principle, that governs our ostensive communication. The relevance model contrasts with Grice's main notion – the Co-operative Principle. Unlike Grice's claim, the notion of relevance is not presented as the communicator's goal to achieve in ostensive communication, but rather, a descriptive claim about the content of a given act of ostensive communication (Sperber & Wilson 1995: 271).

Governed by these two principles, several notions of relevance have been developed, including relevance in a context, relevance to an individual, relevance of a phenomenon, maximal relevance and optimal relevance. In the following, I will focus on the notion of context and relevance to an individual, which directly concerns the discussion of metaphor in Section 2.2. Relevance of a phenomenon, though important in ostensive communication over all, is beyond the scope of this chapter, and will not be discussed in detail here.

The notion of context has been closely related to the relevance model throughout. In the relevance model, a context does not have any cognitive function until it has certain (especially positive) effects in a cognitive system, and contributes positively to the fulfilment of cognitive functions or goals. More importantly, there is an intimate interaction with contextual effect and relevance in discourse processing. Chafe (1987: 48), for example, has supported this point by saying that:

> It is more rewarding, I think, to interpret a piece of discourse in terms of cognitive process dynamically unfolding through time than to analyse it as a static sting of words and sentences.

In defining the relevance to an individual, and optimal relevance, Sperber & Wilson have stated that there is an inverse proportion between the contextual effect and processing effort in ostensive communication. It is a crucial movement in recognizing the important role played by the context in meaning processing, yet it also raises a question about the relation between relevance and context in the relevance model – a problem of circularity.

It seems that the notion of relevance (especially relevance to an individual) and the notion of contextual effect (i.e. positive cognitive effect) have been used largely to define each other. According to the relevance model, an assumption is relevant to an individual if it has a certain contextual effect, and the selection of a particular context is determined by the search for relevance (See Sperber & Wilson 1995: 141, 265). Further more, Sperber & Wilson believe that an ostensive communication will be based on the communicators' assumption that what is being processed is relevant, and such an assumption will be (or will hope to be) justified by the selection of a certain context to achieve maximal or optimal relevance (Sperber & Wilson 1995: 142). If the context is not given but chosen according to relevance, yet relevance is depended on contextual information, then where and how does comprehension start? This problem is especially relevant when dealing with metaphoric comprehension, which involves the possible interpretation of literal meanings and metaphoric meanings. It seems that the resolution of the circularity calls for a 'starting point', i.e. a comparatively stable and reliable understanding, to serve as the basis for an act of ostensive communication. In the following, this 'starting point' will be further examined in the discussion of applying the relevance model to metaphoric understanding.

## 2.2 The relevance model in metaphoric processing and some of its potential problems

The relevance model, as proposed by many relevance theorists, can be applied to analyse figurative language, including metaphoric expressions in different contexts. Sperber & Wilson have outlined explanations of metaphoric comprehension in their works, and suggest that metaphor can be seen as 'loose talk' which only communicates weak implicatures conveyed in a metaphoric expression (see 1986, 1995, 2003).

This relevance account of metaphor contradicts Grice's Standard Pragmatic View in the sense that metaphoric meanings can be accessed directly by achieving optimal relevance rather than by processing the metaphorical meaning indirectly only after the literal meaning has been accessed and rejected in the first place. This view has been supported by empirical findings (Gibbs 1984; 1994; Giora 1997) that metaphoric meanings can be accessed directly.

However, though there is a consensus among relevance theorists that metaphoric comprehension does not demand a special cognitive mechanism, different perspectives have emerged when talking about the distinction between literal meanings and non-literal meanings (i.e. metaphoric meanings in particular).

There are two main relevance accounts of the distinction between literal and metaphoric meanings: the implicature account (represented by Sperber & Wilson 1995, 2003, and Pilkington 2000) and the *ad hoc* concept account (proposed by Carston 1997, 2002).

Pilkington has developed Sperber & Wilson's relevance model particularly in its treatment of figurative language used in poetic contexts. Following Sperber & Wilson's argument, Pilkington regards the propositional form of an utterance as the crucial element in deciding whether an utterance is literal or non-literal. The implicature account sees an utterance as strictly literal if and only if it has the same propositional form as the speaker's thought.

(3) This place is a dump.

In one of Pilkington's (2000: 93) examples (3), for instance, the proposition that 'this place is literally a dump' is not communicated, but its implied meanings that 'this place is untidy', 'this place is smelly', etc. are instead comprehended. The central claim of this implicit account is that literal utterances communicate the propositions expressed by the utterance, as well as implicature; metaphorical utterances, however, do not communicate the proposition, but the implicatures only (Pilkington 2000: 96).

The implicature account, however, is questioned by Carston's *ad hoc* concept account (1997, 2002). While both the implicature account and the *ad hoc* concept account regard metaphoric utterance as a loose use of language, the *ad hoc* concept focuses on the new *ad hoc* concept formed in the comprehension process rather than on the relation between the speaker's thought and the propositional form of an utterance.

The term '*ad hoc* concept' refers to 'concepts that are constructed pragmatically by a hearer in the process of utterance comprehension' (Carston 2002: 322). An *ad hoc* concept is based on a certain lexically encoded concept, but is used to communicate a non-lexicalised concept, which shares a certain elements of its logical and encyclopaedic entries.

(4) Mary is a bulldozer.

In example (4) above, Carston argues, that the lexicalised concept 'bulldozer' is broadened into an *ad hoc* concept BULLDOZER* which contains a contextualised meaning implying certain personality traits of Mary. Once the new *ad hoc* concept BULLDOZER* is formed, the proposition of the utterance 'Mary is a BULLDOZER*' can be communicated explicitly as well. In this sense, metaphorical utterances can convey its propositional form as well as literal utterances.

The *ad hoc* concept account thus suggests a double shift in comprehension processing: from one between proposition expressed and thought communicated to one that is between lexicalised concept and proposition expressed, i.e. thought communicated, and one that from a global relation between whole propositional forms to a local relation between constituent concepts (Carston 2000: 339).

Though different from each other on the issue of communication of the propositional form, the implicature account and the *ad hoc* concept account both take the view that communication (especially metaphorical expressions) is achieved by seeking relevance with the aid of contextual information in discourse. This demonstrates that the problem between meanings and relevance mentioned in Section 2.1 above still remains unsolved. Also, each of the accounts has its own potential problems in analysing metaphoric expressions.

The *ad hoc* concept recognizes a newly constructed metaphoric meaning (the new *ad hoc* concept) in processing a metaphoric expression. Yet by replacing the original concept (e.g. bulldozer) with the *ad hoc* concept (e.g. BULLDOZER*), and used the *ad hoc* concept as the actual proposition being communicated, it seems that the cognitive bond between the original concept and the *ad hoc* concept is lessened, especially when the *ad hoc* concept has been constructed very differently from its original base. Emphasizing the *ad hoc* concept in metaphoric utterances might overlook the interaction between the original source domain (e.g. bulldozer) and the modified source domain, and the newly constructed metaphoric meaning (e.g. BULLDOZER*).

The implicature account sees the modified source domain and the metaphoric meaning largely as a subset of the original concept, i.e. a loose use of the original concept. In the discussion of the emergence and selection of metaphoric meanings, Pilkington (2000) argues that certain salient features or meanings are suggested by the relevant context. However, these 'salient features' do not come with any fixed hierarchy, and different assumptions will become highly salient in different contexts (94-5). This, however, does not provide a cognitive insight into which contextual information is relevant and which meanings are more salient than others. It thus sounds arbitrary to claim that a certain saliency occurs in metaphoric understanding while there is no way to qualify or quantify such a property.

The above discussion so far has shown that the relevance model is a useful pragmatic approach in analysing verbal communication, especially metaphoric utterances. However, problems occur when simply applying the relevance model (either the implicature account or the *ad hoc* concept account) to metaphoric comprehension. It seems that a relatively stable 'starting point' is needed at least in the initial phase of comprehension. Such a 'starting point' can serve as a reliable 'source domain' in comprehending metaphor, and implies a cognitive connection with the newly constructed metaphoric meanings. In the following, I will introduce a salience account proposed by Giora (1997; 1999; 2003), which can work together with the relevance model in analysing metaphoric expressions, especially in a rich context.

## 2.3 A salience approach: graded salience hypothesis

As discussed above, 'salience' can work out well with the relevance model, but a systematic study is needed to exemplify the notion of salience. Giora's graded salience hypothesis provides such an account, where 'salience' is examined and supported by empirical research. In the following, I will briefly review graded salience hypothesis, and suggest an alternative account that combines the notion of salience and relevance together in analysing metaphoric expressions in a rich context.

Giora (1997; 1999; 2003) has been interested in finding out how meaning is processed in comprehension, especially at the initial stage of cognition. Empirical results have shown that there exist 'salient meanings', which are encoded lexical meanings or a word or an expression that are decided by usage frequency, familiarity, conventionality, and prototypicality (Giora 1997, 2003; Giora & Fein 1999). Giora *et al.* further propose graded salience hypothesis, which assumes two parallel approaches at the initial stage of meaning processing: a top-down approach of processing the contextual information, and a bottom-up approach of processing the salient lexical meanings. These two approaches are activated simultaneously in the initial comprehension. Contextual information, however strong and apparent, cannot suppress the contextually inappropriate salient meanings. However, in the subsequent processing stage, salient meanings will be either rejected if interfering with the contextual information, or will be sustained otherwise (even they are contextual-inappropriate).

In the case of cognitive metaphor, Giora et al (Giora 2003; Giora & Fein 1999; Giora & Balaban 2001) have found out that metaphor comprehension varies with its conventionality as well. For conventional metaphor, both literal and metaphorical meanings are salient, and thus will both be activated in the initial phase of processing, regardless of the context. For novel metaphor, however, the literal meaning is still salient and will be activated regardless of the context, the metaphoric meaning is not salient (due to its novelty and thus not lexicalised), and will not be activated in a literally biasing context, but will be activated in a metaphorically biasing context.

Graded salience hypothesis provides a psychologically-based account for cognitive metaphor, especially in the initial phase of processing. The initial activation of salient lexical meanings answers some unsolved questions in the Standard Pragmatic Account, which holds an indirect access view for metaphoric understanding, and in the relevance model, which assumes a direct access to metaphoric meanings without the activation of literal meanings.

Having reviewed these two approaches, the relevance account and graded salience hypothesis, I can now propose an alternative account, which applies both the notion of relevance and salience in analyzing metaphoric expressions. As mentioned above, salient lexical meanings, on the one hand, can be used as a 'starting point' for construction of metaphoric meanings. Relevance, on the other hand, can take into account the contextual information when interpreting metaphors. In Section 3 below, I will illustrate how this alternative account works by emphasizing both relevance and salience. This alternative account will be further applied to analyze a short story, *Chest* (Sell 1994), to demonstrate how the notion of salience and relevance are represented by the use of metaphor.

## 3 An alternative account and its application to a literary text

Sperber & Wilson (1995: 63-4) have mentioned briefly the relationship between relevance and salience ('importance', in their term). They suggest that the more 'important' or 'interesting' the information, the greater the contextual effects, and the more efficient in processing, and hence the greater the relevance.

The notion of 'salience' discussed in this paper, however, is somewhat different from what Sperber & Wilson mean by 'importance', and also different from Pilkington's understanding of 'salience'. In Section 3.1, I will illustrate the version of 'salience' referred in this paper. More importantly, it will be shown that how the notion of 'salience' can be working alongside the relevance model. This salience account will then be applied to one of Will Self's short stories in Section 3.2.

## 3.1 An alternative account: combining salience and relevance

Based on the graded salience hypothesis, the alternative account is salience oriented. This salience account acknowledges the lexical salience proposed in the graded salience hypothesis. (Giora 1997, 2003; Giora & Fein 1999). However, besides applying the notion of lexical salience in discourse processing, the salience model also takes into account salience in contexts, which is closely related to the relevance model. Also, the salience account divides metaphoric processing into the initial phase and subsequent phase. Degrees of conventionality are important in the salience account as well. Furthermore, when put in a discourse level, metaphors can be seen as individual metaphors, group metaphors, and extended metaphors.

In the initial phase of comprehension, a metaphoric expression will be activated with its salient meanings first. These meanings are salient lexical meanings of both the target domain and the source domain. Since the meanings of these two domains may be changed in the processing, I will call them the 'original target domain', and the 'original source domain'. The degree of saliency of these two original domains will be decided by their usage frequency, familiarity, conventionality, and prototypicality/stereotypicality (Giora 1997, 2003; Giora & Fein 1999). Besides the activation of the salient lexical meanings, the salience in contexts will emerge simultaneously from contextual information as well. As argued by Sperber & Wilson (1995: 15), contextual information is not

> 'limited to information about the immediate physical environment or the immediately preceding utterance: expectations about the future, scientific hypothesis or religious beliefs, anecdotal memories, general cultural assumptions, beliefs about the mental state of the speaker, may all pay a role in interpretation.'

Following this argument, contextual information referred to this paper include a more general notion, which contains a wider range of relevant information that concerns the reader's social, cultural knowledge and sense of value, her personal experience and understanding, etc. Besides this general context, contextual information can also have a narrower referent, which occurs in the immediate context in the discourse. In the following analysis, the term 'context', if not pointed out specifically, will be referring to the actual text being processed, i.e., the narrower version of context.

Salience in the context in the initial phase of metaphor comprehension will depend on the overall coherence achieved by contextual information. Generally speaking, the immediate contextual information will be more salient than distant contextual information, considering that the immediate context provides the latest contextual effect on the text processing. It should be noted that the reader's ability and preference will influence the salience in context as well, and this accords with the presumption of optimal relevance (Sperber & Wilson 1995: 267).

In the subsequent stage of processing, salient lexical meanings of the original target domain and source domain will be sustained if they are not interfering with the salience in the context. The sustained salient meanings will then be transferred from the source domain to the target domain for construction of metaphoric meanings. If the metaphoric meanings are further supported by the contextual information, they can be sustained and even develop throughout the text. If there is such a constant development, then the metaphoric meanings may be 'implanted' into the original target domain, which becomes a 'modified target domain'. Such a modified domain accords to Carston's (2002) newly emerged *ad hoc* concept in metaphoric processing.

In the following, I am going to apply this alternative account to analyse a short story written by Will Sell - *Chest* (1994).

### 3.2 Application of the alternative account in literary text

Will Self's short story *Chest* (1994) is chosen here for demonstration because it is a literary text with reasonable level of contextual information for this paper's analytical purpose. More importantly, it is a story that can be read metaphorically. It is not the intention for this paper to provide a new interpretation for this text. Rather, analyzing the text by using a pragmatic and cognitive approach can represent the notion of 'salience' and 'relevance' in discourse processing. Also, the construction of the metaphoric meanings in the text can show us how creativity and metaphoricity are developed in the discourse.

The plot of the story is simple, but the place and characters are unusual. The story takes place in either the contemporary time or the near future when everywhere has been polluted by poisonous fog. People are suffering from respiratory disease and have to wear masks outdoors. Ironically, while people are using high-tech radars to test the movement of the fog, they adopt a Victorian style of life and sense of value, and the distinction of social classes. The protagonist, Simon-Arthur Dykes, is an icon painter. He longs for the redemption of his present life but dies of cancer caused by the fog.

The contextual information of the story has constructed a fictional world for the reader. It is different from our every world in two striking ways: the ever-lasting and poisonous fog, and the life style of the characters. Detailed descriptions have been given of the dangerous fog, the pretentious and affectless manner of the characters, people's constant cough, and even sputum on the street. While this rather strange world reminds the reader of the fictionality of the story, it creates an easily accessed analogy between itself and our present world. Like many other fictional narratives, this story evokes a general contextual effect in the reading process as well. In the light of the relevance model, fictions can be relevant to a reader if truth of the output is what matters (Sperber & Wilson, 1995: 265).

Echoing the contextual information, the text is abundant in metaphoric expressions, from individual metaphors to group metaphors and extended metaphors. One of the pervasive group metaphors is 'sputum metaphor' which will be discussed in detail below (Self 1994: 127):

> The pavement outside Marten's the newsagent was streaked with sputum. In the outrageously dull light of a mid-afternoon, in midwinter, in middle England, the loops and lumps of mucus and phlegm appeared strangely bright, lurid even, as if some Jackson Pollock of the pneumo-thorax had been practising Action Hawking.

This is the very first paragraph in the story, telling the reader the time, place, and some first impression of the fictional world. There are several conventional metaphors in this paragraph (e.g '…the newsagent was *streaked* with sputum', and 'in the outrageously *dull* light of'). These conventional metaphors, as discussed in Section 2.3, have the salient metaphorical meanings and can been understood without much support from the context. However, a novel metaphor in this paragraph should draw the reader's attention:

> (5)…the loops and lumps of mucus and phlegm appeared strangely bright, lurid even, as if some Jackson Pollock of the penumo-thorax had been practising Action Hawking.

This metaphor has the original target domain 'sputum', and the original source domain 'Jackson Pollock's action painting'. The salient contextual information, i.e., the immediate context in the first sentence, has told the reader that sputum can be seen everywhere. In the metaphor itself, the salient lexical meanings of the original target domain, 'sputum', have been indicated by words such as 'lumps', 'mucus' that indicate the shape and status of the domain. Other words modifying the target domain, e.g. 'bright', 'lurid', describe other properties of the sputum (or phlegm), such as the object's light and colour. These properties mentioned by the modifiers are coherent with the salience lexical meanings of sputum and phlegm. Even applied to a wider context, these properties can still easily fit in the reader's mental image of sputum and phlegm, which is quite a negative one. However, the original source domain, Jackson Pollock's painting, may very likely arouse a positive feeling. Consider Jackson Pollock's action painting is a well-known style and the word 'practising' has indicated a certain kind of exercising, the salient meaning of the source domain should be the style of action painting, an artistic performance.

The initial activation of salient meanings in the context and in both of the original metaphoric domains, however, is not yet sufficient to account for the metaphoric meanings. The metaphoric mapping takes place in the subsequent processing stage when the salient meanings in the original source domain are transferred to the original target domain, which is therefore modified accordingly. It should be noted that not all the transfer of salient meanings from the original source domain will make a change in the original target domain. Some of the meaning transfer can enhance rather than alter the target domain, and some transfer can be rejected if it is impossible or inappropriate for the target domain to be accommodated in the context.

In the subsequent processing stage, the salient meanings, such as 'action painting', 'heavy and thick paint pouring', 'the use of colour and light', 'artistic' and 'aesthetic', etc., are transferred from the original source domain to the original target domain. Some of these can be matched to the salient meanings of the target domain, and others are new to the target domain. 'The use of colour and light', for example, can be matched with the properties of 'bright' and 'lurid' in the original target domain, and enhance the comparability between the two domains. The action of 'painting' is invited to match the action of 'hawking' by the expression of 'Jackson Pollock of the penumo-thorax had been practising...' which emphasizes the action and its result (or production). It should be noted that the concept of 'Action Hawking' is a newly constructed one, and can be interpreted as an *ad hoc* concept according to Carston's account (2002). When applying the alternative account here, I am inclined to regard this new concept as a modified target domain, which is still closely related to the original target domain. Another important transferred meaning is the positive evaluation of Jackson Pollock's painting into the original target domain, where negative evaluation is dominant. Given the salient meanings of 'sputum' and 'phlegm' in both of the immediate context and a wider context are negative, the positive transferred meaning cannot override this tendency, but can create a sense of irony and sarcasm, which echoes the weak implicatures of the relevance model (Pilkington 2000).

Overall, the use of metaphor in the first paragraph of the story has constructed a salient meaning – sputum displayed in the street in an 'artistic' way. When the reading process moves on to the following text, it can be seen that this metaphorically modified domain 'sputum' sustains its newly transferred meaning, and further interacts with other metaphorically modified domains such as 'cough' and 'fog' (Self 1994: 129-33):

> (6) Soon, both of the men were hacking away, producing great caribou-cry honks, followed by the rasping eructation of tablespoon-loads of sputum, which they dumped, along with the rest of the infective matter, on the pavement fronting the newsagent's.

> (7) Darkness was coming; and with it the great bank of fog, that had hung two hundred feed above the ground all day, was beginning to descend, falling around the shoulders of the grey stone houses like some malodorous muffler.

> (8) As he pulled out and drove off down the road Simon-Arthur avoided looking at the fog too closely. He knew from experience that if he peered into it for too long, actually concentrated on its twistings, its eddies, its endless assumptions of insubstantial form, that it could all too easily draw him down a darkling corridor, into more durable, more horribly solid visions.

The above examples are metaphoric usage from the 'cough metaphor' and 'fog metaphor', which are grouped by different metaphoric target domains. Example (5) and many other metaphors in the story have described the characters' cough in detail. One striking effect of these descriptions is that coughing and spitting have become a common social act, which can be done by decent characters in public without feeling ashamed. This accords to the 'sputum metaphor' described in the beginning of the story. In such a fictional world, it is possible to regard sputum in an artistic way, and therefore the metaphorically modified concept can be sustained in such a context. This deformed version of 'sputum' and 'cough' is caused by the poisonous 'fog' (Example (8)), which is dangerous and seducing. The protagonist Simon-Arthur is finally killed by such 'fog'.

Throughout the text, the reader can experience the development of the key concepts in a metaphorical way. Key concepts, such as sputum, cough, fog, treatment, etc., while constructed and modified as target domains in individual and group metaphors, can serve as source domains for extended metaphors that are built upon the overall contextual information of the story. Sputum and cough, for example, are symptoms of respiratory disease, and they can also be seen as symptoms of the whole society which is decaying and dying. The concept of fog is the source of contamination, and it is also the unseen social environment which is suffocating and dangerous for people who live within it. Simon-Arthur's failure to find treatment is an individual tragedy, but it can also be interpreted as the failure of the society and humanity. Though the modification or alternation of these concepts may be large, the salient meanings, such as suffering, dysfunction, contaminating, suffocating, dangerous, and failure, etc. are transferred from one domain to another, and are implanted in the modified domains according to the relevant contexts.

It seems that the analysis of the text by using the alternative account proposed in Section 2.3 and 3.1 can provide with us a better understanding of the emergence and development of salient and relevant meanings in metaphoric expressions. This alternative account emphasizes the initial activation of salient lexical meanings of the original metaphoric domains, and illustrates how these salient meanings are transferred and implanted from the source domain to the target domain for the construction of a new metaphoric meaning (i.e. the *ad hoc* concept). Furthermore, the alternative account explains how contextual information takes effect in metaphoric processing, and how a series of weak implicatures are created in the reading process. As it is put by Pilkington (2000: 102-4), the expressive power and aesthetic force of metaphor depends on 'the spontaneous, rapid way in which implicatures are processed', and a theory of value is suggested by the idea that creativity and metaphoricity can be described in terms of the communication of a wide array of implicatures. The strength of the relevance model, as has been argued in this paper, can be enhanced by combining the notion of salience when dealing with metaphoric expression in a rich context.

## 4 Summary

In this paper, I have reviewed the relevance model for its pragmatic stand and cognitive insight. Yet when analysing metaphoric expressions, I have argued that neither the implicature account nor the *ad hoc* concept account can be served as a sufficient approach alone in revealing the construction of metaphoric meanings. In order to solve this problem, I further review the graded salience hypothesis, and suggest that a resolution can be made by combining the relevance model with the salience account.

This alternative account has been illustrated in the analysis of Will Self's story *Chest*. It is shown that the alternative account can trace the development of a certain salient and relevant meanings in the discourse context. One important point that has been made in this paper is that a pragmatic and cognitive account can help us understand better how our cognitive system works in comprehending and interpreting figurative language, especially cognitive metaphor in a literary context.

## References

Carston, Robyn. 2002. *Thoughts and Utterances: The Pragmatics of Explicit Communications*. Oxford: Blackwell.

Carston, Robyn. 1997. 'Enrichment and Loosening: Complementary Processes and Deriving the Proposition Expressed' in *Linguistische Berichte* 8: 103-27.

Chafe, Wallace. 1987. 'Cognitive Constraints on Information Flow' in Tomlin, Russell. (ed.) *Coherence and Grounding Discourse*. Amsterdam: John Benjamins: 21-51.

Fauconnier, Gilles, and Mark Turner. 2002. *The Way We Think*. New York: Basic Books.

Gibbs, Raymond. 1984. 'Literal Meaning and Psychological Theory' in *Cognitive Science* 8: 275-304.

Gibbs, Raymond. 1994. *The Poetics of Mind: Figurative Thought, Language, and Understanding*. Cambridge: Cambridge University Press.

Giora, Rachel. 1997. 'Understanding Figurative and Literal Language: The Graded Salience Hypothesis' in *Cognitive Linguistics* 7: 183-206.

Giora, Rachel. 1999. 'On the Priority of Salient Meanings: Studies of Literal and Figurative Language' in *Journal of Pragmatics* 31: 919-29.

Giora, Rachel. 2003. *On Our Mind*. Oxford: Oxford University Press.

Giora, Rachel, and Noga Balaban. 2001. 'Lexical Access in Text Production: On the Role of Salience in Metpahor Resonance' in Sanders, T., J. Schilperoord, and W. Spooren (eds). *Text Representation*. Amsterdam: John Benjamins: 111-24.

Giora, Rachel, and Ofer Fein. 1999. 'On Understanding Familiar and Less-Familiar Figurative Language' in *Journal of Pragmatics* 31: 1601-618.

Grice, Paul. 1989. *Studies in the Ways of Words*. Cambridge, MA: Harvard University Press.

Lakoff, George. 1990. *Women, Fire, and Dangerous Things, What Categories Reveal About the Mind*. Chicago: University of Chicago Press.

Lakoff, George, and Mark Johnson. 1980. *Metaphors We Live By*. Chicago: University of Chicago Press.

Pilkington, Adrian. 2000. *Poetic Effects: A Relevance Theory Perspective*. Amsterdam: John Benjamins.

Self, Will. 1994. 'Chest' in *Grey Area*. London: Penguin Books:125-64.

Sperber, Dan, and Deirdre Wilson. 1986. *Relevance: Communication and Cognition*. Oxford: Blackwell.

Sperber, Dan, and Deirdre Wilson. 1995. *Relevance: Communication and Cognition* (2nd ed.). Oxford: Blackwell.

Wilson, Deirdre, and Dan Sperber. 2003. 'Relevance Theory' in Horn, Laurence, and Gregory Ward (eds). *Handbook of Pragmatics*. Oxford: Basil Blackwell: 607-32.

# Challenging our World View: The Role of Metaphors in the Construction of a New (Text) World

María Dolores Porto Requejo

## Abstract

This paper analyses how a text world is built, how it relates to the cognitive and cultural models of the real world and the role of metaphors in this construction. Because the processes by which we construct worlds, whether real or fictional, are automatic, we are usually unaware of them, but the construction of a fantastic text world, where the usual cognitive, cultural and social models do not apply, will allow us to evidence the role of metaphors in that construction. In order to do, several metaphors from a Fantasy novel are collected and analysed so that the *megametaphor* and the most basic image schema underlying the text are revealed. Finally, the question will be addressed of whether the final representation of the text world reinforces or refreshes the readers' previous schemas of knowledge and so affects their perspective on and their interpretation of the real world.

Keywords: text worlds, metaphor, megametaphor, schema refreshment, magic, fantasy.

## 1 Introduction

Whenever we read a text, we get a mental representation of it. This representation is not just a static image and does not include only visual elements. In fact, it is more like a complex conceptualization of how things go and happen in the text, i.e. it is a text world.

Obviously, there is much of the real world in a text world. We rely on our knowledge of reality to fill the gaps of anything that is not specified in the text. Some text worlds are mimetic to the real one, others are as different as possible from what we know and they require a bigger cognitive effort to be constructed. Finally, some text worlds challenge our view of reality and force the readers to pay attention to some values and truths they used to take for granted. The effects of this challenging are usually temporary and are only active for the time of the reading, but sometimes the changes in the readers' conceptual system may be permanent and so they can acquire a different perspective on the world they know.

This paper analyses how a text world is built, how it relates to the cognitive and cultural models of the real world and the role of metaphors in this construction. Metaphors are a powerful tool to interpret reality, and also a powerful tool to understand new ideas and concepts in terms of what we already know well. However, most of the metaphors we live by are unconsciously learned and convey the conventional cultural models in the community of speakers that use them. Consequently, the creation of new metaphors in a text can produce significant, even if transitory, changes on the way we perceive and understand the world around us.

The processes by which we build a text world are the same ones we follow to construct the real world, since all worlds 'are the product of our mental processes, even those which we think of as very real and concrete'. (Werth 1995: 49). Because we are mostly unaware of these processes, I have chosen a Fantasy novel for the present analysis. In Fantasy, everything we know about the real world –science, economics, social rules, etc. – does not apply and so the readers of the novel must make an additional effort in order to construct the specific world presented by the author. This way, the strategies employed to construe the novel metaphors and to interpret the text are more demanding and so more evident than those in a realistic world.

The title of the novel is *Forging the Darksword* (Weis & Hickman 1988), and it is the first volume of a trilogy: *The Darksword*. It is one of those stories of *sword and sorcery* that take place in an imaginary world inhabited by fantastic creatures like dragons, wizards, faeries... This novel in particular depicts a fantastic place called *Thimhallan*, where magic, and not science, rules. Everybody in this world is born with some magical powers, and they are assigned their position in society depending on the amount and the sort of magic they are born with. To decide on this point, there is a religious ceremony held after birth, a sort of baptism, in which all babies must pass some tests. Depending on the results of the tests, the child will become a wizard of one kind or another (a healer, a warrior, a craftsman, an enforcer, an artist...). However, one day a baby fails all tests, which is absolutely abnormal because that means that he has been born without any magic in him. In this world of wizards, living without any magical powers is impossible and the birth of this child is seen as a threat for the harmony of this magic world.

In the following sections, I will first examine text worlds and how they are constructed and then I will consider the role of metaphors in the interpretation of both real and fictional worlds. Next, I will analyze some of the main metaphors in the novel, namely those that compose the concept of MAGIC, to see how they contribute to the process of text world construction in the novel. Those metaphors will eventually be reduced to the *megametaphor* (Werth 1994, 1999) that runs through the whole text, as megametaphors 'represent the most prototypical and primitive frames in our culture and are the basic building-blocks of our world-view' (Werth 1994: 101). Once the text world has been constructed, we will consider if the final representation of the text can affect our view of the real world.

## 2 Text worlds

'Text processing is also "world creating"' (Hidalgo 2000: 12). This world creation is not only part of the reading process but is its final aim. Paul Werth defined a discourse as 'a deliberate and joint effort on the part of the producer and the recipient(s) to build up a world within which the propositions advanced are coherent and make sense' (Werth 1999: 51). Therefore, the reader of a text is an active part of the process, as he/she must collect the 'clues' given by the text and combine them with his/her previous knowledge in order to create the world evoked by the text.

It would be impossible to provide all the necessary information to create a world in a single text, apart from the evident difficulty of conceiving a world that is completely brand-new. Thus, when reading a text, we follow the principle of *minimal departure* (Ryan 1991), that is, everything that is not explicit on the contrary must be assumed to be the same as in the real world. This applies to physical features of the world as much as to the social values and cultural models.

This is also the way we manage our knowledge about the real world. We cope with everyday situations in terms of fixed structures derived from past experiences and cultural models that have been extensively studied as *frames* (Fillmore 1985), *schemata* (Rumelhart 1980), *scripts* (Schank & Abelson 1977), *Idealised Cognitive Models* (Lakoff 1987). And whenever a deviation of the expected *script* or *frame* takes place, we make the necessary adjustments on it to fit the new situation.

Similarly, when constructing a text world, we interpret anything that is not overtly different as being the same as in the real world. So our mental representation of the text world starts with an exact copy of the real world on which, during the reading, we make all the required changes as indicated by the text. Elena Semino explains the process in the following way:

> The particular circumstances where an expectation failure occurs must contribute to determine whether we ignore it completely, we take note of it pending further evidence, or we incorporate it immediately within an existing schema (Semino 1997: 145)

This involves a sort of permanent comparison between fictional and real worlds. So, even if we virtually place ourselves in the fictional world, our cultural models and everything we know about reality is still partially active at the background, and there is a continuous flow of projections between both domains. This permanent comparison will have significant consequences for potential *schema refreshment* (Cook 1994) in our conceptual system, that is, for our habitual perspective on the real world.

As stated above, the reader of a text must combine this previous knowledge of the world with the elements provided by the text for the text world construction, namely deictic and referential elements (Werth 1999).

As regards the first, the deictic elements of the text, it must be said that, among the features of the genre of Fantasy is the fact that time and space in these stories are usually undetermined. Most of the time it is impossible to decide if the story takes place in a remote past, an imaginary future, or even in a sort of parallel reality in the present time. Nor is it always possible to determine if it happens on the earth, a distant galaxy or just some magical world inhabited by fantastic creatures. So, deictic elements are not so relevant in the genre.

Consequently, it is usually the referential elements that shape a fantastic text world. In Fantasy, there are always new concepts that must be acquired by readers, for this reason, neologisms and neosemes are typical of the genre, as they are also in science-fiction (Stockwell 2000). Another way to introduce new concepts in a text world, and a very powerful one indeed, is by taking advantage of what we already know and project it on the new reality presented by the text, that is, by means of metaphorical projections.

We will now see how metaphors can introduce new referents into a text world, in particular, how they can explain an important concept for this novel, MAGIC, and eventually how what we learn about MAGIC in the text world can affect our view of the real world.

### 3 The metaphors of Fantasy

One of the mechanisms we use to interpret reality is the metaphor. In the last 20 years there has been extensive research investigating how metaphorical projections allow us to understand abstract concepts in term of physical entities (Lakoff & Johnson 1980; Lakoff & Turner 1989; Sweetser 1990; Kövecses 2000). Typical examples are concepts like LIFE that we can understand in terms of A JOURNEY, A FLAME, or A FLUID.

Mark Johnson (1987) claims that anything beyond our physical experience can only be apprehended metaphorically. Therefore, we make use of metaphors to understand not only abstract concepts, but also anything we cannot experience directly. Any novel (i.e. new), difficult concepts are better comprehended in terms of something else we know well. For example, we commonly conceptualize ELECTRICITY as a FLUID running through the wires as if they were pipes (Gentner & Gentner 1983).

Most of the metaphors that constitute our cognitive system have been acquired unquestioned and they reflect the cultural models of a specific community of speakers, e.g. MORE IS BETTER or TIME IS MONEY (Lakoff & Johnson 1980: 22; As is the convention in cognitive metaphor theory, small capitals are used here to indicate conceptual metaphors). For this reason, unconventional metaphors can provide a different perspective on the world around us. Also, new concepts are better introduced through metaphors so that they are assimilated in an automatic way, almost unnoticed. In Lakoff and Johnson's words 'much of our cultural change arises from the introduction of new metaphorical concepts' (Lakoff & Johnson 1980: 145; regarding the understanding of new concepts through novel metaphors, see the metaphors that shape the concept INTERNET in Porto Requejo, in press). Consequently, creating new metaphors may result in 'new ways of understanding the world' (Lakoff & Turner 1989: 203).

In the novel we are dealing with, it seems obvious that MAGIC is the most important referent, since everything in this text world has to do with it. It is a basic concept to interpret the novel, but it is also a concept we do not know much about from our own experience, even if we are devoted readers of the genre, because magic works differently in every fantastic world. For this reason, readers will need a number of metaphors to learn what MAGIC is and how it works in this particular story (for a more extensive analysis of the metaphors that shape the concept MAGIC in this novel, see also Porto Requejo, 2003). In fact, because the concept is so central for the story, the novel provides a large number of metaphors to construct the concept from different perspectives. The more complex and important a concept is, the more metaphors are required to understand it, as evidenced by the number of metaphors by which we comprehend the most central concepts in our world like LIFE, DEATH, LOVE (Lakoff & Turner 1989: 18). So, depending on the aspect highlighted at a particular moment, a different metaphor will be employed to refer the concept MAGIC in the novel. For example, MAGIC IS ELECTRICITY can help us understand how it works, whereas MAGIC IS LIFE will evidence how precious it is in this fictional world.

These metaphors are evidenced in the metaphorical expressions on the surface of the text and we probably are not very aware of the way we process them. In the following lines, I will present some of the metaphors that shape the concept MAGIC for the present text world through the surface metaphorical expressions. (The numbers in brackets indicate the page of the quotation in the novel and all the italics are mine to highlight the expressions that reveal the underlying metaphor).

### 3.1 MAGIC IS A MATERIAL POSSESSION

(1) Field Magi are allowed only *enough* of the catalyst's transference of magical Life force to work efficiently, the reason for this being that magi have *the ability to store this Life force* within them and *use it whenever they need.* (74)

This sentence reveals that MAGIC is conceptualized as a measurable physical entity and people can possess more or less of it. Therefore, it becomes a valuable commodity that can be spent, transferred, stored, saved, wasted, etc.

## 3.2 MAGIC IS A FLUID

(2) Drawing a deep breath, Saryon summoned the magic The catalyst felt it *flow into his body, filling him* with the Enchantment and, at the same time, demanding an outlet. (350)

(3) Magic *flowed through him* like blood from an open vein and then he was *empty, drained.* (217)

(4) The magic of the world *flows through them like wine*, they live in a constant state of *intoxication*. Neither rules nor morals govern their actions; no conscience guides them. (201)

These examples present MAGIC as a FLUID that can flow through conduits, fill up a container, be drained. Also, the conventional metaphor THE HUMAN BODY IS A CONTAINER is adopted in this fictional world, so that magic can fill a human body as if it were blood, for instance. As a matter of fact, there are also examples in the story that specify this metaphor further as MAGIC IS WINE or MAGIC IS BLOOD as evidenced in (3) and (4).

## 3.3 MAGIC IS ELECTRICITY

(5) The conduit of magic, normally not visible to the eye, *flared brilliantly* between the two of them, *arcing with a blinding white light* as, with a motion of her hand, the Empress sent the Bishop flying backward five feet in the air. [...]. *Words of magic crackled.* [...] "Never! Get out!" she shrieked, her voice *searing like the heat of the fire.* (13)

ELECTRICITY is something we know well from our experience, even if we do not know exactly what it is in strict scientific terms. We know it flows through conduits, but it is not usually visible unless an overflow makes the cable flare or an accident produce some sparks. We also know that electricity makes it possible to move objects at a distance as it happens with a remote control or have effects at a distance, as when switching on a light. Much of what we know about ELECTRICITY is projected onto MAGIC, and so we learn that MAGIC also flows through conduits, is usually invisible, but can be visible as it happens in a lightning or a voltaic arch, that it can produce sparks and a sound of crackling... As a result, we can agree that MAGIC, like ELECTRICITY, provides light and heat, can move objects at a distance, etc.

### 3.4 MAGIC IS LIFE

This is the most important metaphor in the story, to the point that both terms *magic* and *life* become synonyms in this text. MAGIC, like LIFE, is a sort of latent energy that can be found anywhere around us (7), it is also a divine gift (8) and also the same as with LIFE, those who lack MAGIC are dead (9).

> (6) But, as their feet touched the ground, *the people felt the magic stirring and beating* beneath them, *like a living heart. They could feel it, sense it*; (26)
>
> (7) *Life, the magic, comes from all around us,* from the ground we walk, the air we breathe, the living things that grow to serve us ... (139)
>
> (8) *You* have *the Gift of Life.* Thank the Almin! Some are born without it. Therefore, be *grateful for this gift* and use it wisely, never wishing for more than you have been blessedly allotted. (19)
>
> (9) *I am Dead. Truly Dead. No magic stirs within me* at all, less than what is in a corpse, if we believe the legends of the ancient Necromancers, who were able to communicate with the souls of the dead." (310)

In fact many of the other metaphors can be considered as mere elaborations of this one, since we also conceive that LIFE IS A POSSESSION, LIFE IS A FLUID that fills the body and runs through the veins, and even LIFE IS ELECTRICITY, as we use expressions like *the spark of life*.

### 3.5 MAGIC IS LIGHT

As a result of the projection MAGIC IS ELECTRICITY; we have already seen that it provides light and heat. But the metaphor goes further and so everything related with magic is light and brilliant, whereas anything that lacks magic, namely handmade instruments, is dark. Thus, when someone in the story forges a sword using his hands and not by magical means, it is not a bright glowing sword, but the *darksword* appearing on the title of the novel.

> (10) At last they found it, the source of the magic —a mountain whose fire had burned out, *leaving the magic behind to glow like a diamond* beneath the bright, unfamiliar sun. (26)
>
> (11) The *metal did not gleam*. It was a *streak of darkness* slashing through the moonlight, as though Joram held the embodiment of night. (379)

### 3.6 MAGIC IS THE NATURAL ORDER (and TECHNOLOGY IS CHAOS)

In the world of *Thimhallan*, magic rules. It is something natural and everybody is gifted with it from their birth. Only those unable to use magic must resort to the use of instruments, i.e. TECHNOLOGY, which is considered a dark art, something unnatural, against the laws of nature:

> (12) Everything that exists in this land exists *either by the will of the Almin*, who placed it here before even the ancients arrived, *or has since been either "shaped, formed, summoned, or conjured,"* these being the four Laws of Nature. (23)

> (13) "You mean *the Dark Arts are nothing more than using sticks to move stones*? From the way everybody fears them, I thought they must at least sacrifice babies —" "Don't talk like that, Joram," Mosiah remonstrated in hushed tones, glancing about nervously. *"They deny the magic. They deny Life*. By their Dark Arts, *they would destroy it*. (107)

As a consequence, there are also a number of metaphors that shape the concept of TECHNOLOGY in this text world, namely the opposite metaphors to those that develop the concept of MAGIC. And so we can find in the text that TECHNOLOGY IS DEATH, TECHNOLOGY IS DARKNESS (14), TECHNOLOGY IS CHAOS…

> (14) Saryon was surprised he recalled the illustrations with such clarity, having told himself repeatedly that these were *tools of darkness, instruments of Death*. (347)

These are just some of the metaphors that develop the concepts of MAGIC and TECHNOLOGY in the novel *Forging the Darksword*. In fact, the total number may vary depending on the level of abstraction we decide to get to. Some of these metaphors can be further specified, as is the case of MAGIC IS A FLUID, which can be considered at a subordinate level as MAGIC IS A FLUID INSIDE THE BODY, MAGIC IS BLOOD, MAGIC IS WINE. Or else, we can go up to higher levels of abstraction and take into account more ontological metaphors like MAGIC IS A MEASURABLE SUBSTANCE.

## 4 The Megametaphor

During the reading of the novel, we have acquired a quite definite idea of what MAGIC is and how it works, and at the same time, we have made up a complex mental representation of this fantastic world where magic is essential, as much as life is. But, according to Paul Werth (1994, 1999), the obvious surface metaphors in a text can combine to point to a compelling subliminal message, which is not explicit in the linguistic expressions (1994: 85). So there is a *megametaphor* underlying the whole text, a metaphor that already belongs to our conceptual system, on which we unconsciously rely to interpret the text world, and which makes the text world credible for the reader since it is automatically processed and remits to the same conceptual system by which we interpret reality.

It is quite straightforward, as can be seen from the metaphors collected in the previous section, that all the source domains of the metaphors that build the concept of MAGIC are positive, whereas those that construct the concept of TECHNOLOGY are negative, that is, they all involve the lack of something. As Kövecses (2000) puts it 'good things in general (like life) are metaphorically UP, LIGHT, WARM and VALUABLE, while bad things (like death) are DOWN, DARK, COLD and maybe also NONVALUABLE'(Kövecses 2000: 44). Thus, the opposition between MAGIC and TECHNOLOGY comes to a very basic one in our world, the one between LIFE and DEATH, POSITIVE and NEGATIVE, or the opposition between GOOD and EVIL. As a result, we can reduce all the metaphors to MAGIC IS GOOD / TECHNOLOGY IS EVIL. This opposition reflects the main theme of the novel. As a matter of fact, this is also the main theme of the Fantasy genre, the fight between Good and Evil, only this time, the opposition takes the form of Magic versus Technology.

Still, we can go even further. If MAGIC IS *GOOD* and MAGIC IS *ORDER*, we can conclude that ORDER IS GOOD. Similarly, if TECHNOLOGY IS *EVIL* and TECHNOLOGY IS *CHAOS*, it is quite obvious that CHAOS IS BAD. These two metaphors, ORDER IS GOOD and CHAOS IS EVIL, are not specific for this fictional world, but quite common in our conceptual system. They do reflect the way in which we perceive the world. Also, they both are very basic ones in the sense that they derive from our physical experience, from the BALANCE schema (on the reduction of the metaphors of a text to a basic image schema, see the work by Freeman (1993) on *King Lear*). Consider, for instance, that we often speak of a *physical disorder* or even a *mental disorder* to mean a disease, that is, everything in its place is good, and anything that threatens that order is bad and must be suffocated.

We must conclude, then, that ORDER IS GOOD (and its due opposite CHAOS IS EVIL) is the *megametaphor*:

> [Megametaphors] appear to be close to the primal metaphors of our conceptual life, since they represent the most prototypical and primitive frames in our culture and are the basic building-blocks of our world-view. Because they are so fundamental, their origins presumably go back many generations; they are often, in modern terms, far from "politically correct"…

Nevertheless they covertly underlie much of our everyday language and thinking (Werth 1999, 328)

## 5 The challenge to our world view

The text world of *Forging the Darksword* is fantastic. Apparently there is nothing in it that resembles the real one, as it lacks everything that is common for us: industry, science, technology. However, we have just seen that it is based on the very same schemas as the real world. Both in *Thimhallan* and in our experience of the world, ORDER IS GOOD and CHAOS IS EVIL. There is only a surface minor difference, i.e. in the text world, MAGIC takes the place that TECHNOLOGY has in the real world. We can then assume that under an apparent reversal of these two concepts, the text world is quite conventional after all, as the megametaphor used to interpret both of them is but the same. Thus, there seems to be a *schema reinforcing* effect after the reading of the novel. As Elena Semino points out:

> ...insofar as metaphorical connections exploit obvious or conventionally accepted similarities between two different domains, they will reinforce the readers' existing knowledge and contribute to the creation of a text world that the readers recognize as conventional and familiar; on the other hand, insofar as metaphorical connections lead to the attribution of new properties to the tenor domain, they will challenge and potentially refresh the readers' existing sets of beliefs and assumptions, and contribute to the creation of a text world that the readers will perceive as unconventional and novel. (Semino 1997: 197)

However, as the plot advances, the reader will find out that the real threat for the magic of this fictional world comes from the magic itself. The newborn child who lacked any magical powers is considered by the inhabitants of *Thimhallan* as a threat for their harmonious world, an element that can disrupt balance and bring about chaos. But this child will grow up to become the hero of the novel, the one who will save the fictional world from destruction by using an instrument, the *darksword*, instead of magic. He would save *Thimhallan* not only form chaos but from an 'excess of order'.

The conventional metaphors that the reader was drawing on from experience for the interpretation of the text are later belied by the text itself and so, ORDER, the usual state of affairs, the authority, IS EVIL, whereas CHAOS, regarded as the subverting elements introduced in the text world, IS GOOD. This way, the readers' schemas have been eventually challenged, at least for the scope of the reading.

In conclusion, we have seen that the role of metaphors in the construction of text worlds has to do with the connection between previous knowledge schemas of the world and the schemas presented by the text, and also that the potential for *schema refreshing* in a text world can be developed by metaphors. Nonetheless, whether the changes in the conceptual system are permanent or not will depend heavily on every individual reader and his/her previous experience and knowledge background (Semino 1997: 213). It is possible that only those who had already suspected that the conventional metaphor ORDER IS GOOD may not apply for all situations are ready to accept the challenge.

## References

Cook, Guy. 1994. *Discourse and Literature*. Oxford: Oxford University Press.

Fillmore, Charles J. 1985. 'Frames and semantics of understanding' in *Quaderni di Semantica* 6(2): 222-54.

Freeman, Donald C. 1993 '"According to my Bond": *King Lear* and Recognition' in *Language and Literature* 2(1): 1-18.

Gentner, Dedre, and Donald R. Gentner. 1983. 'Flowing waters or Teeming Crowds: Mental Models of Electricity' in Gentner, Dedre and Albert L. Stevens (eds). *Mental Model*. Hillsdale, NJ: Lawrence Erlbaum Associates: 99-129.

Hidalgo Downing, Laura. 2000. *Negation, Text Worlds and Discourse: The Pragmatics of Fiction*. Stamford, CT: Ablex Publishing Co.

Johnson, Mark. 1987. *The Body in the Mind*. Chicago: University of Chicago Press.

Kövecses, Zoltan. 2000. *Metaphor and Emotion Language*. Cambridge: Cambridge University Press.

Lakoff, George. 1987. *Women Fire and Dangerous Things What Categories Reveal about the Mind*. Chicago: University of Chicago Press

Lakoff, George, and Mark Johnson. 1980. *Metaphors We Live by*. Chicago: University of Chicago Press.

Lakoff, George, and Mark Turner. 1989. *More than Cool Reason*. Chicago: University of Chicago Press.

Porto Requejo, M. Dolores. 2003. 'Del Significado de la Palabra a la Interpretación del Texto: ¿Qué es la Magia?' in *Annual Review of Cognitive Linguistics* 1. Amsterdam. John Benjamins: 121-37.

Porto Requejo, M. Dolores. (in press) 'The Construction of the Concept INTERNET through Metaphors' in *Language, Culture and Representation.*

Rumelhart, David E. 1980. 'Schemata: The building blocks of cognition' in Spiro, Rand J., Bertram C. Bruce and William F. Brewer (eds). *Theoretical Issues in Reading Comprehension: Perspectives from Cognitive Psychology, Linguistics, Artificial Intelligence and Education.* Hillsdale, NJ: Lawrence Erlbaum Associates: 33-85.

Ryan, Marie-Laure. 1991. *Possible Worlds, Artificial Intelligence and Narrative Theory.* Bloomington: Indiana University Press.

Schank Roger C. and Robert P. Abelson. 1977. *Scripts, Plans, Goals and Understanding.* Hillsdale, NJ.: Lawrence Erlbaum Associates.

Semino, Elena. 1997. *Language and World Creation in Poems and Other Texts.* London: Longman.

Stockwell, Peter. 2000. *The Poetics of Science Fiction.* London: Longman.

Sweetser, Eve. 1990. *From Etymology to Pragmatics.* Cambridge: Cambridge University Press.

Weis Margaret, and Tracey Hickman. 1988. *Forging the Darksword.* New York: Bantam Books.

Werth, Paul. 1994. 'Extended Metaphor. A Text World Account' in *Language and Literature* 3(2): 79-103.

Werth, Paul. 1995. 'How to Build a Text World (In a Lot Less than Six Days, and Using Only What Is in Your Head)' in Green, K (ed.). *New Essays on Deixis: Discourse, Narrative, Literature.* Amsterdam: Rodopi: 49-80.

Werth, Paul. 1999. *Text Worlds: Representing Conceptual Space in Discourse.* London: Longman.

# The Attraction of Opposites: The Ideological Function of Conventional and Created Oppositions in the Construction of In-groups and Out-groups in News Texts

## Matt Davies

## Abstract

This article seeks to investigate the relationship between binary opposites (such as 'us/them') and news values as instantiated in the British press. Opposites can range from the canonical ('young/old') to the unconventional ('placard/banner'). Identification of these latter, textually specific oppositions requires the recognition of a variety of syntactic frameworks, identified by Jones (2002), which generate oppositions such as 'X not Y' and either X or Y', where X and Y are each of a pair of oppositional words or phrases. I have utilised and added to these categories of frames to show how unusual oppositions - in a *Sunday Mirror* report of the February 2003 London demonstration against war in Iraq - combine rhetorically to construct groups of protestors as 'acceptable' and 'unacceptable' (e.g. 'dad' and 'traitor' respectively) in the value system of the writer and hence reinforce group stereotypes for the reader. Oppositions are simultaneously used to show the wide range of 'ordinary' protestors to give legitimacy to the demonstration. I conclude with an exploration of some of the wider ideological implications of artificially representing the world as if there were 'no shades of grey' and drawing on Chibnall (1977) and Fowler (1991) discuss some typical news values these oppositions exemplify.

Keywords: binary opposites; consensus; ideology; media values; mutual exclusivity; newspapers; syntactic frames.

## 1 Introduction

My aim in this article is to investigate the role of oppositions in news reports, specifically in the UK national press. By *oppositions* I mean words or phrases treated as contrasting pairs, often binary opposites, within specific contexts. I will explore how conventional oppositions (such as **young** and **old**[1]), can be combined with unusual textually specific ones (for instance **dad** and **traitor**) in ways which can construct participants in news events as belonging to mutually exclusive groups. This will involve a brief re-evaluation of theories of opposites (sometimes called *antonyms* depending on the investigator), a consideration of methods for recognising the textual generation of oppositional pairs, and an analysis of a news article that reports a major news event in contemporary Britain - the 2003 'Stop the War Coalition' demonstration in London against war in Iraq. I will argue that a major function of this article is not only to report on the demonstration but also to orientate the reader towards differentiating between two specific groups of demonstrators - those represented as legitimate, moderate and with genuine motives and those represented as illegitimate, extremist, and with suspicious motives. At the same time, the writer employs oppositions *within* the former category to emphasise the range of people on the demonstration, and hence utilises oppositions for inclusive (rather than just exclusive) purposes. I will show how the reader is encouraged to identify with the 'in-group', typically through the use of the **us/them** binary (see Fowler 1991) and, comment on the broader ideological repercussions.

## 2 Studies of opposites

Major studies of opposites include the lexical semantic approach (Lyons 1977, Cruse 1986,) the corpus approach (Mettinger 1994, Jones 2002) and the pragmatic approach (Murphy 2003)[2]. The lexical semanticists focus on decontextualised examples of pairs of words assumed to be opposites well established in the lexicon. The most basic distinction is made between gradable opposites (called 'antonyms' by Lyons and Cruse), and non-gradable 'complementaries'. Gradables involve pairs such as **hot/cold** which lie at two ends of a scale in which there are any number of points in between (such as **warm** and **cool**). Non-gradable complementaries are mutually exclusive non-scalar binary opposites which conventionally have no midway point, such as **male/female**. These studies tend to focus on lexical relations within an abstract canon of opposites, rarely using data from recorded written or spoken sources. Mettinger and Jones use corpora to examine examples of oppositional pairs in the contexts of the sentences in which they appeared. Mettinger (1994) studied 43 predominantly British crime novels, and Jones (2002) 3,000 sentences chosen from a 280 million-word corpus from the British *Independent* newspaper (1988 – 96). Both researchers attempt to categorise the most common syntactic frames in which pairs of opposites are used when in the same sentence, for instance **X** *not* **Y**, or *either* **X** *or* **Y** (where **X** and **Y** are the oppositional pair). This was achieved by searching for conventional oppositional pairs - in Jones' case, for 56 specific pairs – and identifying the common frames around which they appear. The use of pre-conceived conventional pairs however means that potentially unusual and creative oppositional pairings are ignored. Moreover, the corpus approach, while using examples of real data, goes no further than the sentence level, ignoring the potential significance of the repercussion of the use of opposites in the wider context of the texts in which they appear. However, by proposing a taxonomy of common syntactic frames, this does allow the analyst to search for these environments within a text with a view to investigating the words or phrases which are potentially being treated in an oppositional fashion.

Murphy adopts a pragmatic approach, considering opposites and other semantic and lexical relations 'with reference to their use and their status in the human mind within a human culture'. (2003: 5) This 'contrasts with strictly formal or descriptive accounts of semantic relations, in which words are considered only with reference to their definitional meanings and those definitions' relations with each other'. (2003: 5) Murphy recognises the potential of using what she calls 'canonical' (conventional) opposites to help classify the syntactic frames in which they manifest themselves, but then to take this a step further:

> 'Awareness of these frames and their functions gives us a means for recognizing context-dependent cases of antonymy. So, while Jones has used canonical antonyms to demonstrate the existence of these functions, other pairs, including non-canonical opposites and words that are not antonymous in neutral conditions, function as antonyms in these frames.....Jones' taxonomy of antonym functions and collateral syntactic frames provides a means to identify situational or context-bound antonymy ...'. (2003: 204)[3]

A classic example of a 'situational or context bound antonymy' would be the much quoted response by George W Bush to the attack on the World Trade Centre in 2001 when he announced, 'Every nation, in every region, now has a decision to make. *Either* you are with **us** *or* you are with the **terrorists'**.[4] Here Bush utilised an *either* **X** *or* **Y** framework (labelled 'coordinated antonymy' by Jones, 2002[5]), to place the words **us** and **terrorists** in a position of unconventional opposition. The opposite of **us**, conventionally **them**, is reformulated here as **terrorists**, and in other announcements as **enemy**. Bush sought to unite both the US public and much of the rest of the world against a common enemy, using a soundbite which represented society as one made up of 'goodies' and 'baddies'. This and other formulations were designed to present to his addressees a stark choice between supporting one of these two camps, presented as mutually exclusive non-gradable complementaries. The *either/or* frame provides no possibility of a middle way, the implication being that if you do not support the US administration then you automatically align yourself with people who commit atrocities. Research by Coe et al. (2004) showed that in the weeks and months that followed September 11th, this construction of the world into the oppositional superordinate categories of **good** and **evil** (and **security / peril**) were often mirrored by the US news media, specifically in the editorials of leading US newspapers, responding to Bush's proclamations on the 'war on terror'. They also claim (2004: 236) that the news discourse of post-September 11 echoed that of the Cold War. They quote Medhurst who noted, 'The discourse of cold war pictured a Manichean world of light and darkness, with no shades of gray. Communism was a demonic force unalterably opposed to all that was good'. (2000: 466) Medhurst argues that with 'such a force there could be no compromise, no halfway measures. Clearly this was the rhetoric of polarisation.' (2000: 466) This Cold War rhetoric involved, according to Medhurst, constructing the Soviet enemy as 'communistic', 'atheistic', 'barbaric', 'secretive' and 'violent' and all the connotations of these terms (see 2000: 466), whilst America was 'democratic', 'God-fearing', 'civilized', 'open' and 'peace-loving'. The way politicians and news reports can construct the world into mutually exclusive binaries and consequently omit any 'shades of grey' is a significant feature of 20th and 21st century rhetoric and continues to have potent ideological implications (see for instance van Dijk 2006, Sonwalker in Allan, S. (ed.) 2005, Ch 7 in Allan 2004 and Raum & Measell 1974).[6]

## 3 Data

The Bush example shows how you can identify non-canonical oppositions from common frames and this is my approach in the following analysis, building on the methodology proposed by Murphy in the quote above. In a report of the anti-war demonstration in the British national newspaper, the *Sunday Mirror* (dated 16th February 2003) I have identified frames commonly associated with oppositions and discovered a number of mainly non-canonical oppositions which are 'triggered' by the frames. Sometimes these manifest themselves as phrases rather than just individual words. I will examine how it is possible to justify treating, for instance **placard** and **banner**, as opposites in the context they appear, and how these might influence the reader towards privileging one of the pair over the other.

Firstly it is necessary to provide some brief context to the news article. Although figures vary, the *Sunday Mirror* reported an estimated two million protestors on the anti-war march through London on 15th February 2003. The event dominated the British news media, being at the time of writing, still the largest ever recorded protest march on British soil. The *Mirror* newspaper was unusual in that it took a consistent overt anti-war stance and thereby publicly backed the aims of the demonstrators. For instance, its front page 'Valentines' headline the day before the demonstration was 'Make Love not War' alongside a mocked up photograph of Tony Blair and George Bush locked in a passionate kiss. However, as I will show, the main news report of the demonstration takes great pains to avoid aligning the writer, and hence the *Sunday Mirror* editorial board and its readership, with groups of protestors whose aim it is implied, may be to see the demonstration as a means of bringing down the Blair government (who the *Mirror* previously consistently backed) rather than being a warning shot across the bows.

The 1,400-word report is on Page 2 of the *Sunday Mirror*, is supported by a whole page of captioned photographs on page 3, and is the lead report of the day. The front page consists of a photograph showing the impressive size of the demonstration. Superimposed over this, at the bottom of the page in block capitals is the headline '2M SAY NO'. This is in white lettering on a black box, within which also contains a head shot of Tony Blair with his hands over his ears and the unattributed words 'Are you deaf Mr Blair?' in a smaller typeface to the headline. Underneath, in an even smaller typeface is 'THE BIG DEMO: SEE PAGES 2, 3, 4, 5, 6, 7, 8 & 9'. The article itself is headed 'LISTEN TO US' in large capitals, underneath which are two bullet pointed declarations (smaller typeface) '2m join historic demo' and 'Britain says no to war'. Running along the top of pages 2 & 3 is the strapline 'THE PEOPLE'S MARCH: (on page 2) and 'A TIDE OF PROTEST (page 3), and further down 'Britain says no to War' Both the newsworthiness and the positive stance towards the protest are easily signalled by these headlines. It will be important to identify the *us* that Blair is being encouraged to listen to and who is positioned in the text for instance under the categories of *Britain* and *people*.

The report is a description of the event from the point of view of journalist Tony Rennell.[7] Here, he celebrates what he represents as the genuine voice of the 'British people', in which people of all ages, races and creeds make a legitimate moral stand again the elected government of the day. However, certain people on the march are represented as not being eligible to be categorised this way, and are thence excluded from being celebrated as legitimate protestors. Table one illustrates the oppositional pairings which are constructed for the purpose of this specific text. It is clear - even without seeing these examples in context – to see how words with negative connotations (**The Mob, anarchists, traitors, cowards, fainthearts, extremists**) are contrasted with those who *Mirror* readers would feel comfortable aligning themselves (**ordinary people, worried mums and dads, Joe Public**).

**Table 1**

| | Acceptable protestors (US) | Unacceptable protestors (THEM) |
|---|---|---|
| 1 | sheer power of numbers | The Mob…..thoughts of violence |
| 2 | ordinary people | militants, anarchists, anti-capitalists and anti-Americans….. "the great unwashed" |
| 3 | Worried mums and dads of all ages, all races and religions…..people who have come to express a genuine feeling….. | traitors….cowards….fainthearts |
| 4 | cobbled together | professionally-produced |
| 5 | banners | placards |
| 6 | Notts County supporters | protest groups |
| 7 | "Notts County Supporters say Make Love Not War" | fierce messages – "Blair and Bush – Wanted for Murder" |
| 8 | Joe Public | extremists |

I will analyse each of these examples in their context and show how they are treated as oppositions, and the consequences of this. Below I reproduce the paragraphs I analyse in the order they appear in the news article along with the paragraph number (the article is 37 paragraphs long). Note however that for structural purposes, my analysis will not follow this sequential order.

In years gone by, governments were always wary of what they called The Mob. Governments should still be frightened, very frightened. *Not* by **thoughts of violence**...*but* by the **sheer power of numbers**. (Paragraph 4)

*While* it was true that **militants, anarchists, anti-capitalists and anti-Americans** – what one weary PC called **"the great unwashed"** – were out in force, the heart and mind of the protest was **ordinary people**. (Paragraph 8)

**Worried mums and dads of all ages, all races and religions**. *Not* **traitors or cowards**. *Not* **faint-hearts**. *But* **people who had come to express a genuine feeling they cannot ignore** – that the Prime Minister is wrong. (Paragraph 9)

Dozens of causes were represented. The **professionally-produced placards** of the **protest groups** with their **fierce messages – "Blair and Bush – Wanted for Murder"** – *contrasted* with **cobbled-together banners**. **"Notts County supporters say Make Love Not War",** said one. (Paragraph 11)

The answer came as people flooded in. **Young** *and* **old**, all wrapped up against the cold. Children in buggies, invalids in chairs. *Some were* scruffy in **denims** and **fleeces**, *others wore* **fur-collared coats** and **Barbours**. (Paragraph 15)

"I know there are **extremists** here whose opinions I disagree with, *but* they could *not* summon this number of people. This is **Joe Public**." (Paragraph 29)

## 4.1 Inclusive oppositions  1 - when *placard* is the opposite of *banner*

Dozens of causes were represented. The **professionally-produced placards** of the **protest groups** with their **fierce messages – "Blair and Bush – Wanted for Murder"** – *contrasted* with **cobbled-together banners**. **"Notts County supporters say Make Love Not War",** said one.

In this first example, the writer is overtly stating his intention to emphasise the differences between two types of protestors in order to illustrate the range of people represented on the demonstration. His method here is to distinguish between two quite distinct types of protestor – those who have plenty of experience of attending demonstrations and those for whom it is probably a novel experience. It is apparent that he is choosing to describe two sets of protestors from the opposite ends of a spectrum because he uses the trigger *contrasted* as the pivot between which both descriptions rest, which overtly indicates to the reader that there is an opposition being utilised. Jones creates a category he labels 'Distinguished Antonymy' whereby 'a distinction between antonyms is overtly referred to' (2002: 82). Frames covered by this category include *the difference between X and Y, polarised between X and Y*, and *distinguish between X and Y*. These explicitly indicate a level of contrast between the **X** and **Y** of the pair. Although Jones has no example of the trigger *contrasted* as such, it is likely he would include this under the same heading. The crucial point is that the writer is drawing attention to the distinction. The syntactic arrangement also plays some part in helping to realise the contrast. The text either side of the trigger is roughly structurally parallel in that each section consists, in this order, of 1) Description of level of skill involved in displaying messages and slogans – **professionally-produced** / **cobbled-together**; 2) Type of medium utilised to display messages – **placards** / **banners**; 3) Types of groups carrying the messages – **protest groups** / **Notts County Supporters**; 4) The messages themselves – **"Blair and Bush – Wanted for Murder"** / **"Make Love Not War"**. Jones notes parallelism as an 'important contrast-generating' device (2002: 56), as does Short who claims that 'they invite the reader to search for meaning connections between the parallel structures' (1996: 14) and 'make us look for parallel or contrastive meaning links between those parallel parts' (1996: 15). However, just because there is a kind of (inexact) formal symmetry here it does not necessarily follow that the reader is encouraged to treat each side with equal respect. In my analysis below I will show how one of the sides is privileged over the other in terms of the writer's attitude towards them, which contributes towards his overall construction of 'good' and 'bad' protestors. This example is particularly fascinating because it takes in, I would argue, four separate examples of contrast, mirroring the list of four above.

The contrast between **professionally-produced** and **cobbled-together** is perhaps the most conventional of the four. Both are compound adjectives pre-modifying nouns referring to media on which slogans can be displayed. The conventional opposite of **professional** would likely be **amateur**, of which **cobbled-together** is synonymous. It is possible however that **cobbled-together** has been chosen because **amateur** or **amateurish-looking** may have the effect of mocking the less experienced protestors as it can often have negative connotations. Moreover, the colloquial nature of **cobbled-together** may elicit the sympathies of the reader more in an article whose emphasis is on aligning itself with 'Joe Public' (see section 5.3) whose demonstration this is represented to be, and hence more informal forms of lexis might reflect this, as is common in the popular tabloid press. The formal tone of **professionally-produced** distances the reader from this type of group. These groups are anonymous, carrying manufactured, mass-produced placards and therefore lacking the individual touch of, in this case, a banner made by Notts County Supporters. It would be much more difficult to justify as conventional oppositions the nouns which these terms modify – **placard** and **banners** – if you take them on their own out of context.[8] However, the writer has differentiated the two extremes of protestors by choosing to describe one group as holding mass produced placards and the other individually crafted banners. This does place **placard** and **banner** in a position of opposition, partly by being associated with the more conventionally oppositional adjectives pre-modifying them. Jones calls this kind of opposition 'Ancillary Antonymy' whereby 'a familiar antonymous pair is effectively acting as a lexical signal that we should interpret a non-antonymous pair contrastively'. (2002: 38) In this way many unconventional oppositions can be generated. A simple example would be from a sentence taken from Jones' corpus which puts **change** and **die** in a position of opposition in '**change** quickly or **die** slowly' (2002: 36) because of the conventional opposites **quickly** and **slowly** attached to them. In this case, because the opposite of **die** is usually **live** and not **change** it is possible we process change as synonymous with **live** in this particular context, and associate dying with an inability to change. The complication with the **placard** / **banner** pair is that they are virtually synonymous, so how can they be opposites? One answer to this is to refer to the minimal difference rule that applies to defining opposites, i.e. that opposites have everything in common apart from on one particular dimension.[9] They are similar in that they both refer to materials on which words and images can be placed to draw attention to their messages and are usually held aloft by human beings. They are different however (otherwise we would not need two words). Placards are usually cardboard or wood, and therefore mass-produced messages can be printed on them. The photographs of the demonstration in much of the data I have perused, plus TV images of demonstrations, show hundreds of placards with the same messages and the name of the group sponsoring them, usually at the top, presumably in order to promote the name of that group in media images. Banners however are usually made from soft material like cloth. They are difficult to mass-produce and more commonly associated with the specific groups of people who actually carry them at demonstrations. They usually have a more individual local or regional name and design, such as that of individual trade union branches, or in this case supporters of a football team and therefore have a unique bespoke design. Usually it requires more than one person to carry them attached as they are across two poles, whereas placards are designed for the individual. So in this context there are dimensions of difference which casts **placards** and **banners** as contrasting concepts.

This is supported further when we look at the third pair of opposites referring to the people who are carrying the messages - **protest groups** and **Notts County supporters**. Both **groups** and **supporters** belong to the same lexical field in that they refer to collections of individuals bound by some kind of common factor. They are not therefore conventionally cast as contrasts. There are differences however. Notice that the term **protest group** usually connotes a collection of people who are against something whether it be against war, against mobile phone masts, or against the takeover of a football team by American businessmen. **Supporters** however are in favour of something and more specifically associated with like-minded watchers of sport or some other definable interest. So it is possible we might understand the contrast in terms of an underlying binary of 'general political anti-something' (**protest groups**) opposed to 'specific non-political pro-something' (**Notts County Supporters**).[10] We only know that the banner carriers are Notts County supporters because their name forms part of the message being held aloft .The writer's decision to choose these specific messages – **'Blair and Bush Wanted for Murder'** and **'Make Love not War'** - out of the thousands on the march reinforces who the reader is encouraged to align themselves with, a position built in several other places in the text as I will illustrate shortly. The message of the protest groups sounds negative, even hate-filled. The decision to evaluative their message as **fierce**, hints at the writer's stance towards them, as the word has aggressive connotations as opposed to **defiant** or **emotive** for instance. The inclusion of the word **murder** in the placard, although aimed as an accusation towards Bush and Blair may associate the protest groups with violence (as they are elsewhere in the report, see section 5.4) whether it is of their doing or somebody else's. The writer has chosen not use an evaluative adjective to contrast with **fierce**, probably because the message itself is promoting love and by implication peace (which the former is not). Potential conventional opposites of **fierce** might be **gentle**, **docile** or **tame** and if used make the banner carriers sound too ineffectual. Of course, there is an element of passivity implied in the message itself which harks back to the peace movements of the 1960s. However, grammatically, it has active elements, being an imperative and thus instructing somebody to do something, whereas the declarative of the protest group's message is passive, semantically and grammatically, neither encouraging anybody to do anything nor showing who it is that wants Blair and Bush for murder.

To summarise so far, this paragraph picks on two sets of anti-war marchers whose difference is signalled both by the word *contrasted* and elements of syntactic parallelism. Its function in the context of the rest of the article is to celebrate the diversity of the demonstration by choosing two ends of an artificial scale of protest 'types', between which, the reader must assume, there may be a whole range of other diverse groups of people. However, the writer points us favourably towards one group more than another in ways which are much less subtle in other constructed oppositions which I will deal with later.

## 4.2 Inclusive opposites 2 – you are what you wear

Another example where oppositional pairings contribute towards highlighting the inclusive nature of the protest, hence helping to justify the *Sunday Mirror's* support, is in the following paragraph:

> The answer came as people flooded in. **Young** *and* **old**, all wrapped up against the cold. Children in buggies, invalids in chairs. *Some were* scruffy in **denims** and **fleeces**, *others wore* **fur-collared coats** and **Barbours**.

The writer seems keen to emphasise the attendance of protestors from a wide range of ages and classes who quickly fill what previously was an empty Embankment in London. **Young** and **old** is straightforward enough, an example of what Jones calls 'Co-ordinated Antonymy' whereby coordinators are used to link two ends of a scale (2002: 61 – 74). Here the conjunction *and* links both ends of a gradable scale along a semantic dimension of 'age'. The inclusion of the extreme ends of the scale, apart from indicating the attendance of the biggest range in between, also suggests the writer is deliberately focussing on those most vulnerable, the description of them being all wrapped up against the cold possibly drawing attention to the fact their commitment is even more impressive considering the bitter weather conditions. The last sentence of the paragraph moves away from age as a way of categorising the range of marchers, and implies a heterogeneous mix of social classes, without mentioning class specifically. Two types of dress are contrasted potentially acting as an index of the social class of the wearers – **denims** *and* **fleeces** associated with casual wear, and **fur-collared coats and Barbours**, the apparel of the more affluent. In case the reader misses the distinction, we are helped by the writer's evaluation of the former group's attire with the inclusion of the complement *scruffy*, potentially evoking an image of the latter as smart, to imply another kind of gradable opposition. A form of syntactic parallelism is used here which contributes towards triggering the opposition:

| Some | were | scruffy | [in] denims | and fleeces |
|---|---|---|---|---|
| others | wore | | fur-collared coats | and Barbours |
| *Subject* <br> plural pronouns | *Predicate* <br> past tense verbs | | plural clothing-related nouns… | ….joined by coordinating conjunction *and* |

Although the two halves are not a perfect match, there is sufficient parallelism here, combined with the semantic relationships between **denims, fleeces, fur-collared coats** and **Barbours**, to make a strong case for the two sets of clothing to be set up as contrasts. Both clauses start with third person indefinite plural Subject pronouns, followed by predicating past tense verbs, which coincidentally or not, also have a phonological relationship, varying only by the second vowel phoneme (*were/wore*). The variation occurs where the writer's use of *scruffy* means the stative verb *were* is followed by a Complement and Adverbial, whilst the dynamic verb *wore* is followed by an Object. However, the two noun phrases which constitute the last two elements of each clause correlate well. Semantically there is a good match in that the clothing referred to can all be coats (although *denim* can have a broader meaning). So here the writer turns into opposites clothes chosen more for their looks – **denim / fur-collared coats,** as well as those which are more practical, designed to protect against the weather – **fleeces / Barbours**. Again, one would presume that if there were a scale on which to place clothing in terms of its value or prestige status, there would be a whole range of middle-range attire which would also be represented on the demonstration which is not mentioned. But, by focussing on the two ends of the spectrum (and ignoring the middle range), a picture of two usually mutually exclusive and antagonistic classes collaborating against a common enemy is constructed.

The examples I have investigated so far mostly show how the report of the demonstration uses oppositions *inclusively*. This draws attention to the diversity of marchers in order to show it is representative and has the support of a vast number of the general public and hence has legitimacy in the view of the *Sunday Mirror,* as opposed to being dominated by people who tend to regularly attend demonstrations. This latter point is only implied in the first example I gave, but is more strongly and overtly emphasised in the following examples.

### 5.1 Exclusive oppositions 1 – soapboxes or soap?

It is in paragraphs eight and nine of the report that we find the most explicit expression of the way the text differentiates between the acceptable and unacceptable groups of protestors.

> *While* it was true that **militants, anarchists, anti-capitalists and anti-Americans** – what one weary PC called **"the great unwashed"** – were out in force, the heart and mind of the protest was **ordinary people**.
>
> Worried mums and dads of all ages, all races and religions. *Not* traitors or cowards. *Not* faint-hearts. *But* people who had come to express a genuine feeling they cannot ignore – that the Prime Minister is wrong.

There are two sets of oppositions here which I will deal with one at a time but they need reproducing together because they refer to the same groups of people and their juxtaposition connects them grammatically and semantically.

The first of these paragraphs contrasts a list of four types of groups and an evaluation of them with **ordinary people**. The syntactic framework for this is *while* **X, Y**. Jones has no mention of the function of the subordinator *while* in the generation of oppositions, and this reveals one of the flaws in the ways he develops his taxonomy. His corpus of opposites is based purely on pre-selected individual words. However some oppositional concepts are expressed in terms of phrases expressing *circumstances* which utilise frameworks unsuitable for individual words, *while* **X, Y** being one of them. It makes no sense to say, for instance, *while* **militants, ordinary people**. This framework however does generate a contrast. Quirk *et al.* (1972) call subordinators such as *while*, *although*, and *even*, 'concessive conjuncts', and the clause they operate in 'concessive clauses'. Their function, according to Quirk et al., is to 'imply a contrast between two circumstances; *ie* that in the light of the circumstance in the dependent clause, that in the main clause is surprising.' (1972: 745) From this point on I will add the category of 'concessives' to the list of potential oppositional triggers.[11] The circumstances in this case are that groups who it is implied usually turn out to demonstrations are overwhelmed in numbers by 'ordinary people', therefore differentiating between the two. Each of the labels **militants, anarchists, anti-capitalists and anti-Americans** are all related in terms of their anti-establishment stance and are often used by the media to portray groups in a negative light. The labels would not necessarily be used by the individuals in these groups to refer to themselves. Neither is it necessary to specifically list four categories of protestor. Doing so suggests they are distinct groups with separate agendas, although none of them are named at any point in the article. Neither is it implausible for the values and beliefs of one particular individual to coincide with all four categories. The writer has therefore constructed the list for rhetorical purposes and created an opposition to it for a similar reason. The list emphasises their 'outsider' status with terms it is assumed will have a derogatory effect. So while they are given separate categories, at the same time they are all disparagingly tarred with the same brush when the writer chooses to quote the *weary PC* who calls them **the great unwashed.** Traditionally the term is often used to refer to the 'masses' or the 'working class'. Here however it may be drawing on the stereotype of the political activist who has neither the time nor the inclination to waste precious energy on matters of personal hygiene. This may serve to reinforce the idea that the non-conformity of these people keeps them permanently outside of the mainstream. The description of the PC as *weary* implies that the experienced (but unacceptable) protestors are something the police are resigned to have to put up with on every protest march as an inevitable nuisance or irritant.

On its own, the subordinate clause within which all this information is held would not have the strength of the implications it does, without the contrasting main clause which counterpoises **the great unwashed** (and its list of referents) with **ordinary people**. Here, being 'ordinary' is a compliment. It is often used in the news media to refer to those people who lack any kind of special status or talent and are therefore not prone to extreme lifestyles, behaviour or opinions. They therefore do not threaten to upset the status quo. Of course, in other contexts being **ordinary** is far from flattering. Canonical opposites like **extraordinary** or **out-of-the-ordinary** apply to people whose behaviour and lifestyles is usually the staple diet of news stories celebrating the special or rare talents of certain individuals or groups. So the two extremes of the opposition scale in that instance would involve being special at one end and bland at the other. However, here it is ordinariness which is being celebrated. The conventional opposite of **ordinary** in this paragraph relates to 'abnormality' or 'extremism' hence the scale on which this contrast rests has moderation and acceptability at one end (to be embraced) and unacceptable extremism on the other. The irony is that the writer suggests that this particular protest is out-of-the-ordinary precisely because it is dominated by those the writer represents as ordinary.

Another potential contrast alluded to in this paragraph which reinforces the positive status of the 'common' people is a more abstract one which aligns them with spiritual power, and the 'undesirables' with physical power. This is expressed by the fact that ordinary people are cast as the **heart and mind** of the protest whilst the other groups were **out in force**. **Hearts and minds** (in themselves sometimes treated oppositionally based on an **emotional / rational** binary) are here connected as they relate to the abstract field of ideas or things possessing spiritual qualities, implying love, warmth and genuine emotion (in the case of **heart**) and thought, intellect and identity (in **mind**). Of course, in this context, the hearts and minds are not specifically those of individual protestors but of the protest itself. This is expressed as a singular entity using singular abstract nouns preceded by the definite article (*the* **heart and mind**) suggesting that the protest spiritually and legitimately belongs to the ordinary people. This represents them as having a morally acceptable, dignified and peaceful claim to take on the government whilst their antithesis, **out in force**, are associated with a physical (and therefore potentially more aggressive, even violent) presence, something to be expected and even tolerated, but whose motivations are suspect. This is suggested even more explicitly in another example later on (see Section 5.4).

### 5.2 Exclusive opposition 2 – traitor *or* dad?
The paragraph directly following this one reinforces the paper's alignment with the less experienced protestors.

**Worried mums and dads of all ages, all races and religions**. *Not* **traitors or cowards**. *Not* **faint-hearts**. *But* **people who had come to express a genuine feeling they cannot ignore** – that the Prime Minister is wrong.

This time the writer is reinforcing the notion of ordinariness by focussing on the protestors' family status as **worried mums and dads**, whilst also ensuring the reader is clear they cannot be aligned with other types of anti-war groups whose motives could be questioned in terms of their loyalty to their country (**traitors, cowards, fainthearts**). Before I examine the significance of this distinction, it is necessary to explore the syntactic framework which triggers the artificially created opposition.

This involves what Jones calls 'Negated Antonymy' which he defines as 'the co-occurrence of an antonymous pair within a framework that negates one antonym as a device to augment the other.' (2002: 88) Examples he gives from his own *Independent* newspaper corpus include, 'We are striving for the withdrawal to facilitate the re-establishment of **peace**, *not* **war**' and 'If you look at **employment**, *not* **unemployment**, that too fell in the first quarter of the year.' (2002: 35-6) Here of course the pairs **peace** / **war** and **employment** / **unemployment** are conventional ones that Jones has pre-chosen and subsequently found examples of in his search for common frames.

Jones says that negated antonymy is 'arguably the "purest" form of antonymy' (2002: 88), as using a negator like *not* makes *explicit* the antonymy between the two of the pair. He also argues that negated antonymy sentences (especially those hinging on *not*) 'tend to reflect spoken rather than written English' (2002: 89), including being involved in sentences starting with, according to Jones, *in my opinion*, and those with a 'strong colloquial style.....reminiscent of political rhetoric'.(2002: 90) Jones goes on to claim that this 'suggests that Negated Antonymy is more common in speech and speech-like, persuasive writing, than it is in formal writing [because] negating the antonym of a word is strictly tautological'. (2002: 90) By this he means that a construction like X *not* Y implies a mutual exclusivity within the context in which the opposites are instantiated. If you describe or label some thing in terms of one state of being and use something else as a contrast to emphasise it is *not* another state of being, you are likely to choose something which falls at the opposite end of the spectrum upon which this specific dimension of meaning lies. So for instance, taking Jones' own examples - 'facilitate the re-establishment of **peace**' and 'if you look at **employment**' - are logically equivalent to 'facilitate the re-establishment of *not* **war**' and 'if you look at *not* **unemployment**' (although it is unlikely the latter would ever be formulated this way). So the rhetorical, speech-like style Jones refers to is a result of the emphasis placed on essentially repeating the same point, for if **X** is equivalent to *not* **Y** then on a logical level **X** *not* **Y** entails **X** and **X** again! It is of course quite usual to reinforce utterances by including both **X** and **Y** in an **X** *not* **Y** statement. If I say, 'Alex is a **boy** *not* a **girl**' when talking about a boy called Alex who it seems my addressee thinks is a girl, then I am merely clarifying the situation by emphasising what Alex is not.

There are two points to make here. Firstly, according to Jones' database instances of 'negated antonymy' count for a mere 2% of his 3,000 examples. This is much lower than the percentage in the *Sunday Mirror* article. This may support Jones' theory that the use of an **X** *not* **Y** structure is more typical in rhetorical styles, which the *Sunday Mirror* article does employ, as we have seen. However, even more pertinent to my study is that the examples Jones uses consist of *canonical* opposites whereby, for instance, we are assuming that **war** is the opposite of **peace**. This is *not* the case in other textually specific examples, for instance on anti-war slogans on the aforementioned demonstration, which include 'make **love** *not* **war**' and 'make **tea** *not* **war**'. In these cases, **love** and **tea** can both be the opposite of **war** if we take for granted that the **X** *not* **Y** frame is triggering an opposition. Crucially, the more unconventional the **X/Y** pair in an **X** *not* **Y** frame, the more essential it is that the **Y** element is included, as for instance making **tea** would not conventionally entail or trigger the concept of *not* making **war**. So an **X** *not* **Y** frame could be used for emphatic rhetorical purposes with canonical opposites and/*or* because the form of the Y element cannot automatically be taken for granted in the case of more non-canonical pairings. The latter is certainly the case in the *Sunday Mirror* example quoted above. A conventional opposite of **worried** might be **calm** (or unworried), and **mum** and **dad** are conventional opposites between themselves. If we take **mums** and **dads** in their sense as co-hyponyms of the superordinate 'parents', the opposite of this might be **children**, or **childless couples** (depending on the context). What is certain is the unlikelihood of **traitor**, **coward** etc. being triggered in anything other than a very specific context such as this. So the inclusion of the *not* **Y** element of the framework is essential in representing to the reader what not being **worried mums and dads** is, in the unlikely event that **calm, childless couple** is evoked!

The significance of this is as follows. Firstly, if an **X** *not* **Y** frame signals mutual exclusivity then the writer is proposing the peculiar notion that one cannot both be a **worried mum and dad** and a **coward** at the same time. You are either one or the other. This is clearly ludicrous, but has a certain coherence within the rhetoric of the report. If you are *not* a **traitor**, **coward** or **faintheart** then you are a 'brave patriot', which in this context is synonymous with being a **worried parent**. Moreover – and this is why it is necessary to explore this sentence alongside the one that precedes it – the **ordinary people** in the previous paragraph correlate with the **worried mums and dads**, and hence those labelled the **great unwashed** by implication must be the **traitors, cowards** and **fainthearts**. This is because all four sentences in Paragraph 9 are minor sentences. The **worried mums and dads** *of all ages, races and religions*, which forms a complete, non-standard verbless sentence only makes sense if it acts as a noun phrase in apposition to the end of Paragraph 8 - *the heart and mind of the protest was* **ordinary people**. What is more, those deemed acceptable protestors are described in the same paragraph as **people who had come to express a genuine feeling they cannot ignore**. This point is expressed using an added trigger for contrast, the coordinating conjunction *but*. This often acts alongside *not* in constructions like *not* **X** *but* **Y**. For convenience I will call this a 'negated contrastive'.[12] Quirk et al. say '*but* denotes a contrast' (1972: 564), and Jones that '*but* acts unambiguously as a signal that what comes next should be contrasted with what went previously' (2002: 57). So if these people hold **genuine feelings** it follows that the unacceptable protestors have **non-genuine** (fake?) **feelings** and moreover must be 'unworried, childless, anarchist traitors'! It also follows that you cannot simultaneously be a serious anti-capitalist and a cowardly parent. Despite these evidently absurd lines of thought they do consistently follow the logic of what seems to be the writer's value system in this report – i.e. planned, organised, experienced protest is a real threat to democracy and is not to be tolerated, whilst inexperienced, impulsive, one-off protesting is fine, as long as it only goes so far as expressing discontent and not disrupting the balance of power too radically.

So here we can see that the writer has been heavily implying that the kinds of protestors worth supporting are of a particular type who represent a consensual norm, outside of which any other types are on the fringes of society and to be treated with suspicion. This is most overtly expressed in the next example, which occurs a few paragraphs from the end of the report.

### 5.3 Exclusive oppositions 3 – extremist or ordinary Joe

> That was the thought that led so many ordinary people to flood the streets of London yesterday. One Lancashire mother explained how it had meant taking her toddler out of school early the day before and travelling overnight.
>
> She cradled her five-month-old baby son to her as she said: "It was a huge decision to come. I've never been to London to a march before.
>
> "But when the bloodshed starts I don't want to feel it is in my name. When the children are older I want to be able to tell them we played a part in trying to stop it."
>
> "I know there are **extremists** here whose opinions I disagree with, *but* they could *not* summon this number of people. This is **Joe Public**." (Paragraphs 26 – 29)

Here I have reproduced the three paragraphs preceding the one under analysis to help contextualise it. Paragraph 29 constructs **extremists** and **Joe Public** as unconventional opposites. The Lancashire mother quoted is reluctantly acknowledging the presence of a body of people she labels **extremists**, claiming however that they have had little influence on the organisation of the demonstration, using a version of a negated constrastive framework, **X** *but not* **Y**. The negator applies to what it is the woman claims those she labels as **extremists** could not have done i.e. '*summon up this number of people*', rather than simply denying there were none there (as this is evidently not the case, whoever they are). What is clear is that the *could not* [summon this number of people]…*is* [Joe Public] frame again presupposes the existence of two mutually exclusive categories of people (note the categorical nature of the claim *this is* **Joe Public** i.e. with no modal verbs of possibility like *might* or *maybe*). The term **extremist** tends to have negative connotations whatever it is applied to, and its canonical opposite would be **moderate** in most cases. The woman is asserting that the demonstration is made up of ordinary people using a common colloquial term for this - **Joe Public**, who hence by implication are moderate (therefore acceptable).

Evidently, the writer has chosen this woman as a kind of prototypical 'ordinary' person, one with whom he clearly aligns himself, and therefore the *Sunday Mirror* readers. This is clear in the first paragraph of the group quoted above – *the thought that led so many* **ordinary people** *to flood the streets of London yesterday. One Lancashire mother …* .She herself makes it clear that she includes herself in the category of **Joe Public** by distancing herself from '*the* **extremists** *whose opinions I disagree with'*. She is the only person from the demonstration who is given any voice in the form of direct speech, presumably having spoken to the journalist himself. The only other people quoted are celebrities speaking to the crowd at the concluding rally in Hyde Park. No member of the groups labelled **extremist** are given a voice in the article, and if so, it would be interesting to know whether they would refer to themselves in the same way the *Mirror* writer does. The mother however is accorded great unchallenged authority in claiming to know who has and has not participated in organising the demonstration despite the fact the writer is simultaneously taking great pains to emphasise her ordinariness. She is in effect a conduit through which the writer can reinforce his polemic about unacceptable protestors. He is trying to give his values added force by expressing them through a member of the **Joe Public** he supports -  regional, female, mother of baby, who has made sacrifices to attend the demonstration, and hence has not made her decision to support it lightly. Again, this may give the impression that those labelled **extremists**, being seasoned protestors, are somehow prepared for this kind of situation, and moreover are not young mothers from Lancashire. This whole section involves a kind of self-perpetuating consolidation of the values approved of by the writer. He aligns himself with one kind of protestor, whose existence he effectively constructs through the employment of group categories placed in positions of opposition. He then chooses to quote one of those protestors who labels herself as one of the types the writer supports and who is quoted as distancing herself from the groups he disapproves of. The reader therefore is positioned in way which means if they do not align themselves with the writer and/or quoted mother then they are in effect supporting 'extremists' (see Bush example in Section 1).

One last example should illustrate how a reader, who may be unclear of the significance of these negative labels, is encouraged into this position.

### 5.4 Exclusive opposition 4 – the mobs become the masses

In years gone by, governments were always wary of what they called **The Mob**. Governments should still be frightened, very frightened. *Not* by **thoughts of violence**...*but* by the **sheer power of numbers**.

This comes from early on in the text (paragraph 4) and is the reader's first encounter with the writer's attempt to distance himself his readership from certain protestors. It is therefore immediately clear that this is potentially a major theme running through the article and designed to reassure the reader that the newspaper is not supporting people who they perceive as a potential threat. In the sentence prior to this the writer has celebrated the *awesome feeling when the people take over the streets of the capital*, clearly expressing his belief that there are at least *some* circumstances in which mass protest is to be applauded. The opposition here associates **The Mob** with **thoughts of violence** and contrasts them with **sheer power of numbers**, again using form of the negated contrastive syntactic frame, in this case *not* **X** *but* **Y**.

If we presume that a conventional opposite to **violence** is **peace**, then **peace** is being treated as synonymous with **sheer power of numbers**; a mass of people who we don't expect to be violent. This meaning is intensified by pre-modifying **power of numbers** with **sheer** which implies that the concept to which it is attached (the noun phrase) can do what it does unaided by outside interference from anything else, in this case **violence**, which the writer associates with **The Mob** in the first sentence. Interestingly, both **The Mob** and **sheer power of numbers** are closely synonymous, in the sense that they both refer to bodies of people who hold some potential power. Of course **a Mob** often connotes a group of people with sinister, often violent (if unorganised) motives. Here however, early on in the article the writer is keen to distance this particular mass of people from anything which may be construed as having violent potential, hence sets up **sheer power of numbers** in opposition to **Mob/thoughts of violence**, presumably because protests are often associated in the mind of the news consumer with rioting and threats to democracy (e.g. the 1990 Poll Tax riots in Trafalgar Square, in a movement which contributed to the resignation of Prime Minister Margaret Thatcher later in the year). The fright that the writer declares the government should feel is something to be proud of owing to the legitimacy of the protest rather than because it is dominated by groups out to cause trouble.

To summarise so far, the examples I have explored perform interlocking functions. The writer is using oppositions to emphasise the range of people on the demonstration, using both ends of mainly constructed semantic dimensions of opposition, whether it be a conventional one of age, or less conventional ones based on clothing, or the kinds of medium employed and the messages on them. This *inclusive* function allows the *Sunday Mirror* to feel comfortable with supporting a movement which in other circumstances has led to riots and in the case of Eastern Europe in the late 1980s, peaceful revolutions which brought down governments. At the same time however, the writer is bending over backwards to cordon off these protestors within a boundary of acceptability, and hence *exclude* those which a reader might associate with more radical intentions. The reader can feel it is fine to support peace-loving, brave, patriotic, genuine, moderate, banner-carrying, football supporting, Joe Public parents of young children of all races and creeds, as long as they do not have to sympathise with violent, extremist, cowardly, traitorous, unwashed, childless, anarchist, placard-wielding anti-capitalists!

## 6 Conclusion – media constructed oppositions and ideology

The construction of binary oppositions in the press has been the subject of much scrutiny (see for instance van Dijk 2006, Thetala 2001, Leudar, Marsland & Nekvapil 2004, Bishop & Jaworski 2003). Even the unlikely figure of the Bishop of Liverpool, James Jones, made the following point in the British newspaper *The Guardian*:

> ' … the most alarming feature of the media-dominated universe is that it presents the world in terms of opposites and polarises every issue into extreme positions. For every view the media seek the extreme opposite to present the debate as dramatically as possible … it reinforces entrenched positions and becomes the enemy of understanding of the truth of an issue or a policy or a situation … the source of alarm … is the way that such polarisation sets us a dynamic in society that resists reconciliation'. (*Guardian*, 10th January 2005)

Fowler (1991)[13] conducted one of the first important systematic studies of the relationship between language choice in the news media and the embedded ideological stance taken. He argued that news articles often presuppose readers' alignment with a consensual view of society, i.e.

'the theory that a society shares all its interests in common, without division or variation'. (1991: 16) This is commonly instantiated by first person plural pronouns *we* or *us*, which are used especially in opinion and editorial columns, to speak on behalf of and simultaneously include their readership and sometimes 'the Nation' in general. This is clearly apparent in the *Sunday Mirror* article whose headlines include 'Listen to **Us**' (my emphasis) whereby **us** will be ostensibly referring to the protestors, with the support of the *Mirror* and hence the presumption of that of the readership. Similarly in a separate headline, 'Britain says no to war', 'Britain' here clearly cannot be referring to everyone in the UK or even everybody on the demonstration, but those whom the newspaper deem the voice of reasonable protest and hence acceptably representative of 'the nation'. So Britain is equivalent to **us** which equals the *Sunday Mirror* and its readership which yet again equals the acceptable protestors on the demonstration. However, according to Fowler, for **us** to be meaningful, there has to be a **they/them**, which in the case of the right-wing press especially includes 'trade unionists, socialist council leaders, teachers, blacks, social workers, rapists, homosexuals etc.' (1991: 16) To update this list we might add Muslims, asylum seekers, paedophiles, travellers, 'chavs' and 'hoodies', who regularly appear as falling outside of the consensual norm in news reports. Fowler goes on to explain how news values often rely on these categorisations, of which stereotyping is one of the effects, to:

'create a socially-constructed mental pigeon-hole into which events and individuals can be sorted, thereby making such events and individuals comprehensible: 'mother', 'patriot', 'businessman', 'neighbour' on the one hand, versus 'hooligan', 'terrorist', 'foreigner', 'wet [Tory], on the other …'. (1991: 17)

Crucially, these categories are socially constructed by discourse, and are not directly reflective of a much more complex external reality. But their use in the media reinforces the reader's tendency to want to fit people into these groupings as a way of comprehending events. Furthermore there is a dialectical relationship between news events and news values, in which the 'occurrence of a striking event will reinforce a stereotype, and reciprocally, the firmer the stereotype, the more likely are relevant events to become news'. (1991: 17) Similarly, Sonwalker (2005) argues that mainstream journalism is predicated upon the centrality of the *us-them* binary and was particularly prominent after the attack on the Twin Towers. This 'banal journalism' as he calls it, is hegemonic in that:

> 'it caters to the 'us' and presents one view as *the* worldview of an entire society or nation. After 11 September, this omnipresent but unstated sense of 'us' and 'them' came out of the closet' (2005: 263).

Fowler (1991), citing Chibnall (1977), claims that the relationship between consensus and pronoun use reflects a set of abstract news values often manifesting themselves as simple binary pairs.[14] Chibnall's binary pairs fall under the headings 'positive legitimating values' and 'negative illegitimate values'. Although some of the categories under these headings may need updating 30 years later (Fowler adds **self –reliance/dependence** to the list), many of them relate very aptly to the *Sunday Mirror* report analysed above including most of the pairs of opposites which act to differentiate the two types of protestors. Figure 2 illustrates this[15]. The fact that Chibnall chooses to categorise these values in relation to legitimacy is apt, as this covers both the obsession with the 'rightness' and 'wrongness' of staying within the boundaries of the rule of law, as well as the broader moral concepts of legitimacy (e.g. *that is a legitimate course of action*). This presupposes of course that the values in the left column are legitimate and those in the second are not. Fowler claims that the liberal position would be to accept variety and departures from the norm as long as they are within tolerable boundaries and hence containable within what is deemed the consensus (fitting under the 'tolerance' heading in Chibnall's list), what he calls 'tolerant pluralism' (1991: 52). This, I would argue, is the position *partially* taken up by the Sunday Mirror, especially at the points in which the writer focuses on the diversity and inclusivity on the demonstration. The more conservative stance would embrace the **us/ them** dichotomy much more enthusiastically. According to Fowler:

> 'Law and public opinion stipulate that there are many ideas and behaviours which are to be condemned as outside the pale of consensus: people who practise such behaviours are branded as 'subversives', 'perverts', 'deviants', 'dissidents', 'trouble-makers', etc. Such people are subjected to marginalisation or repression; and the contradiction returns, because consensus decrees that there are some people outside the consensus. The 'we' of consensus narrows and hardens into a population which sees its interests as culturally and economically valid, but as threatened by a 'them' comprising a motley of antagonistic sectional groups: not only criminals but also trade unionists, homosexuals, teachers, blacks, foreigners, northerners, and so on'.
> (1991: 52-3)

This is the side of the *Mirror* article which focuses on constructing groups as excluded from the consensus. Fowler's claim that the 'consensus decrees that there are some people outside the consensus' is epitomised by the decision to quote the Lancashire mother whose words are used to reinforce who is and is not deemed 'acceptable' and who represents herself and is represented by the writer as falling into the 'acceptable' category.

Fowler goes on to argue that despite the fact that the news media tend to align themselves and strengthen the consensual ideology, they rely on the 'negative, illegitimate values', as without them there would be little news. They often form the staple of what are considered newsworthy stories such as those that:

> 'exemplify the negative attitudes and behaviours thought to be characteristic of 'them'; so the newspapers fill their columns with murder, rape.....freaks: stories of 'the other', 'them' rather 'the familiar', 'us'.' (1991: 53)

The *Mirror* example is a curious one as its primary surface purpose might not seem to be such a voyeuristic fixation with the lives of those on the margins of society, highlighting as it does the power of the people whose desire it is to register a protest. But the very nature of protest, especially against a government elected by the 'legitimate' ballot box , threatens to align the *Mirror* with the values on the right of Chibnall's column, especially when they can be the catalysts of or equivalents to revolution. So they have to stress their distance from this position by showing that its stance falls firmly within the consensus. They achieve this by consistent reference to and disparagement of those who, if they were seen to be sympathetic towards, may alienate their readership, as well as giving ammunition for their competitors.

According to Carr & Zanetti,

> 'Western thought is imbued with a style of thinking based on dichotomy and binary opposition ... Embedded in this fundamental style of thinking, however, are not only oppositions but also hierarchy, in that the existence of such binaries suggests a struggle for predominance. If one position is right, then the other must be wrong' (1999: 324).

Table 2

| 'Positive legitimating values' | 'Acceptable' protestors US | 'Negative, illegitimate values' | 'Unacceptable' protestors THEM |
|---|---|---|---|
| moderation | ordinary people worried mums and dads no boos for the old warlord Joe Public | extremism | extremists, militants, anarchists, anti-capitalists, anti-Americans, traitors, unwashed |
| co-operation | worried mums and dads of all ages, races and religions Make Love not War Young and old, children, invalids, denims/fleeces, fur coats/Barbours | confrontation | violence, fierce messages , Blair and Bush wanted for murder |
| order | little frivolity high spirits not the order of the day, | chaos | violence |
| peacefulness | Make Love not War | violence | The Mob, violence, out in force, fierce messages, murder |
| tolerance compromise | all ages, races, religions no boos for the old warlord | intolerance dogmatism | Blair and Bush wanted for murder |
| constructiveness | Make Love not War | destructiveness | traitors, Blair and Bush wanted for murder |
| realism | genuine feeling Notts County Supporters | ideology | anti-capitalist, anti-American, anarchist |

The *Sunday Mirror* report is one of many very examples of the portrayal of, in this case, group hierarchies based on binary oppositions whereby celebrated in-groups and stigmatised out-groups are constructed in a position of mutually exclusive antagonism.

This chapter has been an attempt to contribute towards our understanding of how we can use theories of oppositional frameworks to recognise and subsequently evaluate the consequences of opposites in context, in this case in a news report of a significant event. There are further studies to be done on frameworks for opposition generation and the cognitive elements of how we might understand non-canonical oppositions. What I hope to have shown, however, is that where oppositions are employed with a measure of concentration in a medium which has a mass readership, there can be serious implications. And if the conflict which still envelops many parts of the world continues to be represented and treated as if there were 'no shades of grey' then we have still a long way to go before there is much chance of a resolution.

## Endnotes

[1] Throughout this article, words and phrases employed as oppositional or *potential* oppositional pairs are in bold typeface, whilst the oppositional triggers (like *not*) are italicised. Where a bold or italicised typeface appears in cited newspaper text, this has been inserted by myself, unless otherwise stated. Where bold or italics appear in cited academic texts, these are in the original, unless otherwise stated.

[2] Other useful introductions to opposites in books on semantics include Jeffries (1998), Lobner (2002), and Kreidler (1998), whilst more detailed examinations of 'antonymy' can be found amongst others in Lehrer & Kittay (eds). (1992), and Lehrer & Lehrer (1982).

[3] Jones and Murphy use the term 'antonymy' in a broader sense than Lyons and Cruse, meaning all instances of oppositions, not just gradable ones.

[4] Made before a joint session of the US congress on 20 September 2001.

[5] I am using Jones's terms for convenience here, however it has to be noted that I find his system of categorisations problematic, and this will be dealt with in a forthcoming paper.

[6] Also see Achugar (2004), Edwards (2004), Edwards & Martin (2004), Lazar & Lazar (2004), Keenan and Dowd (2004) and Martin (2004), for a discourse analytic approach to media responses to September 11th.

[7] It is worth pointing out that the convention of the journalistic 'eye-witness' account is, according to Van Dijk (1988: 86) 'the ultimate warrant of truthfulness ... The immediacy of the description and the closeness of the reporter to the events is a rhetorical guarantee for the truthfulness of the description and, hence, the plausibility of the news.'

[8] In the many informal word association exercises tried at various talks and seminars, nobody has ever come up with **banner** as the opposite of **placard**, and the vast majority of respondents rarely come up with a word, just a look of bewilderment!

[9] There is no space here to explore how it is claimed opposites rely on the interaction between features of equivalence and difference. In many cases the difference is just one minor component, such as the oft-used example between **man** and **woman** whereby they only differ on one semantic dimension i.e. that of gender. In all other comparable ways they are the same i.e. human adults. See Murphy (2003), Jeffries (1998) and Mettinger (1994), amongst others for a discussion on this. When it comes to **placard** and **banner**, 'make **tea** *not* **war**' and many of the examples used in this article, this theory makes for a fascinating investigation.

[10]In a forthcoming paper I will argue that it is possible we might only be able to process non-canonical oppositions by reference to higher level, more general and abstract canonical oppositions.

[11]There are some difficulties with Jones's categories including some omissions, which is a result of his methodology.

[12]Jones (2002) has no category for versions of the *not* **X** *but* **Y** framework, and indeed his system seems flawed when any of the triggers are combined. For instance, which category should this frame be assigned to? This should not matter if one is simply using them as descriptive tools to conduct an analysis, but if producing quantitative statistics based on these categories then this seems highly problematic.

[13]See Fairclough (1989, 1995) for other important work on the relationship between discourse and power in the news media.

[14]For more reading on news values, see Hartley (1982) and Price & Tewksbury (1997).

[15]I have included a few more examples from the report which I have not mentioned in this article for reasons of space.

## References

Achugar, Mariana. 2004. 'The Events and Actors of 11 September 2001 as Seen from Uruguay: Analysis of Daily Newspaper Editorials' in *Discourse and Society* 15 (2–3): 291-320.

Allan, Stuart. 2004. *News Culture.* Milton Keynes: Open University Press.

Allan, Stuart, (ed.). 2005. *Journalism: Critical Issues.* Milton Keynes: Open University Press.

Bishop, Hywel, and Adam Jaworski. 2003. 'We Beat 'em: Nationalism and the Hegemony of Homogeneity in the British Press Reportage of Germany versus England during Euro 2000' in *Discourse & Society* 14(3): 243-71.

Carr, Adrian, and Lisa A. Zanetti. 1999. 'Metatheorizing the Dialectic of Self and Other' in *American Behavioural Scientist* 43(2): 324-45.

Chibnall, Steve. 1977. *Law-and-Order News.* London: Tavistock.

Coe, Kevin, et al. 2004. 'No Shades of Gray: The Binary Discourse of George W. Bush and an Echoing Press' in *Journal of Communication* 54(2): 234-52.

Cruse, Alan. 1986. *Lexical Semantics.* Cambridge: Cambridge University Press.

Edwards, John. 2004. 'After the Fall' in *Discourse and Society* 15 (2-3): 155-84.

Edwards, J., and J. R. Martin. 2004. Introduction: Approaches to Tragedy' in *Discourse and Society* 15 (2–3): 147-54.

Fowler, Roger. 1991. *Language in the News: Discourse and Ideology in the Press*. London: Routledge.

Fairclough, Norman. 1989. *Language and Power*. London: Longman

Fairclough, Norman. 1995. *Media Discourse*. London: Edward Arnold

Graham, Phil., Thomas Keenan and A. Dowd. 2004. 'A Call to Arms at the End of History: A Discourse-historical Analysis of George W. Bush's Declaration of War on Terror' in *Discourse and Society* 15 (2-3): 199-221.

Hartley, John. 1982. *Understanding News*. London: Routledge.

Jeffries, Lesley. 1998. *Meaning in English: An Introduction to Language Study*. Basingstoke: Palgrave.

Jones, Steven. 2002. *Antonymy: A Corpus-based perspective*. London: Routledge.

Kreidler, Charles. W. 1998. *Introducing English Semantics*. London: Routledge.

Lazar, Annita, and Michelle M. Lazar. 2004. 'The Discourse of the New World Order: 'Out-casting' the Double Face of Threat' in *Discourse and Society* 15 (2-3): 223-42.

Lehrer, Adrienne, and Eva Feder Kittay (eds). 1992. *Frames, Fields, and Contrasts: New Essays in Semantic and Lexical Organisation*. Hillsdale, NJ: Lawrence Erlbaum Associates.

Leudar, Ivan., Victoria Marsland and Jiri Nekvapil. 'On Membership Categorization': 'Us', 'Them' and 'Doing Violence' in Political Discourse' in *Discourse and Society* 15 (2-3): 243-66.

Lehrer, Adrienne, and Keith Lehrer. 1982. 'Antonymy' in *Linguistics and Philosophy* 5: 483-501.

Löbner, Sebastian. 2002. *Understanding Semantics*. London: Arnold.

Lyons, John. 1977. *Semantics*. Cambridge: Cambridge University Press.

Martin, J. R. 2004. 'Mourning: How we get Aligned' in *Discourse and Society* (15) 2-3: 321-44.

Medhurst, Martin J. 2000. 'Text and Context in the 1952 Presidential Campaign: Eisenhower's "I shall go to Korea" speech' in *Presidential Studies Quarterly* 30: 464-84.

Mettinger, Arthur. 1994. *Aspects of Semantic Opposition in English*. Oxford: Oxford University Press.

Murphy, M. Lynne. 2003. *Semantic Relations and the Lexicon*. Cambridge: Cambridge University Press.

Price, Vincent, and David Tewksbury. 1997. 'News Values and Public Opinion: A Theoretical Account of Media Priming and Framing' in *Progress in Communication Sciences* 13:173–212.

Quirk, Randolph, et al. 1972. *A Grammar of Contemporary English*. London: Longman.

Raum, Richard. D., and James S. Measell. 1974. 'Wallace and His Ways: A Study of the Rhetorical Genre of Polarization' in *Central States Speech Journal* (25): 28-35.

Rennell, Tony. 2003. 'Listen to Us; The People's March: A Tide of Protest – Britain Says No to War' in *Sunday Mirror* (16 Feb. 2003).

Short, Mick. 1996. *Exploring the Language of Poems, Plays and Prose*. London: Longman.

van Dijk, Teun A. 1988. *News as Discourse*. Lawrence Erlbaum Associates

van Dijk, Teun A. 2006. 'Discourse and Manipulation' in *Discourse & Society* 17(3): 359-83.

# The Same Old Story: Uncovering Archetypal Narrative in 'Real Home' Magazine Features

Diane Davies

## Abstract

The role of linguistic style in the construction of shared meanings can be usefully explored through the analysis of the many media discourses today that represent, construct and 'sell' lifestyle concepts. Kress & Van Leeuwen (2001) have noted how, from a social-semiotic point of view, lifestyle has become 'the culturally dominating paradigm in the public domain'. In the marketing context, lifestyle is now seen as having largely replaced the traditional demographic segmentation based on class, age and gender (Vyncke, 2002). Lifestyle discourses have thus come increasingly to define how people see themselves and the social networks to which they belong.

Keywords: media discourse, lifestyle, social networks, social semiotics, multi-modality

## 1 Introduction

Work by Giddens (1991) and others have drawn attention to the way the concept of lifestyle allows individuals in late modern society to align and realign themselves to others according to shared attitudes and values, aesthetic tastes and media preferences. However, while creating the sense of shared aspirations, lifestyles are, at the same time, 'sold' to us as part of the expression of individuality. Consumers know that the products they buy in high street shops and department stores (e.g. clothes) are the same as those bought by millions of other people around the world, yet they are still persuaded that they can have such a thing as a personal style and 'are making creative use of the whole range of semiotic resources made available to them by the culture industries' (Machin & van Leeuwen 2005:585). In this sense, the power of lifestyle discourse appears to lie in its capacity to appeal in different ways to both personal and group aspirations, suggesting how we can identify with others while trying to persuade us that we can still be ourselves.

Homes and decoration magazines are classified, according to National Readership Survey data, as women's monthly periodicals, most of their readers being female (generally over 70%), and the average readership age ranges from late 30s to late 40s. What I am calling *real home* narratives for the purposes of this paper are the main features of these publications, appearing in the contents pages under generic headings such as 'readers' homes', 'inspiring homes' (or indeed 'real homes'), and narrating how specific homeowners have designed, decorated, furnished and generally transformed the houses they live in. Unlike shorter 'makeover' articles which focus on the improvement of a specific area of the home, such as a hallway, spare bedroom or kitchen, 'real home' narratives give an account of a complete home, aiming to construct a coherent 'story' around the social identities, actions and aspirations of the homeowners and their families.

Magazine reading has become increasingly popular in the UK over the past decade or so. According to *PPA Marketing* consumers increased their expenditure in the magazine sector between 1994 and 2004 by 67%, the number of consumer magazines grew by 25% and magazines were, in spite of this, able to increase their cover price by 62%. The time devoted by the public to magazine reading also increased at the expense of newspapers, which saw a marked decline. Combined results from the National Readership Survey (NRS) and Quality of Reading Survey (QRS) have shown that, as a medium, the consumer magazine is strongly targeted, with regular readers appearing to identify strongly with their chosen magazines, making their purchase decisions on the basis of individual attitudes, interests and values, and seeing their favourite magazine as a 'trusted friend'.

Here I discuss a selection of features from a sample of popular home magazines on sale in the UK in 2005. My main aim is to explore how these texts use linguistic style to construct meanings likely to be shared, or aspired to, by their target readership. I suggest that they do this not simply through aspects of discourse and style that they have in common with magazine features in general, but, more especially, through their use of narrative, and in particular their adaptation and exploitation of an archetypal narrative structure. I also argue that, from a social cognition perspective, some useful points of comparison can be made between this genre of magazine discourse and literary narrative. To consider the main characteristics of the *real home* narrative, I compared six features, one from each of the following magazines:

*BBC Good Homes* (March 2005): 'Renovated Edwardian Home', by Neil Davis (Photographs), Teresa Ward (Feature) and Mary-Rose Fox-Ness (Styling).

*Country Homes and Interiors* (November 2005): 'River Life', by Anthea Gerrie (Feature) and Robert Sanderson (Photographs).

*House Beautiful* (April 2005): 'It's modern but full of charm'. [Names of feature writer and photographer not shown.]

*Ideal Home* (July 2005): 'I've learned a lot about living in a small space', by Pat Garratt (Feature), Jennifer Morgan (Styling) and Winfried Heinze (Photographs)

*Livingetc* (December 2005): 'Home for the Holidays', by Mary Weaver (Words); Bob Smith (Photography) and Mette Johnson (Styling)

*Real Homes Magazine* (March 2005): 'I'm so glad I was brave enough to go for bold colours', by Alice Moro (Words) and David Giles (Photography)

In a highly competitive market, each magazine has a well researched and defined reader profile. For example, while *Ideal Home* readers are described as 'practical, family oriented DIYers' who apparently 'love to indulge themselves', readers of *Livingetc* are thought to be 'stylish shoppers, confident in their modern tastes' who 'love their gadgets and appliances' [source: www.ipcmedia.com]. Of course, it is worth noting that the target readers of home magazines are always supplemented by 'accidental' readers, those who pick up copies in friends' homes, health centres, hotels and the like, who may or may not share some of the characteristics of the 'ideal' target consumer group.

## 2 The multimodal dimension

Before discussing the stylistics of the *real home* feature, I should point out that these narratives do not rely solely on language to encourage an identification of the reader with the 'characters' being written about and their projects. In home magazines visual and linguistic texts jointly construct the 'stories' being told. The photographs, with or without the homeowners, are designed to convey attractive, reassuring images of home as a place of refuge from the pressures of daily life, a place of renewal, calm and, usually, family togetherness. They may, for instance, show a prepared bath surrounded by candles, a shopping basket left at the foot of the stairs, washed strawberries in a bowl in the kitchen, an open book on a sofa, a cat waiting in a hallway. When homeowners appear in them, they are often shown seated on sofas with their children or partners, reading books, holding cups of coffee, frequently smiling at someone in or outside the picture. A framework for analysing the structure and meaning of visual representation can be found in Kress & van Leeuwen (1996), who adapt a systemic-functional model of language to describe the narrative and conceptual processes conveyed in images, the positioning of the viewer, modality, and the placing of different elements in an image in terms of 'given' and 'new' information structure. To illustrate one of these dimensions, modality, with regard to the use of colour in 'real home' narratives, most images in home magazines are glossy photographs, rich in colour differentiation, detail, brightness and image depth etc, features which mark high modality according to this model and, appropriately in such a commercially driven domain, high 'credibility'. In more recent work Kress & Van Leeuwen (2001) have noted with reference to an article about a child's bedroom makeover in *House Beautiful* (September 1996), that language and image have 'complementary specialist tasks' and have distinguished between the roles of images and language in this context still more clearly.

In spatial matters, language comes a poor second to image. But then, language is used for other things: to tell the story of the way the house was acquired and the room decorated, to link the layout of the room to the child's activities, to reinforce the meanings of the colour scheme by means of evaluative adjectives, and to bring out, however implicitly, the pedagogic 'message' of the room (Kress & van Leeuwen 2001: 18).

In my own sample texts it is clear that language and image have these distinct but complementary functions. It is the linguistic text rather than the photography that provides the ongoing story, since the main images focus only on the finished product. We do not (as in TV shows about home improvement) see photographic records of any of the decorating or design setbacks described in the words, for instance, or any incomplete stages in the process. Nevertheless, the images do reinforce the narrative in effective ways, for instance by letting us see more of the homeowners (only the images show what they look like, how they dress etc, aspects which the viewer interprets socially and culturally) .This can be best illustrated with reference to an image from the feature in *Livingetc*, which shows, alongside a view of the décor in the young homeowners' spare bedroom, a smaller image of the couple outside the home altogether, wearing scooter helmets and looking totally unburdened by the responsibilities of their home project. This seems very much in tune with the magazine's targeting of confident consumers with fashionable tastes.

### 3 The magazine feature as discourse type

Delin (2000) discusses the discourse structure of magazine features as a genre, noting that they typically have a title and then a shorter text called a 'standfirst', which has a summarising function, followed by an intro to the main body of the feature. Titles, she writes, are meant to be 'intriguing rather than descriptive' and are usually 'semantically incomplete' in that they invite us to read on to work out what they are actually referring to. This structure is generally what we find with *real home* features. Looking at my sample, all except one ('Renovated Edwardian house', *BBC Good Homes*) use a title which in some ways 'intrigues' and invites further reading. An example is 'River Life' (*Country Homes and Interiors*) which uses a phrase we might initially associate more with the natural life of the river and riverbank, fish and animal (or perhaps with people who live on canal boats), than with the owner-occupiers of houses situated nearby. Of course, the intention here is to highlight the close proximity of nature to the elegant and upmarket home being described. Another example is the title 'Home for the holidays' (*Livingetc*), which we soon learn focuses on a 'globetrotting couple' whose jobs give them the opportunity to spend their time in a number of different places. Thus the chosen titles are in keeping with the underlying aims of the narrative.

Drawing on manuals for feature writers, Delin (2000) notes that three key 'values' in the writing of features are 'evidentiality', 'discursivity' and 'point of view'. By *evidentiality* she refers to the use of authoritative and diverse sources of information, which can be illustrated, for example, by the direct quoting of the words of people interviewed by the writer. By *discursivity* is meant that 'what is presented is not just plain facts, but explanation and elaboration', and by *point of view* the fact that magazine features convey opinions and do not remain neutral. A feature writer will use vocabulary conveying 'affective meaning' and through this will also appeal to the target reader's own beliefs and assumptions.

## 4 Direct representation of speech

Looking at the typical *real home* feature from the perspective of Delin's three values, we see that *evidentiality* is achieved in this sub-genre mainly through a frequent use of direct speech representation. In my sample every feature makes significant use of direct speech. In the feature from *Ideal Home*, for example, 45% of the sentences contain direct speech, most of them being 'untagged' or not used with a reporting clause. Unusually, the body text of the feature from *BBC Good Homes* is written entirely as a sequence of direct questions (in bold typeface) and answers, with only the answers in inverted commas and (because the identity of the homeowner answering the questions is established at the beginning) with no tagging used at all:

*Who lives here?* 'I'm Sally Begg, 36, and I live here with my husband Steve, 38, who works as a crude oil trader in the City of London. I used to work in the City, but now look after our children, Alice, six, and one-year-old Poppy.'

Taking the sample as a whole, I found that an average of 53% of the sentences used contain direct speech, with varying use of tagging, depending on whether more than one of the homeowners are quoted and on how much narration intervenes between the quotations. Interestingly, in three out of the six cases, direct representation of speech is also used in the title of the feature, suggesting that it is considered an effective stylistic device for attracting the reader's attention. Wherever used, direct speech is not only attention-catching, however, but also a means of reinforcing the 'truth value' of what is being communicated about the home transformation. Readers tend to assume that speech represented between inverted commas is an exact report of what was said, though this may not always be the case. As we can see in the example from *BBC Good Homes* quoted above, the actual words spoken are inevitably subject to some journalistic compression and 'styling'. The real give-away here is the insertion of the ages of the speaker, her husband and one of their children in the form of single phrases following the proper nouns (as in typical newspaper reporting). In everyday speech the use of an additional independent or relative clause would be far more likely (i.e. 'my husband Steve, *who's* 38' or 'my husband Steve, *he's* 38'). And of course the hesitations, reformulations and other non-fluency features of spontaneous speech are not recorded at all.

## 5 Authority and expertise

While considering *evidentiality*, it is worth looking at whether *real home* features achieve this quality through the use of direct speech alone, or whether they also construct a sense of authority in any other ways. There is an interesting difference in this regard between magazine features and TV programmes about home makeovers, where the role of the 'expert' has considerable prominence through its merging with the role of presenter (and where expert presenters are indeed celebrities). *Real home* features do not seem to foreground the writer as expert or authority in any way. Instead the writer is often no more than an appreciative, complimentary reporter, while it is the homeowners themselves whose training and skills are, directly or indirectly, showcased:

> 'We were looking at Georgian architecture for the proportions and the symmetry,' says Clare, who studied interior design before taking a career break to have sons Sam and Toby. (*Country Homes and Interiors*)
>
> As a dealer in decorative antiques, she was itching to get her hands on a house that would be a suitable backdrop for her particular style of shabby French chic – and this small cottage, with its big potential, was ideal. (*Ideal Home*)
>
> 'We approached it as if Chris were the client and I the designer,' explains Rebecca, who, in between modelling jobs, is nearly through an interior design diploma. […]
>
> In between work on their home (which took around 14 months), Rebecca has started her own company, Interior Desires, and picked up some interesting work. She is furnishing a smart house in Kensington, as well as designing a spa for a men's basketball team in   Detroit. (*Livingetc*)

No doubt homeowners with professional design training and their own design companies are likely to welcome the publicity of having a feature published about their home as it is an indirect form of advertising (indeed they may well actively court the interest of magazine editors). From the point of view of the magazine's readers, however, this may not always be welcome. Reacting to the fact that many of the homes featured are those of people 'in the trade', a reader of *Livingetc* makes this point unequivocally on the Letters page of the magazine, writing: '… I have just one small rant: is it possible to feature great homes that aren't the finished result of couples who are either architects or interior designers or, worse, both? Go on, give Joe Public a chance'. Predictably, the editorial response to this criticism does not attempt to justify the bias towards the use of professional designers' homes but states: *We're always looking for new homes to feature, Rowan, so why not send some snaps of your home to livingetc@ipcmedia.com.*

In lifestyle discourse across different media a careful balance is usually struck between recourse to expertise and the need for a central narrative that encourages empathy and engagement on the part of the target audience. In TV lifestyle programmes, expert presenters carefully avoid sounding over-authoritative or formal, instead appearing to act in an easygoing partnership with their 'clients' and to be open to negotiation. Referring to experts on gardening programmes, Taylor (2002) writes that they 'strive to establish empathy with viewers by lowering the differences in knowledge, personality and outlook between themselves and audiences'. In *real home* features, where some direct expert advice to the reader (e.g. about furniture, fabrics, colour choice) may accompany the article, this is kept visually separate from the main narrative within specially dedicated columns or boxes on the margins of the main story (and in a much smaller font). And even with the benefit of such presentational distinction, these more peripheral texts can still betray an apparent reluctance to use exclusively informative or instructional language. They do this by referring back to the main narrative and inviting us to emulate the 'look' achieved by the featured homeowners or to 'steal' their ideas. It is thus the resonating power of the central story that is meant to hold our attention, while any further guidance provided often appears to operate like footnotes to that story.

**6 The Domestic 'Quest'**

We only need to read a few *real home* features to see that they usually begin with an account of the homeowners' recognition of something they would like to achieve, followed by their decision to fulfil this ambition through a particular set of actions. The narrative then moves on to the challenges and setbacks in the process itself, and finally its successful completion and the homeowners' evaluation of it. Although readers of home magazines are not likely to be consciously aware of it, this narrative structure has much in common with the archetypal 'quest' story:

> Far away, we learn, there is some priceless goal, worth any effort to achieve: a treasure; a promised land; something of infinite value. From the moment the hero learns of this prize, the need to set out on the long hazardous journey to reach it becomes the most important thing to him in the world. Whatever perils and diversions lie in wait on the way, the story is shaped by that one overriding imperative: and the story remains unresolved until the objective has been finally, triumphantly secured. (Booker 2004: 69)

The hunt for treasures and journeys through perilous lands may seem a far cry from the concerns of home living magazines, but the stories we find in them exploit many of the basic elements of the quest plot. Usually, the *real home* narrative refers early on to the homeowners' feeling of dissatisfaction - what Booker (2004) calls 'constriction' - and the recognition of an urgent need to pursue a valuable goal (i.e. the goal of a more attractive home). However, the challenge of finding the right property and/or transforming it proves more threatening than expected (there are time or money problems; temptations to give up or to lower ambitions; distractions from the main tasks; expensive mistakes etc). In spite of these pitfalls, our heroic homeowners, aided by a small band of close companions and helpers (usually friends and relatives), manage to keep their sights on the original goal and, despite their ordeals, eventually triumph, having a sense of achievement and renewal. These different stages of the 'domestic quest' can be illustrated with the following extracts:

## Sense of constriction

'When Ian and Lara Lay learned that their second child was on the way, they knew that living on a busy junction with no off-street parking and a tiny garden would no longer do.' (*Real Homes Magazine*)

'After a decade of having to make do with a cramped and dated bathroom in their 1930s three-bedroom semi in Surrey, Kate and Paul Stratton decided to tackle the problem.' (*BBC Good Homes*, March 05)

'...for years their dreams of owning this imposing riverside mini-mansion just outside London seemed dashed'. (*Country Homes and Interiors*)

## Companions and helpers:

'Now, seven years on, after modelling their way around Asia and the States and doing up individual places, this is the first home they've created together....' (*Livingetc*)

'Her father, an electrician and skilled craftsman, volunteered to do most of the work and, with Kev, tackled a vast list of electrical, plumbing and structural jobs'. (*Ideal Home*)

*Threats and ordeals*

> 'Despite its grand appearance, the house posed big challenges to bring it up to date after years as a rental property.' (*Country Homes and Interiors*)

> 'Not long after they moved in, part of the Lays' roof was damaged in a storm.' (*Real Homes Magazine*)

> '"It wasn't until I finished the last room that I realised it was totally dreadful, and we had to buy gallons of paint to cover it all up again!"'. (*House Beautiful*)

*Life renewal:*

> 'Now that all the work is complete the McMasters are glad they followed their instincts and took on the dark terrace. 'Everything turned out as we hoped – probably one of the advantages of taking our time and thinking things through,' says Maria. (*House Beautiful*)

> 'There's always a new project in the offing,' says Lara. 'We're delighted to be living in such an adaptable and constantly evolving house.' (*Real Homes Magazine*)

> 'We've done pretty much everything we want to do to this house now, so we're happy to relax for a while'. (*BBC Good Homes*)

Interestingly, the 'life renewal' phase does not typically produce a sense of permanent resolution in *real home* narratives; instead the homeowners are often quoted as saying they have yet further goals and projects in mind for the future. This can be linked with changes in domestic life and patterns of consumption that lifestyle media and related industries have in part brought about. As Chapman (1999) points out, the many home magazines on the market, along with such phenomena as the growth in DIY and the accessibility of large, edge-of-town furniture and decorating stores, have actively encouraged people to want to change the look of their homes far more often than they did in the past. Today the concept of the constantly evolving house is not only taken for granted in this competitive area of lifestyle media but is no doubt vital to its commercial survival.

## 7 From Discourse to Narrative

Since the most important stylistic characteristic of *real home* features is, in my view, their use of a narrative framework, I prefer to substitute the concepts of 'discursivity' and 'point of view', as used by Delin (2000) with reference to magazine features in general, with the concepts of 'narrative organisation' and 'narrative viewpoint' respectively. In this context, it can be suggested that discursivity is more than simply a rhetorical structure that shows the writer to be variously 'elaborating', 'describing' and 'explaining' etc. Because the discourse has narrative form it automatically has the potential to recall and exploit known patterns of storytelling that can subconsciously affect readers wherever they occur. Likewise, looking at 'point of view' as '*narrative* point of view' allows us to investigate more than just the presence of a commenting and evaluating 'journalistic' voice; for example, we can discover whether the perspectives and viewpoints of the story's 'characters' (in this case the homeowners) are represented through possible shifts in viewpoint or 'focalization' (Genette 1972). The possibility of such shifts in point of view also suggests that the *real home* feature may have some stylistic affinity with narratives in other domains, such as literature, and that readers may, to some degree, read *real home* narratives in the way they read fictional narratives. This may seem paradoxical, given that the homeowners are real people. However, unless we happen to know them, the fact that they are real individuals and not fictional characters may not be as important as might at first be assumed. After all, they 'exist', as far as the reader is concerned, only within the limits of the narrative about them (in that sense they are similar to fictional characters), and we can imagine their story only in the way intended by the narrating voice (that is, we have no other version of the story to draw on, as we might have in the case of, say, a biographical account of a famous person). This has an important implication too, I think, in establishing how style and social cognition may be related. The reader recognises the homeowners as both *social* actors in a specifically contemporary discursive context (reinforced by the photographic images), and as *archetypal* actors in a story which has, despite having many possible forms, guises and variations, one basic underlying shape.

## 8 Narrative Viewpoint and Focalisation

As noted earlier, *real home* narratives make substantial use of direct speech representation. This can create, for the reader, the illusion of hearing the speaker's voice and even of being the addressee of the words spoken. However, like fictional narratives, they also represent some of the *thoughts* of their characters. If we think of thought as 'mental utterance', indirect thought 'offers the sense but not the precise grammar or wording of a character's thought' (Toolan, 2001:120). Here are some examples:

'But Sharon and Dermot were delighted to be homeowners at last and knew the property's potential would make it a good investment.' (*House Beautiful*)

'As the building work had been so expensive, Lara knew she couldn't afford
to make            mistakes with the aesthetics and took care to get the colours
just right.' (*Real Homes Magazine*)

'Chris was suitably impressed'. (*Livingetc*)

'Anne-Marie is thrilled with the end result' (*Ideal Home*)

Unlike the writer of fictional narrative, though, the writer of the *real
home* feature can only represent thoughts or feelings based on what
the homeowners have made explicit (or at least suggested) in their
speech. As a result, the use of indirect thought is quite limited in this
genre. And there is certainly no call for a sustained imaginative
representation of thought processes of the kind we associate with
fictional narrative such as the following:

> The dining-room was big, but overfurnished. Chelsea would have moaned
> aloud. Mr Wilcox had eschewed those decorative schemes that wince, and
> relent, and refrain, and achieve beauty by sacrificing comfort and pluck. After
> so much self-colour and self-denial, Margaret viewed with relief the
> sumptuous dado, the frieze, the gilded wallpaper, amid whose foliage parrots
> sang. It would never do with her own furniture, but those heavy chairs, that
> immense sideboard loaded with presentation plate, stood up against its
> pressure like men. The room suggested men, and Margaret, keen to derive the
> modern capitalist from the warriors and hunters of the past, saw it as an
> ancient guest-hall, where the lord sat at meat among his thanes. Even the
> Bible – the Dutch Bible that Charles had brought back from the Boer War –
> fell into position. Such a room admitted loot.
>
> 'Now the entrance hall.'
>
> The entrance hall was paved.
>
> 'Here we fellows smoke.'
>
> We fellows smoked in chairs of maroon leather. It was as if a motor-car had
> spawned. 'Oh, jolly!' said Margaret, sinking into one of them.
>
> (E. M. Forster, *Howards End*, 1910)

This extract occurs at the point in the novel where Mr Wilcox is
showing Margaret Schlegel round his London house with a view,
ostensibly, to letting the property to her and her family. However, his
real intention is to use the occasion to make her a proposal of
marriage. Margaret is herself aware of the growing intimacy between
them and realises that a proposal is a possibility. These feelings
influence her thoughts strongly at this point in the narrative and she
views the room and furniture as clues to the character of the man she
may marry. While the text has an omniscient third-person narrator, the
focalization or 'angle of vision' (Rimmon-Kenan, 1983) of the
narrative is clearly that of Margaret for most of this extract. We are

aware of her physical, cognitive and emotional orientation throughout: she interprets the room in gendered and colonialist terms, preferring to see in Mr Wilcox the figure of a feudal 'lord' than a 'modern capitalist'. In 'It would never do with her own furniture…' and 'We fellows smoked in chairs of maroon leather' we find examples of 'free indirect thought', a blending of focalizer and narrative voice that brings the character's subconscious to the foreground.

Clearly, the use of free indirect thought is not a feature we would associate with *real home* narrative, and so here the two genres obviously diverge markedly. The narrator of the *real home* story simply does not have the potential 'omniscience' of the fictional narrator in the representation of a character's thought.

## 9 Conclusion

The use of narrative is not the only stylistic feature that encourages shared meanings in *real home* stories. For example, words and expressions of volition (i.e. wishes, intentions, insistence etc) also play a part, as does idiomatic and clichéd language. However, the use of narrative is, I would argue, a more fundamental stylistic choice than these, since it frames the whole text and, as noted above, even influences the shorter, peripheral texts that may accompany the narrative, often making them virtual extensions of the main story.

As we have seen, the fact that the *real home* feature exploits the basic narrative structure of the quest means that it constructs shared meanings through using one of the main archetypal patterns of storytelling through the ages. But we can take this still further and make a more direct connection to readers themselves by adding that life, too, can be seen as a narrative. The philosopher Paul Ricouer argues that personal identity is only really understood as 'narrative identity' within the narrative of life, achieving closure when that life is interpreted by others, just as literary narratives are 'completed' by the interpretation of readers (Simms, 2003). We might argue, then, that stories about others' lives (whether in popular media or literary discourse) are powerful because they remind us, as it were, of the ongoing narrative of our own lives. While, in post-structuralist terms, it is true that the social meanings constructed by media narratives can be seen as myths and ideologies that we may wish to resist (Fulton et al, 2005), the power of narrative itself in giving structure to experience is far harder to reject.

# References

Booker, Christopher. 2004. *The Seven Basic Plots: Why We Tell Stories.* London: Continuum.

Chapman, Tony. 1999. 'Stage Sets for Ideal Lives: Images of home in contemporary show homes' in Chapman, Tony and Jenny Hockey (eds) *Ideal Homes? Social Change and Domestic Life.* London: Routledge: 44-58.

Delin, Judy. 2000. *The Language of Everyday Life: An Introduction.* London: Sage.

Forster, E. M. [1910] 1941. *Howards End.* London: Penguin.

Fulton, Helen, et al. 2005. *Narrative and Media.* Cambridge: Cambridge University Press.

Genette, Gerard. 1972. *Figures III.* Seuil: Paris (tr. 1980 *Narrative discourse*, Basil Blackwell).

Giddens, Anthony. 1991. *Modernity and Self Identity: Self and Society in the Late Modern Age.* Oxford: Polity.

Kress, Gunther and Theo van Leeuwen. 1996. *Reading Images: The Grammar of Visual Design.* London: Routledge.

Kress, Gunther, and Theo van Leeuwen. 2001. *Multimodal Discourse: The Modes and Media of Contemporary Communication.* London: Arnold.

Machin, David, and Theo van Leeuwen. 2005. 'Language Style and Lifestyle: The Case of a Global Magazine' in *Media, Culture & Society* 27(4): 577-600.

Rimmon-Kenan, Shlomith. 1983. *Narrative Fiction: Contemporary Poetics.* London: Methuen.

Simms, Karl. 2003. *Paul Ricoeur.* London: Routledge.

Taylor, Lisa. 2002. 'From Ways of Life to Lifestyle: The 'Ordinari-ization' of British Gardening Lifestyle Television' in *European Journal of Communication* 17 (4): 479-93.

Toolan, Michael. 2001. *Narrative: A Critical Linguistic Introduction.* (2nd ed.) London: Routledge.

Vyncke, P. 2002. 'Lifestyle Segmentation: From Attitudes, Interests and Opinions, to Values, Aesthetic Styles, Life Visions and Media Preferences' in *European Journal of Communication* 17(4): 445-63.

# Forms of Address: Social Value and Expressive Potential

Iryna Tryshchenko

## Abstract

By studying the use of metaphoric forms of address in a number of works of fiction, this article concludes that they may be classified according to the lexical composition of the transferred names and frequency of their usage (clichéd, belonging to a certain style or register, individual). The article also explores the possibility that their vocative position facilitates greater variation in connotative meanings of metaphoric forms of address which leads to the increase of their expressive potential, including the possibility that their connotations may either match or contrast with those of the context in which they occur. It is noted that adjectives used in the vocative position have a vital influence on the expressive potential of metaphoric forms of address. The connotations of these adjectives may both reinforce the connotations of nouns and weaken them. Metaphoric forms of address often serve as means of evaluative reaction to a situation and its various components. They are also used for creation of the ironic or humorous narrative tone and characterization.

Keywords: forms of address, zoometaphors, vocative, metaphorization

One of the main characteristics of human communication is its 'addressness', i.e. its orientation toward the addressee. This was emphasized by a numbers of philosophers and linguists. Thus Volosinov claims that

> Word is a two-sided Act. It is determined equally by whose word it is and for whom it is meant. As a word it is precisely the product of the reciprocal relationship between speaker and listener, addresser and addressee. Each and every word expresses the 'One' in relation to the 'Other'. I give myself verbal shape from another's point of view… (1973:86).

So speech 'addressness' is a universal category and has a vast arsenal of means for its manifestation (both verbal and non-verbal). Forms of address may be considered to form the core of verbal means.

The aim of this paper is to show how forms of address contribute to different aspects of literary communication. The data for my analysis were taken from novels and plays by British and American authors mainly from the 20th century. However, I think that these samples from fictional discourse reflect phenomena occurring in real speech situations. I also intend to demonstrate that forms of address may acquire a great variety of connotative meanings. In this paper I focus on metaphoric form of address.

There exist different theories of metaphor, a multifaceted phenomenon (Black: 1962, Kittay : 1987, Kovecses : 1986, Lakoff & Johnson : 1980, Miall : 1982, Ortony : 1980). I agree with those scholars who highlight the anthropometricity of metaphor or stress the importance of human factor in metaphorization process. I value the interpretative concept of metaphor suggested by a Russian scholar Teliya V.N. (1988). Metaphors in the vocative position can be distinguished according to the degree of their originality. Thus some metaphors are more frequently used and after a certain period of time can be found in dictionaries, others are less frequent and belong to one of the stylistic registers. There are also the metaphors that exist only in a certain context. Occasional formations, metaphoric forms of address including, have greater expressive potential than the trite ones. Therefore I am particularly interested in the usage of metaphor and other stylistic devices based on the stylistically marked occasional nominations. So I am interested in the usage of secondary nominations acquiring stylistic markedness in the context as address forms.

Zoosemic metaphors constitute the bulk of metaphoric forms of address. Such forms of address are used to express the attitude of the speaker to the addressee more vividly and expressively. A great number of zoometaphors have become clichéd and are fixed in the dictionaries. Accoding to the data of M.A.Olikova out of 578 names of different species and subspecies of animals fixed in Roget's thesaurus, 98 names of animals in the vocative function are found in English-English dictionaries and confirmed by informants. Out of 98 names of different animals 83 have a vividly expressed negative character and only 15 of them a positive one (1979: 53-54).

Clichéd zoometaphors are based on the stereotypes established in society and known to all the speakers of this or that language. But certain deviations from these norms are observed in literary discourse and individual communication. In such cases nontrivial features come into the focus of metaphor. Zoometaphoric forms of address may change their fixed connotations for the opposite ones under the influence of context and communicative situation. In her work M.A. Olikova (1979) gives lists of zoometaphoric forms of address with positive and negative connotations. We have come across a number of animals' names from the negative list used with positive connotations. Let me give several examples:

> (1) "I meant to tell you, Joe," the librarian said, "how much I enjoyed your performance in The Far". "Hell," Teddy said," so did he. I bet he rehearsed those love scenes. Admit it, **you young ram"**. (J. Braine)
>
> (2)"No, **you little goose**. Sharks live in the sea. But you're sharp, Anne. Crocs, that's the trouble." (A. Christie)

The first (1) example contains a fragment of a young man's chat with his friend. The zoometaphor "ram" in the vocative position traditionally has negative connotations. However, in the given example it is not an insult. It sounds friendly and familiar.

In example (2) the zoometaphor "goose" having the meaning "a silly person" fixed in the dictionary with negative connotations accordingly, occurs when a young man addresses his beloved (girlfriend). He points out some example of slow-wittedness of his girlfriend with the help of such form of address, but his general positive attitude to her dominates over this particular evaluation of her behavior. Negative connotations of the noun "goose" are suppressed in its combination with the adjective "little", acquiring the coloring of endearment in this situation.

In the examples given above, the adherent connotation of address forms doesn't wholly suppress the inherent connotation of zoometaphors, but coexists with it, though taking the dominant position. In other words, a general positive attitude of the speaker to the addressee dominates over any particular negative evaluation of the addressee in this or that respect.

However, adjectives defining zoometaphors in the vocative position, may not only suppress their connotations, but also reinforce them. They intensify the feature that metaphoric transfer is based on.

> (3) "She wasn't there. "Where?" At the match, **you silly ass"**.(P.G. Wodehouse)
>
> (4) Ftatateeta (screaming down at one of the porters) Do not step on it. **Oh thou brute beast**. (J.B. Shaw)

In example (3) the metaphoric meaning of the noun "ass" is "a stupid person, a fool". The adjective "silly" has similar meaning. The speaker uses the given form of address to highlight the slow-wittedness of the addressee and emphasize his negative evaluation of this feature.

In example (4) "brute" as an adjective means "like a beast, not sensitive or reasoning". In this case the speaker strives to express her strongly negative attitude to such characteristic features of the addressee as cruelty, insensitivity.

Cases of metaphoric use of birds' names also belong to zoometaphors. Both the generic name "bird" and different species names are used as metaphoric forms of address. Unlike Olikova's data(1979) where the zoometaphor "bird" is included in the list with negative connotations, our analysis shows that this generic name and names of particular birds may also have positive connotations in a certain context.

> (5) "Shall I tell you something?" "Certainly, **old bird**: I said cordially. (P.G. Wodehouse)
>
> (6) Carol: .Isn't it funny you've hit on the truth about me. Val: Well, then fly away, **little bird**, fly away before you - get broke. (T. Williams)
>
> (7) "Now, look here, old friend", I said. ..."Proceed", I said. "You interest me strangely, **old bird**." (P.G. Wodehouse)
>
> (8) Arnie. You're very contained, **my little.sparrow** (D. Storey)

The communication between two close friends is given in example (5). The positive connotation of "bird" in confirmed by the adjacent adjective "old" expressing familiarity and by the adverb "cordially" which is used in the introduction of direct speech and characterizes positively the tone of conversation.

In example (6) the zoometaphor follows the direct nomination of the addressee having positive connotation and intensifies it. The metaphoric form of address expresses the speaker's sympathy with and his positive attitude to the addressee more emphatically. The adjective "little" used in metaphoric vocatives often acquires the meaning of endearment. The metaphoric form of address from example (8) also testifies to it. Example (7) contains the fragment of a friendly chat. The zoometaphor "old bird" is also used as a parallel construction, emphasizing positive connotation of the direct nomination of the addressee.

In the above given examples 1,3,4,6,7,8, metaphoric forms of address render the general positive attitude of the speaker to the addressee, but they don't express the latter's evaluation of this feature.

Unlike zoometaphors, the names of plants used in the vocative position don't usually have fixed connotations. They acquire these or those connotations directly in the context.

> (9)"Tell you, **you cornstalk, you son of a cauliflower**! It's the first time I ever heard such unfeeling remark.... **You turnip** ...You're the looser by this rupture, not me, **pie plant**. Adios." (M. Twain)

> (10) "You shouldn't, he'll just get drunk." "I know. That was his wish. Where can our star sleep, **sweet fern**?" (J.Steinbeck)

> (11) Jerry: ...(he slaps Peter on each 'fight') Fight for that bench; fight for your parakeets; fight for your cats; fight for your two daughters; fight for your wife; fight for your manhood, **you pathetic little vegetable**. (He spits Peter in the face). (E. Albee)

Example (9) is taken from a satirical story by M. Twain. Here the situation of conflict communication is presented. The participants include the editor of an agricultural newspaper and one of the employees temporarily acting for him. This explains the usage of the names of several vegetables and plants by one of the communicants. The speaker uses these forms of address to express his indignation at being fired from the editorial staff and demonstrate his negative attitude to the addressee.

So, in the metaphorization process, neutral plant names used as vocatives may acquire negative connotations in the given situation. The juxtaposition of several vocatives of such a kind and their overlapping meaning components contribute to the strengthening (intensification) of their expressiveness.

Example (10) contains a fragment of a husband and wife's talk. Here the communication is normal. It doesn't have a conflictual character. This example is taken from the novel *The Winter of our Discontent* by J. Steinbeck. Its main character constantly addresses original endearing names (vocatives), including metaphoric ones, to his wife. In this case the metaphoric form of address has positive connotation. Along with the tone of communication, the adjective "sweet", which is used in the vocative position and contains the same of positive evaluation, testifies to it. The speaker wants to express kind, tender feelings to the addressee with the help of this form of address.

In example (11) the communication is of a conflictual and extremely negative character. It's quite natural that in such situation metaphoric forms of address have negative connotations. The adjective "pathetic" used in the vocative emphasizes them. The adjective "little" acquires contemptuous and disparaging meaning in the given context. The speaker uses this metaphoric form of address to badly hurt the addressee's feelings and provoke his retaliation.

Another rather large group of metaphoric forms of address includes names of sweets, pastries and, less frequently, nouns denoting other food products. Metaphorically used names of sweets traditionally have positive connotations. Many of them have become trite (honey, sugar, sweetie).

> (12)...She pulled his head around by one ear and set her cheek against his. "**My old pie,**" he said (F. Scott Fitzgerald)
>
> (13) Marion; Do you know what I saw in the hall just now? In the mirror. My face. My God, I saw my face. It was like seeing my face for the first time. Ronald: Oh, come on. It's not a bad face, **old sausage**.   (A.Ayckborne)
>
> (14) I said seriously, "Look, **cheesecake**, you do think I have a great business brain, don't you?" (J. Steinbeck)

In example (12) a situation of father and daughter's meeting after a long separation is presented. They are both glad to see each other. The father's pleasure and his love for his daughter are expressed by means of a metaphoric form of address. So in this situation the metaphoric form of address has a positive connotation. In addition to the communicative situation, the use in the vocative position of the possessive pronouns "my" and adjective "old" in the familiarizing meaning testify to this.

In example (13) a fragment of the dialogue between husband and wife is given. This metaphoric form of address is not so frequently used. It sounds friendly and familiar. The speaker uses this form of address to calm down and cheer up his interlocutor who is upset because of unpleasant changes in her appearance.

In example (14) a metaphoric form of address is also used in the sphere of family communication. The husband addresses it to his wife. It is clear from the context that the given vocative has positive connotations and expresses benevolent attitude of the speaker to the addressee. This vocative is an individual formation, more original (fresh) than forms of address from previous examples.

I'd like to give two more examples of original metaphoric vocatives. They are used by the main character of the novel *The Winter of our Discontent* by J. Steinbeck. He addresses such vocatives as "my ablative absolute" and "carotene, dear" to his beloved wife. In the first case the term of Latin grammar is used metaphorically and in the second – the name of a substance. They definitely have positive connotations.

According to Russian scholar Yefimov A.I.

> "…The peculiarity of individual (authorial) metaphorization lies in the fact that it is created and understood only in the context of literary works. Therefore it is, as a rule, individual, has its author and characteristic stylistic status" (1961:129).

This claim is relevant to the metaphoric forms of address. Metaphoric vocatives may also be used as means of evaluative reaction to a certain situation, to the utterances, actions, appearance of the addressee. Let me illustrate my point with several examples.

> (15) (Blanche sings) Stanley; Hey, **canary bird**. Toots. Get OUT of the BATHROOM. Must I speak more plainly? (T. Williams)
>
> (16) " What are you going laughing at, **you big hyena**?" said the burglar. "Wipe that smile off your face or I'll plug you." (Th. Wilder)
>
> (17) Abigail (handing him a mug): Here.     Patrick (shuddering): Ugggh. You're a barbarous creature. If 1 had my way, this would be a capital offence. You should be flogged mercilessly with cold, **wet lettuce**.  (A.Ayckbourn)

In example (15), a metaphoric form of address expresses negative evaluative reaction to the addressee's action described in the author's remark. The speaker is irritated by the inability to get into the bathroom because of the addressee. The addressee's singing aggravates the irritation. In this context metaphoric vocative has negative connotation.

In example (16), the addressee happened to be a witness to a burglary. But he doesn't lose his sense of humour even in such a situation. The speaker (the burglar) is irritated by the addressee's behavior. The metaphoric vocative presents the negative evaluative reaction to the addressee's laughter and his appearance which is characterized with the help of the adjective "big". Metaphoric transfer is based on the similarity of sound characteristics of objects of primary and secondary nominations. Thus according to dictionaries the sounds produced by hyena resemble human's laughter. In the given situation the addressee's laughter, being unpleasant for the speaker, reminds him of hyena's cries.

In example (17), husband and wife are the participants in the conversation. Their communication has a conflictual character. The wife got into trouble through her own fault. As a result she's got soaked and is shivering with cold. The husband reproaches her for precipitate actions. The metaphoric form of address expresses the negative reaction of the husband to her behavior and wretched (pathetic) appearance.

Metaphoric forms of address may be used to produce ironic or humorous effect, to crack a joke.

> (18) (Suddenly there comes the sound of a loon calling). Ethel. They must be right in front. Norman. Sound tome they are right behind the couch. Out boy. Billy. Good morning, **loonies**. (E. Thompson)

In the given situation the grandson decided to hide and make fun of his grandparents by imitating the cry of loons that lived on the pond near their house. So he uses metaphorically the name of the birds whose sounds he tried to imitate. This form of address sounds jokingly and good-naturedly and has positive connotations in the given context.

Thus, taking into account all the above-mentioned, I've come to the conclusion that metaphoric forms of address may be classified according to the lexical composition of the transferred names and frequency of their usage (clichéd, belonging to a certain style or register, individual). I claim that the vocative position facilitates greater variation in connotative meanings of metaphoric forms of address which leads to the increase of their expressive potential. Adherent connotations acquired by them may have the same sign as inherent ones, coexist with them being of the opposite sign or completely suppress them. Adjectives used in the vocative position have a vital influence on the expressive potential of metaphoric forms of address. The connotations of these adjectives may both reinforce the connotations of nouns and weaken them. Metaphoric forms of address often serve as means of evaluative reaction to a situation and its various components. They are also used for creation of the ironic or humorous narrative tone and characterization.

## References

Black, M. 1962. *Models and Metaphors* Ithaca. NY: Cornell University Press.

Brain, J. 1986. *Room at the Top*- Harmondsworth: Penguin Books.

Christie, Agatha. 1978. *The Man in the Brown Suit.* Frogman: Triad Panther.

Fitzgerald, F. Scott. 1979. *Selected Short Stories*. Moscow: Progress Publishers.

Kittay, E. 1987. *Metaphor: Its Cognitive Force and Linguistic Structure*. Oxford: Clarendon Press.

Kövecses, Z. 1986. *Metaphors of Anger, Pride and Love*. Amsterdam: John Benjamins.

Lakoff, George, and Mark Johnson. 1980. *Metaphors We Live By*. Chicago IL: University of Chicago Press.

Miall, David. S. (ed.) 1982. *Metaphor: Problems and Perspectives*. Brighton: Harvester Press.

Ortony, A. (ed.) 1980. *Metaphor and Thought*. Cambridge: Cambridge University Press.

Shaw, J. B. 1958. *Selected Works*. Moscow: Foreign Languages.

Steinbeck, John. 1985. *The Winter of Our Discontent*. Moscow: Vyssaja Skola.

Storey, D. 1980. *Early Days. Sisters. Life Class*. Harmondsworth: Penguin Books.

Volosinov, V. N. 1973. *Marxism and the Philosophy of Language*. New-York : Seminar Press.

Wodehouse, P. G 1983. *Life with Jeeves*. Harmondsworth: Penguin Books.

Ефимов, А. И. 1961. Стилистика художественной речи. Москва: Изд. МГУ.

Оликова, М. А. 1979. Обращение в современном английском языке. – Львов: Вища школа.

Телия, В. Н. 1988. Метафора как модель смыслопроизводства и ее экспрессивно-оценочная функция // Метафора в языке и тексте. – Москва Наука

# Telling Stories: Males and Females *Doing* Gender in Personal Narratives about *Trouble*

## Marina Lambrou

### Abstract

This article focuses on whether there are significant gender differences in narrative storytelling and importantly, where those differences can be found. Specifically, which stylistic features do male and female narrators use to construct identity and in some instances, 'save face' in personal experiences. Are male narrators only willing to disclose experiences of themselves in situations where they are cast 'in the most favourable possible light' or what Labov and Waletzky (1967) describe as 'self–aggrandizement' when compared to women, who are less concerned with that aspect of their identity being undermined (Coates, 1995, Johnstone, 1993) ? Furthermore, why is humour often a feature of "Trouble" (Bruner 1987) themed experiences where the crisis or complication describes difficult, traumatic and often violent situations which would be more likely to provoke the opposite reaction. And who uses this device more and for what reason? This paper explores such questions by examining a corpus of spoken personal narratives from males and females from the Greek Cypriot Community in London and uses Labov and Waletzky's (1967) narrative model as the central framework for analysis. The findings show how meaning through identity is constructed and how social cognition develops between narrators and their recipients through the act of storytelling.

Keywords: narrative, gender, competition, co-operation, trouble, identity

## 1 Introduction

Language and gender as a sub-discipline in sociolinguistic study has historically focused on the notion of *difference* in men and women's speech as a reflection of gender difference (Cameron 1998; Coates 2004). In other words, it is through such different discourse strategies that men and women are said to construct their gender identity, show solidarity, or as in the case of male speakers, stress their individuality. One such difference that is said to be enacted in single sex-interaction, and in particular, in conversational interactions, is that men are more likely to be competitive while women are said to be collaborative or co-operative (Cheshire and Trudgill 1998; Coates, 1996, 1997, 1998, 2004, 2004; Nelson 1998).

Findings have suggested that men tend to be competitive as they base their interaction on power and as a result are more likely to interrupt each other, disagree more, ignore each other, and stress their own individuality and hierarchical relationships with others in the group. Other features associated with men's dominance in interactions are taking and maintaining the floor though the use of more numerous and lengthier turns. Women in single sex interactions, on the other hand, are said to be co-operative as they are more collaborative, demonstrated by bringing others into the group; more supportive and encouraging, shown by the use of minimal responses to signal they are listening and generally interrupt less.

## 2 *Doing* gender

Competitive and co-operative gender discourses have since been widely accepted as being the norm in single sex as well as mixed sex interaction to the extent that this type of male and female behaviour is often generalized across a range of speech genres. However, this sociolinguistic approach to looking at differences in men and women's speech behaviour has been criticised for presenting such distinctions as clear-cut and purely at an interactional and linguistic level. Gender, Cameron (1988) argues, is something that people *do* in their social interactions so taking a more performative approach to understanding gender differences provides a more useful model.

The term *doing* gender was first coined by West and Zimmerman (1987), where gender identity is seen as a *social construct*. People are seen as *doing gender* rather than *being* a particular gender; in other words, gender is not static but something we *do*, in that it is enacted or accomplished every time we talk, every time we socially interact and is embedded in all the activities we undertake. As Cameron states (1988: 271):

> Gender has constantly to be reaffirmed and publicly displayed by repeatedly performing particular acts in accordance with the cultural norms (themselves historically and socially constructed, and consequently variable) which define *masculinity* and *femininity*.

## 3 Oral narratives of personal experiences

The telling of personal narratives in single sex interactions provides an interesting corpus of discourse for the analyses of *doing* gender. I had originally set out to analyse narrative structure in personal experiences, using Labov and Waletzky's (1967) six schema model as the central framework for my analyses (see Table 1, below)

| 1 Abstract | signals what the story is about; |
|---|---|
| 2 Orientation | provides the *who?, what?, when?* and *where?* of the story; usually descriptive; |
| 3 Complicating action | provides the *what happened?* part of the story and is the core narrative category; |
| 4 Evaluation | provides the *so what?* element and highlights what is interesting to narrator or addressee; reveals how participants in the story felt; |
| 5 Resolution | provides the *what finally happened?* element of story; |
| 6 Coda | signals the end of the story and may be in the form of a moral or lesson. |

**Table 1** Labov and Waletzky's (1967) six schema model

By looking at patterns of variation in personal experiences at both the macro and micro-structure levels and correlating them to a number of variables, I hoped to comment on the presumed universalism of the narrative model (Lambrou, 2005).

### 3.1 Informants and methodology

My chosen informants are members of the London-based Greek Cypriot community (LGC), who present an alternative speech community to those investigated by Labov and Waletzky (1967) and later, Labov (1972), in their studies. Any differences between their findings and those here would have implications for the existence of a universal model of narrative structure. As well as testing culture as a variable, a number of other factors were also considered: males and females were interviewed in single sex interviews - either in peer groups of between two and four - or in a one-to-one setting. (I was the interviewer throughout the study). Three age groups were identified for the purposes of this study: 9-11; 18-21; 35-49. Story theme or topic of the personal experience was also tested to see how far story genre determines story structure. I asked informants to recall personal experiences about a range of topics besides the classic 'danger of death' scenario. Specifically, the topics are: danger of death, fight/argument, embarrassing, happy, sad and funny experiences. All the interviews took place in English, the native language of all the informants and the interviewer.

In total, 44 LGC informants participated in 25 interviews, resulting in a total of 279 personal experiences from one-to-one and single sex peer group interviews. Of the 279 personal stories: 61% were identified as narratives, that is, according to L&W's definition which requires a temporal sequence of clauses or a *complicating action*; while 39% were identified as recounts (or non-narratives).

## 4 Findings – demythologising language and gender

### 4.1 Collaboration not competition

One significant finding that challenges the competitive versus co-operative differences in gender discourses is that males as well as females in peer group interviews are co-operative. Males and females use a number of different strategies to support, encourage and generally assist each other in the co-construction of personal narratives across the various adult informant groups (see Lambrou 2003). Closer analysis of the spoken data, or more precisely the interaction that took place surrounding the narrations as well as the narratives themselves, showed that this is accomplished through the use of different strategies. These were subsequently categorised under two main sub-headings, *explicit collaboration* and *implicit collaboration*, which are summarised in Table 2.

| 1. Explicit collaboration<br>Direct verbal collaboration with other members in peer group interview | 2. Implicit collaboration<br>No direct verbal collaboration with other members in peer group interview |
|---|---|
| **A. Direct prompt**<br>i. provides abstract: *story topic*<br>ii. provides coda: *evaluative* | **C. Indirect prompt**<br>i. triggers abstract: *story topic* |
| **B. Request for clarification**<br>i. elaborates orientation:<br>*who?*<br>*what?*<br>*where?*<br>*when?* | |

**Table 2** Categories of collaborative storytelling (placed within Labov and Waletzky's 1967 narrative schema model)

The key difference between *explicit* and *implicit collaboration* is that *explicit collaboration* is overt verbal collaboration where members of the peer group interview, including the narrator, directly address each other with *prompts* or *requests for clarification*. *Implicit collaboration*, on the other hand, involves no direct verbal collaboration between members of the peer group and narrator, yet inadvertently helps to co-construct narratives through *indirect prompts*. *Indirect prompts* 'trigger off personal narratives in other informants as a result of the narrator using certain keywords, which they then go on to use to create a sequence of narratives that are thematically linked' (Lambrou 2003: 160).

An example of a *direct prompt* (*explicit collaboration*), which provides an *abstract*, is given in Text 1, below. The excerpt is taken from a peer group interview between adult males (aged 35-49) on the topic of an argument. In ll.4-9, speaker M purposely interrupts speaker G in an act of co-operativeness to assist him with an *abstract* for a possible narrative. At no time does speaker M attempt to take the floor to narrate his own personal experience.

| 1 | Int | Can you think of a particular incident? |
|---|---|---|
| | G | The particular incident? Ha blimey you're asking! Don't forget you're now pushing my mind back 30 ... 33 years |
| | M | = = I've got a good one! I |
| 5 | | give -I go -you can -a story for you what happened to your 2 children when you went to a little ca -a little -you took them to a er a self-service restaurant and ehm and some old lady gave, was it (name of child) some hassle about him being Greek. Was that still -do you remember that one? |
| 10 | G | I remember but I don't remember when that was [clears throat]. That was an incident where we tried to sit down o-or we sat down ahh (name of child) had sat down to get us a table and we went to get, this is true, went to get food from the self-service ... (*continues to narrate experience*) |

**Text 1** Males, 35-49, peer-group interview, fight/argument experience

An example of a *request for clarification* can be seen in Text 2 where speaker G asks a question in l.7. Speaker C waits until the end of speaker G's turn before requesting clarification of when the events took place. The information that follows elaborates the *orientation* (who, what, where, when) by locating events in a specific time as it was omitted in the earlier stages of the narration (see Text 1 above). Moreover, requesting this detail provides a fuller account of the personal experience, which satisfies the audience's needs. Again, speaker C does not attempt to take the floor away from the narrator but waits for his turn to finish.

| 1 | Int | (G) ehm can you tell me about a time that you were involved in a fight or an argument that really upset you? |
| | G | (G recounts an argument ) … and this is in the restaurant and the worse bit about that was again that NOBODY but NOBODY, if you |
| 5 | | think that you're gonna get some HELP from anybody, NO - everybody just LOOKED but nobody made any comments |
| | C | How long ago was that? |
| | G | This is when the kids were about 6 and 8 years old … |

Text 2 Males, 35-49, peer-group interview, fight/argument experience

None of the strategies in male, peer group interviews are attempts to compete for the floor or undermine narrative storytelling. Any interruptions as a result of *direct prompts* and *requests for clarification* help to facilitate and enable storytelling by another member of the group in a co-operative and supportive manner. This contradicts the interactional behaviour previously identified in sociolinguistic research that has come to be associated with male discourse. After all, collaborative storytelling is a way of reinforcing group membership and solidarity through shared experiences.

### 4.2 *Trouble* in narratives by males *doing* gender: constructing identity at topic level

Another finding that has not been commented on previously and appears to be gender specific is the theme of *Trouble* in narratives. The notion of *Trouble* was first coined by Burke (1945), then borrowed by Bruner (1997) with a capital 'T' who used the term to describe an important element in personal narratives. According to Bruner, 'Trouble defines complication':

> L&W take Trouble so much for granted as the heart of complication that they even gathered their corpus of narratives so as to guarantee its presence. Recall that they asked their subjects to tell about a time when their lives were endangered - the ultimate trouble! And, of course, it's virtually in the structure of narrative that if a story contains a troubled complication, it requires some explication about how things were before it got that way - that is, an orientation, telling how things were before the trouble erupted. (1997: 63).

It would appear that *Trouble* guarantees a crisis and this factor is fundamental to a personal experience being described as a narrative and reportable in the first place. Personal narratives about danger of death, fights/arguments and embarrassing experiences - all highly anxious situations – present a crisis of some sort that needs to be resolved, and therefore guarantees the sequence of events that are temporally ordered (i.e. where something happens followed by something else happening and then something else after that etc.). An example of a full personal narrative where *Trouble* is the underlying theme is presented in Text 3 below.

1    Int    And I just wondered if um any other stories in the sort of argument
            danger happy sad or embarrassing kind of genre have come up at all
     L      Em ... fights-s ... I've only had one other experience of a fight and
            that was when someone was chasing me in a car because apparently
5           I'd cut him up I'd the kids in the car ... um I parked the car outside
            my dad's factory he parked in front of me walked up to the window
            and started staring and started shouting at me through the window um
            the kids had got scared so I got fed up of this got out kicked him a
            couple of times... and he drove off so I phoned up the police to tell
10          him what I've done just in case he'd gone as well and never thought
            anything of it. *I'm not a very violent person but I can be if I have to
            be em ...*

**Text 3** Male, 35-49, one-to-one interview, fight/argument experience

Speaker L is clearly not only the protagonist of his experience but also an active participant in the fight that ensues. His evaluative commentary in ll.11-12 (in italics) voice his feelings about fighting in general as an activity that he will *do* if he has to.

*Trouble* experiences are also found in the repertoire of personal narratives by females, which might suggest that males and females across the three age groups have been involved in equal amounts of fights and arguments. Examination of the range of *Trouble* story topics, however, reveals a marked difference in those narrated by males and females. My findings show that males in both adult age groups tell a higher proportion of personal narratives about danger of death and fight /argument experiences as opposed to embarrassing experiences; whereas women tell a fairly equal amount of both. Table 3 and Graph 1 present these findings more clearly.

| | Total number of *Trouble* narratives (danger of death, fight/ argument and embarrassing experiences) | Proportion of danger of death and fight/ argument narratives | Proportion of embarrassing narratives |
|---|---|---|---|
| **Older Adult males (35-49)** | 71% | 11 (73%) | 4 (27%) |
| **Older Adult females (35-49)** | 62% | 10 (55%) | 8 (45%) |
| **Males (18-21)** | 60% | 15 (63%) | 9 (37%) |
| **Females (18-21)** | 69% | 6 (55%) | 5 (45%) |

**Table 3** Danger of death and fight/ argument experiences against embarrassing experiences in the narratives of adult LGC male and female informants

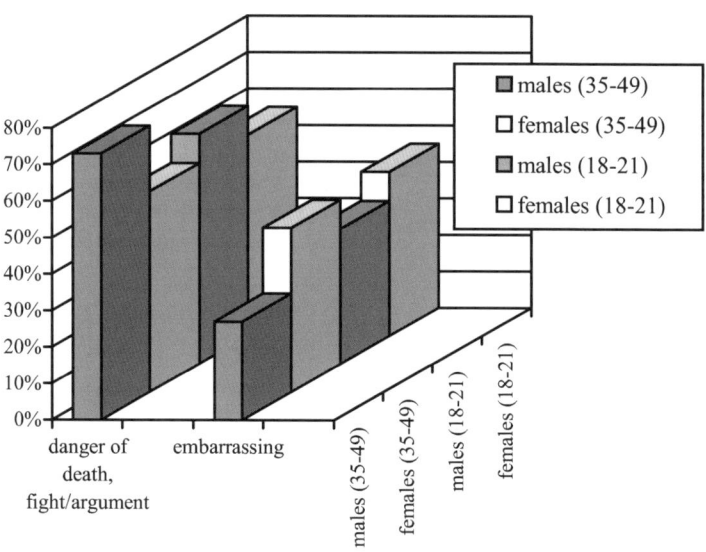

**Graph 1** Breakdown of *Trouble* narratives to show proportion of danger of death and fight/ argument narratives against the proportion of embarrassing narratives, across the adult male and female informant groups

The question this discussion raises is how do males and females *do gender* when constructing identity in their personal narratives.

My findings confirm earlier research which concludes that men like to present themselves as the hero of their experiences (Coates 1995, 1996; Johnstone 1993), and this is evident in narratives about fights and arguments where males are clearly the doers and as such, active and aggressive protagonists. This positioning is also highlighted by the use of *self-aggrandizement* as a common evaluative feature in the personal narratives of males. Conversely, in personal experiences about fights narrated by women, women as the protagonists position themselves as unwilling participants: instead they are the objects of aggression where something is *done* to them. This can be illustrated in Text 4, a peer group interview with two adult females.

| 1  | Int | Okay thank you for telling me something so personal…can you think |
|    |     | of a [ ] incident? |
|    | S   | Yeah yeah yeah there's something something really silly really it was |
|    |     | in Greece and I was driving along and some bad driver behind me |
| 5  |     | overtook me um then he –I said something to him I was –the way he |
|    |     | was driving and he he turned abusive verbally he turned abusive and |
|    |     | I just got really angry I know it sounds silly but that really made me |
|    |     | angry cause of the way he reacted I was like telling him that he was |
|    |     | in the wrong which he was in the wrong em and he just turned round |
| 10 |     | and started calling me all these names under the sun really it was just |
|    |     | so disgusted by him it's just the thought of someone how someone |
|    |     | could be so abusive in such a split second um that really made me |
|    |     | angry we just got into a big argument in the street [laugh] with a |
|    |     | complete stranger |
| 15 | M   | [laughing] |
|    | S   | yeah the way he was so abusive he was just swearing just slagging |
|    |     | me off he didn't even know me he was just insulting calling me all |
|    |     | the names em that REALLY made me angry and sometimes when |
|    |     | you think about things like that it just really annoys me that someone |
| 20 |     | can become so abusive that's it really I know it sounds silly but that |
|    |     | sticks to my mind |

**Text 4** Females; 35-49; peer group interview; fight/argument

In Text 4, speaker S narrates a sequence of upsetting events caused by another person's actions. The narrator positions herself as blameless and is keen to emphasise the abusive nature of the male driver's discourse in contrast to her own disgust at being the one abused. It is also clear that she does not participate in swearing back and becomes angry instead. The narrator may well have sworn at the time of the events, or she may not have, as the above telling shows. In this telling, she is *doing gender* by constructing an identity for herself, her audience and the interviewer as a victim, as non-aggressive and non-verbally abusive, all characteristics associated with female behaviour. One of the effects is to generate sympathy in the female audience. This contrasts markedly with speaker L in Text 3, who enacts masculinity through violence and then uses self- aggrandizement in his evaluative commentary to justify his actions. In both instances, speaker L and speaker S are both *doing gender* in the narration of their personal experiences where *Trouble* is the underlying theme.

### 4.3 Humour, face, and men behaving badly

One further finding that challenges another common generalisation about male and female discourse is that women are more likely to disclose experiences about embarrassing or humiliating events compared to males. Males on the other hand are more concerned with maintaining masculinity and are therefore less likely to narrate embarrassing experiences for fear of losing *face* among other male peers (see Eggins and Slade 1997; Coates 1995b; and Johnstone, 1993).

The notion of 'face', or one's public self-image was first proposed by Goffman (1967) and adapted by Brown and Levinson (1978, 1987) in their study of politeness. They subdivided face into 'negative' (the desire to be unimpeded in one's thoughts or actions) and 'positive' (the desire to be approved) aspects. According to Brown and Levinson (1987) as every interlocutor understands that every other interlocutor has (more-or-less) the identical face wants then it pays to attend to others' aspects of face in interaction as they will, theoretically, be predisposed to reciprocate. In social settings where personal narratives are exchanged, a loss of positive face (the desire to be approved of) can occur not so much as a result of other people's actions or speech acts, but through an individual's own actions or speech. The following two personal narratives from two different adult males reveal that men do tell embarrassing personal experiences that undermine their masculinity, in peer- group interactions. See Texts 5 and 6, below.

| 1 | Int | Okay if you can think –if something comes to to mind later just chip okay so no embarrassing stories |
| | T | There's always the usual one where you're walking down the street fall over flat on your face in front of everybody you know? It's |

5    happened to me many times but I've never admitted it but seeing as my name isn't going to be mentioned on this tape I could say it now and these are my closest friends my closest closest friends so you know walking down the high street on a Saturday everyone's there

Int    Can can you tell me a whole

10   T    All right I'll tell you a specific one I was walking down Southgate high street [laugh] outside the sports shop and there about was three of us three back in a long long time ago I must've been about 13 or 14 and those days you know everything matters much more than now you know now we're a bit older we're a bit more mature walking

15   down the street and we've all got you know our new trainers on you and walking like bowling as you could say you know like walking with style in them days and then [laughing] there was this like for four girls across the road and we were like you know trying to give it you know the large and I tripped on a paving stone and fell flat on

20   my face [claps hand] but I clicked straight away and I started doing press ups [gestures to show press up movement] yeah

All    [laughing]

T

I started doing press ups in the street so I tried to style it but it didn't

Int    quite come over and I just got laughed at for the next six months

T    Ah that's great good at improvising
Oh I tried you know but it didn't didn't come over if it come over then

**Text 5** Males: 18-21; peer group interview; embarrassing experience

1    C    I used to go (name of place) like there's a swimming -we used to go there like every Saturday… I was only like 10? 9? 10? that when I was still at primary innit? 9, 10 … and em … everyone was scared to go on the top board apart from me I was the macho one yeah I

5    thought I'd go on the top board so I just dived I dived off yeah
*an' I never used to buy my my own swimming trunks my mum used to buy my == swimming trunks yeah* So *-they weren't trunks they were like shorts* so I jumped off the top one yeah went to the bottom and I done like a a scissors thing a straight thing I went straight to the

10   bottom yeah  and came back up and see my trunks floating on the thing on the water like that My teacher was in tears I just felt like … I didn't feel like embarrassed it was as I was going like swimming to get em and I knew that everyone was watching me… seriously I felt like drowning an like when you go to the bottom there's like

15   windows there's like windows and they can see people that going down but I was only young though … THEN it was embarrassing

but now when I think I was only young …

**Text 6** Males: 18-21; peer group interview; embarrassing experience

What is interesting in that in both Texts 5 and 6, the narrators use different strategies to help overcome a loss of face amongst their male peers. In Text 5, speaker T uses a great deal of humour which is not only engaging for the audience but helps maintain the narrator's status as a successful storyteller. Text 6, is also funny, but in addition, speaker C uses evaluative commentary in ll.16-17 to justify these events by blaming them on the fact that *I was only young though*, a linguistic device that I call *post-Evaluation*, a structural category or schema found in the in oral narratives of personal experience of members of the LGC's (see Lambrou 2002). Overall, both personal narratives are entertaining, engaging and fulfil the rhetorical functions of being embarrassing and funny. As a result, by allowing their masculinity to be undermined, these narrators are seen as successful and competent storytellers, and can justify taking the floor for an extended turn.

## 5 Conclusion

Research into language and gender and specifically the discourse of males and females in single sex interactions has provided useful insights into *differences* in linguistic behaviour. This has, however, also led to a number of generalisations that are widely accepted as being the norm. My findings, which emerge from oral narratives of personal experiences from members of the London-based Greek Cypriot community, confirm but also challenge some of the previously held assumptions as described in this chapter. To summarise, in peer group interviews:

- Co-operation is not just a feature of female interaction but also a feature of male discourse, where men use *explicit collaboration* strategies to encourage and support peers in the co-construction of personal narratives;

- Males assert their masculinity in *Trouble* narratives about fights and argument experiences and position themselves as active and willing participants. This contrasts with women, who also have a repertoire of fight and argument narratives but while they are the protagonists of their experiences, they are more likely to position themselves as acted upon rather than as the aggressor, which maintains their feminine identity;

- Men on the other hand are more likely to tell a lower proportion of embarrassing experiences but when they do, evaluative strategies such as humour and *post-evaluation* commentary function to help overcome a loss of face and ensure that masculinity is not undermined. Both males and females disclose highly personal and embarrassing events and not just females.

All the above suggests that *doing gender* is complex and how males and females represent themselves in their experiences is not fixed but variable. Analyses of personal narratives about *trouble* provides further insights into an individual's linguistic behaviour in a social setting. Findings show that  males and females have a choice in how they position and represent themselves in their experiences. Gender, i would argue here, is enacted and therefore constructed for the purpose of the interaction, with speaker intent, the audience and the topic of the personal narrative being some of the variables at play.

**Transcription Key**

| ? | question or uncertainty |
|---|---|
| ! | Surprise |
| WORDS IN CAPITALS | emphatic stress and/ or increase in volume |
| " " | indicates direct speech |
| "*italics*" | captures the marked change in voice quality in direct speech of narrator or when narrator mimics another |
| (names and places) | names and locations not given but indicated in brackets |
| [ ] | non-transcribable speech |
| [laughs] | paralinguistic and non verbal information |
| = | Interruption |
| = = | Overlap |
| ... | pauses of under 3 seconds |
| (3.0) | pause of 3 seconds in utterance |
| [3.0] | interval between turns |
| -dash | false start/ restart |
| a-and | elongation of word |

**References**

Brown, Penelope, and Stephen Levinson. 1978. 'Universals in Language Usage: Politeness Phenomena' in Goody, D. (ed.) *Questions and Politeness*. Cambridge: Cambridge University Press: 56-289.

Brown, Penelope, and Stephen Levinson. 1987. *Politeness.* Cambridge: Cambridge University Press.

Bruner, J. 1991. *Acts of Meaning.* Cambridge, MA: Harvard University Press.

Bruner, J. 1997 'Labov and Waletzky Thirty Years On' in *Journal of Narrative and Life History* 7(1-4): 61-8.

Burke, K. 1945. *A Grammar of Motives.* New York: Prentice Hall.

Cameron, Deborah. 1998. 'Performing Gender identity: Young Men's Talk and the Construction of Heterosexual Masculinity' in J. Coates (ed.) *Language and Gender: A Reader.* Oxford: Blackwell: 270-83.

Cheshire, Jenny and Peter Trudgill. (eds) 1998. *The Sociolinguistics Reader. Vol. 2: Gender and Discourse.* Arnold: London.

Coates, Jennifer. 1995. 'The Role of Narrative in the Talk of Women Friends', paper presented at the University of Technology, Sydney.

Coates, Jennifer. 1996. *Women Talk: Conversation between Women Friends.* Blackwell: Oxford.

Coates, Jennifer. 1997. 'One-at-a-time: the Organisation of Men's Talk' in Johnson, S. and U. Meinhof (eds), *Language and Masculinity.* Oxford: Blackwell: 107-29.

Coates, Jennifer. (ed.). 1988. *Language and Gender: A Reader.* Oxford: Blackwell.

Coates, Jennifer. 2004. *Women, Men and Language* (3$^{rd}$ ed.). Harlow: Longman.

Eggins, S. and D. Slade. 1997. *Analysing Casual Conversation.* London: Cassell.

Goffman, Erving. 1967. *Interaction Ritual.* Chicago:AldinePublishing.

Helm, J. (ed.) 1967. *Essays on the Verbal and Visual Arts.* Seattle, Washington: University of Washington Press.

Johnstone, B. 1993. 'Community and Contest: Midwestern Men and Women Creating their Worlds in Conversational Storytelling' in D. Tannen (ed.) *Gender and Conversational Interaction.* New York: Oxford University Press: 62-8.

Labov, William. 1972. *Language in the Inner City: Studies in the Black English Vernacular.* Philadelphia: University of Pennsylvania Press.

Labov, William, and J. Waletzky. 1967. 'Narrative Analysis: Oral Versions of Personal Experience' in J. Helm (ed.) *Essays on the Verbal and Visual Arts*

Lambrou, Marina. 2003. *Story Patterns in Personal narratives: a Variationist Critique of Labov and Waletzky's Narrative Schema Model,* paper presented at the Poetics and Linguistics Association (PALA) at the University of Birmingham.

Lambrou, Marina. 2003. 'Collaborative Oral Narratives of General Experience: When an Interview becomes a Conversation' in *Language and Literature* 12(2): 153-74.

Lambrou, Marina. 2005. *Story Patterns in Oral Narratives: A Variationist Critique of Labov and Waletzky's Model of Narrative Schemas.* Unpublished PhD Thesis: Middlesex University.

Nelson, M. W. 1998. 'Women's Ways: Interactive Patterns in Predominantly Female Research Teams' in Coates, Jennifer (ed.) *Language and Gender: A Reader.* Oxford: Blackwell: 354-72

West, C., and D. Zimmerman. 1987. 'Doing Gender' in *Gender and Society* 1: 125-51.

# You Must Alter Your Style, Madam:
# *Pamela* and the Gendered Construction of Narrative
# Voice in the Eighteenth-Century British Novel

## Larry L. Stewart

## Abstract

In Stewart (2005), I suggest that quantitative analyses of seventeen eighteenth-century British novels reveal telling differences in the ways male and female writers construct male and female narrators. Preliminary data from principal components analyses of word frequencies indicate that female narrators created by male writers use certain items of vocabulary at a rate significantly different than those items are used by male narrators created by male writers or by narrators created by female writers. The language of female narrators constructed by males tends to be more contingent, more self-referential, and more socially engaged than that of male narrators created by men or of male or female narrators constructed by women. These results may indicate shared assumptions, probably both conscious and unconscious, on the part of male writers concerning the language or perhaps mind style of women.

This paper furthers that investigation by considering more closely the male and female letter writers in Samuel Richardson's *Pamela* and finds not only that the vocabulary items accounting for the difference between male and female letter writers in *Pamela* are nearly identical to those accounting for differences in other eighteenth-century novels but that changes in Pamela's voice within the novel are in accord with her gendered positioning at different points.

Keywords: Gender, Quantitative Analysis, Principal Components Analysis, Samuel Richardson, Eighteenth-Century Literature

This study arose from earlier investigations of the use of quantitative analysis to consider narrative voice. The attempt has been to use methods employed by those doing authorship attribution studies - that is, studies looking at differences and similarities in different authors - in order to look at different narrative voices created by the same writer (see Stewart 2003). Probably the most nearly proven of those methods is the so-called Burrows technique in which the relative frequencies of the forty or fifty most frequent words are used as variables in a principal components analysis. The results are then displayed on a scatter graph. Although the technique seems extremely crude, the results on test cases of authorship attribution have shown themselves to be amazingly accurate, and earlier studies have indicated that the technique also serves to separate different narrative voices created by the same writer. (See Hoover 2003, for a cogent discussion of the use of multivariate analysis for the study of stylistic variation.)

In Stewart (2005), I attempted to determine what quantitative analysis might indicate about the construction of male and female narrators in eighteenth-century British prose; more specifically the question was whether one could determine patterns in the way that male writers constructed different voices for male and female characters. Although the research is preliminary, the data indicate some relatively consistent differences between the narrative voices of female and male narrators created by the same writer.

In applying the Burrows technique to seventeen eighteenth-century novels, there seem to be three sets of words that consistently account for the most significant differences between male and female narrators. The first set is comprised of what might be called the diction of contingency - with the word if being the most significant. Female narrators constructed by male writers use the word significantly more frequently than male narrators. (My speculation is that this diction reminds the reader of the female narrator's dependence on outside circumstance. Whether the narrator is Defoe's Moll or Roxanna or Richardson's Pamela or Clarissa, she is dependent on conditions over which she seems to have little control.)

The second set of words is comprised of self-referential pronouns - particularly the first-person pronouns I, me, and my. One might expect males to use such language relatively more frequently than females, but in fact in every case I have looked at female narrators created by male writers use this vocabulary more frequently than male narrators created by the same male authors. Why would male writers create female narrators that have a focus on the self - perhaps because these female characters are in a world in which they must or perhaps because male writers think that readers believe women use such language.

The third set of words is comprised of what we can call the language of social engagement: primarily such third-person pronouns as *he*, *she*, *her, him,* etc. Again, female narrators created by male writers use these words significantly more frequently than male narrators created by the same male writers. Perhaps, male writers saw such social engagement as an aspect of the mind style of women - or perhaps we can even put this together with the greater frequency of the word *if* to suggest that though these female narrators are extraordinarily skilful in managing their lives, eighteenth-century males view them as recognizing that their success depends on their management of others - and these others are always on their lips.

At any rate, these three sets of words seem remarkably consistent as differentiators of the language of male and female narrators in eighteenth-century novels written by males. However - and more research is necessary here - female writers do not seem to construct female narrators in this way. That is, female narrators constructed by female writers use these sets of words with about the same frequency as male narrators.

Although these data allow for certain generalizations and speculations, it seems important to look more closely at the construction of individual narrators and to determine how these differences function within specific texts. Thus, this study is an attempt to consider the language of a single character, Samuel Richardson's Pamela in the novel of the same name. Working with Richardson's epistolary novels is far more complicated than working with novels having a single narrative voice. It is easy enough to compare, for example, one Defoe narrator with another, because each narrator is the voice of a different novel. However, with Richardson's epistolary novels, not only is it necessary to separate male and female letter writers, a relatively easy task, but it is necessary to find ways to deal with letters that are embedded in other letters. As well, at times, female narrators will quote passages or even pages of dialogue from male characters. In this study, only embedded dialogue of a paragraph or more was assigned to the character being quoted. Although attaining precise figures is difficult, the results are relatively clear and unambiguous.

Most readers are aware that *Pamela* is the story of a virtuous servant girl, whose master, Mr. B- makes numerous attempts 'on her virtue'. Ultimately, Pamela wins over Mr. B- by her honesty and virtue. He proffers an honourable proposal, they are married, and Pamela makes Mr. B- into a faithful husband. The plot and themes of the novel clearly raise issues of gender. As Gwilliam (1993:1) says, 'Because gender and sexuality are explicitly contested in the fiction of Samuel Richardson, his works offer an extraordinarily rich - and immense - textual field for the investigation of both gender and sexuality'.

To analyze *Pamela*, I divided the novel between male and female letter writers, Pamela's obviously being the dominant female voice. In looking at words in the three categories, I found basically what I had found in other eighteenth-century novels. The female letter writers, in this case Pamela, use self-referential and socially-engaged language significantly more frequently than do male letter writers - and that seems to hold true no matter who the male or female narrator is. That is, Pamela uses these categories of words more frequently than either her father or Mr. B-. However, the one category that differed from what I had found in my previous research was that the female narrator in *Pamela* did not use the language of contingency with greater frequency than male narrators. This is so far the only instance I have come upon in which this occurs, but I think it is explicable.

In the following chart, *I/me* stands for first-person pronouns, *he/she* for third-person pronouns, and *if* for the vocabulary of contingency.

**Figure 1** The three categories of word usage in *Pamela*

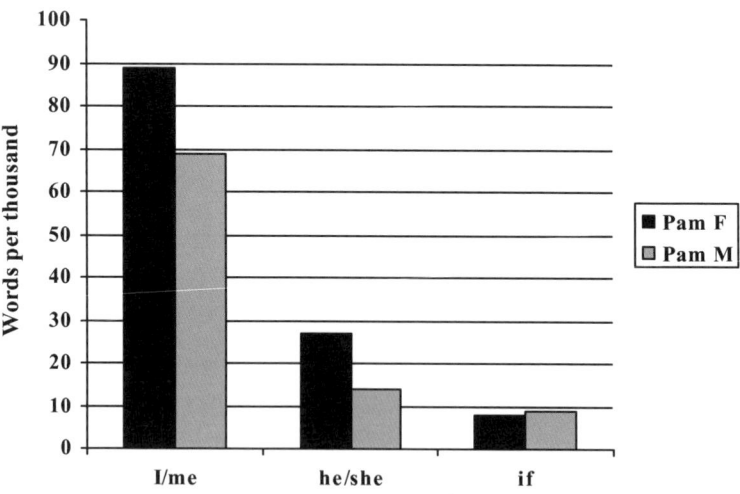

Word usage by female and male characters

What happens, I think, with the vocabulary of contingency is that in this epistolary form, the male writers are continually reminding Pamela of contingencies that await her. As readers are aware, throughout much of the novel, Pamela seems to be at the mercy of Mr. B- and, like other eighteenth-century female narrators, no matter how capable and able, she seems dependent upon the contingencies and vagaries of others and of that outside herself. (I should note that some readers, in fact, do see her in control; they see her as stage-managing throughout the novel; see, for example, discussions in Guilliam (1991) and Roulston (1998). If true, that in itself would supply a reason that Pamela uses the language of contingency less frequently than other eighteenth-century female narrators.) However, my reading suggests that the reason males in this novel use this language as frequently as Pamela does is because they are constantly pointing out these contingencies to Pamela. Time and again, Mr. B- reminds Pamela of what will happen if she continues to act in a certain way and the good consequences that will come about if she conducts herself differently. Her father's letters, too, remind Pamela of consequences that will come about if her conduct is of one kind or another. This explanation seems especially likely since, in fact, Pamela does not use this language less frequently than other eighteenth-century female narrators; what occurs is that male narrators here use it more frequently than others.

These are, of course, crude numbers, and I wanted to look a bit more closely at *Pamela*. Because in this novel female letter writers have about seven times the number of words of male letter writers, I divided the novel into seven approximately equal sections of female narration and one of male. The seven sections correspond to the following parts of the novel:

**Pam1** - from the death of Pamela's lady (Mr. B-'s mother) until Pamela's preparations for leaving

**Pam2** - through most of Pamela's "imprisonment" by Mr. B-

**Pam3** - though the worst of the imprisonment is over, Pamela is still being questioned and held by Mr.B-

**Pam4** - through the Mr. B—'s apology and proposal

**Pam5** - through the engagement and wedding ceremony

**Pam6** - the fight with Mr. B-'s sister Lady Davers and the ultimate reconciliation

**Pam7** - Pamela's full acceptance as mistress of the house and wife

The results of this division reveal a very interesting pattern. Pamela's language changes during the novel. That in itself is not surprising. Others have noted a change in her language. For example, Eagleton (2005: 75) when speaking of language in Pamela writes: '…by the end of the novel [Pamela has] become a docile housewife mouthing moral platitudes, and her language sinks beneath Richardson's own'. Even if one does not agree with Eagleton's formulation, it does indicate a recognition of alteration in language. However, though change itself is not unexpected, the pattern of change is. The scatter graph of a principal components analysis reveals something like a parabola in which Pamela's language moves toward male language and then away (see Figure 2).

The scatter graph showing language change in *Pamela* appears to show Pamela becoming increasingly pulled into the domain and language of Mr. B-; she becomes more and more under his control and her language reflects this male dominance. Pamela's language is furthest from Mr. B-'s in Part 1 as she prepares to leave his household but begins to move toward his in Part 2 as he effectively imprisons her and isolates her from others. By Part 3, her language is statistically almost indistinguishable from his. However, once she becomes engaged, she is freed in a certain way and she regains a language of her own. In Parts 4, 5, and 7, Pamela's language moves increasingly further from the 'male' vocabulary of Mr. B-. That Part 6 seems out of place is not as inexplicable as it might seem. Most of Part 6 reflects Pamela's reaction to being attacked by Lady Davers - Mr. B-'s sister, who does not believe Pamela worthy to be in the family. Lady Davers, in fact, virtually imprisons Pamela in her own home and attempts to isolate her from Mr. B-. The images and circumstances are strikingly are strikingly similar to those early in the novel - and Pamela returns to language much more similar to what she used during her earlier imprisonment.

**Figure 2** Pamela's language change

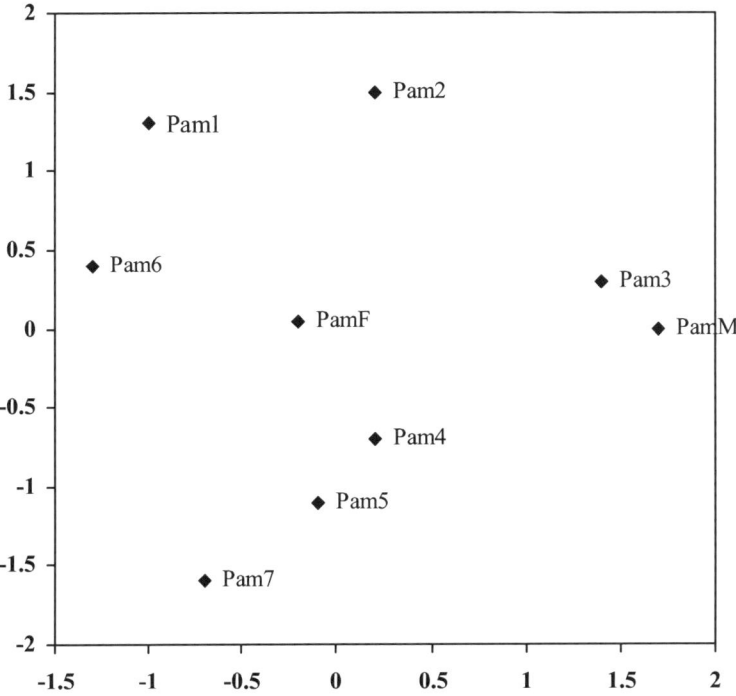

Precisely what elements of language account for this pattern is exceedingly difficult to pinpoint. Clearly, however, one of the relatively consistent changes concerns Pamela's use of first person pronouns. (Again, the frequent use of the first person seems to be a typical element in the way male writers construct female voice.) Early on in the novel, Pamela's father warns her about ego-involvement, about being too interested in herself - and this seems to be the dilemma for women. On the one hand, vanity, ego-involvement, the attention to themselves, and constant use of the first person are negative qualities that male writers seem to assume about female characters, but women are placed in a position of vulnerability in which they must watch after themselves because no one else will do it. It is akin to what Eagleton (2005: 74) says of Pamela: 'She is forced to treat herself as a sexual object in order to avoid being treated as one by others'. However, Pamela's language does, in fact, reflect the admonition toward less self-reference as she moves away from the use of self-referential pronouns once she becomes engaged and moves toward her position as mistress of the house.

As with the earlier chart, only Part 6 resists the pattern, and again the explanation seems to be that when Pamela is most vulnerable and under attack, she has little choice but to become more self-involved and self-referential.

**Figure 3** Pamela's use of first-person pronouns

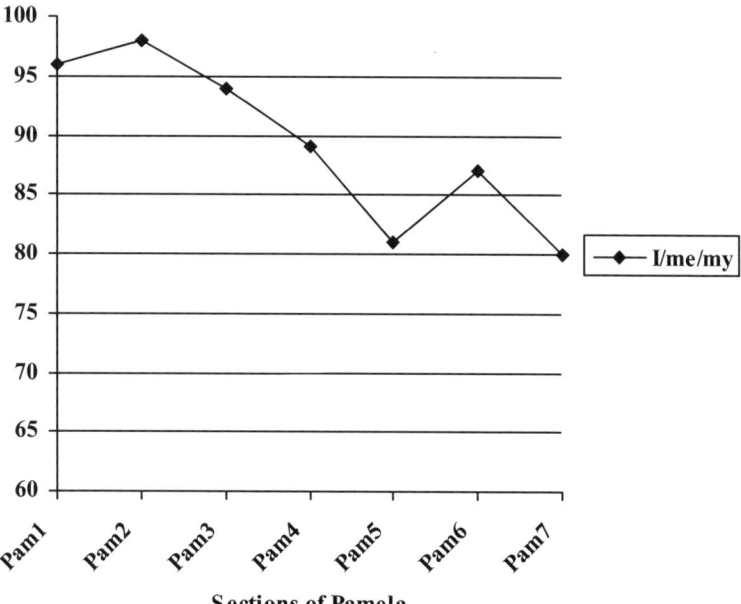

**Sections of Pamela**

Although looking at the first person pronouns suggests one element in the change in her language, it doesn't explain the parabola - why the language as a whole seems to move toward and then away from the male model. Obviously there are complications, but one word that is very significant is one mentioned earlier - *if.* Again with the exception of Part 6, Figure 4 illustrates one element that may help to explain the parabola. Once again, Part 1 begins with a relatively high frequency in the use of if, and the term is used with greatest frequency in Part 3. Obviously, in the first half of the novel, Pamela is constantly aware of the contingencies she faces. With her engagement and wedding, she feels as if she is in a somewhat more stable world - somewhat less vulnerable to outside conditions. The use of if mirrors this.

**Figure 4** Pamela's use of *if*

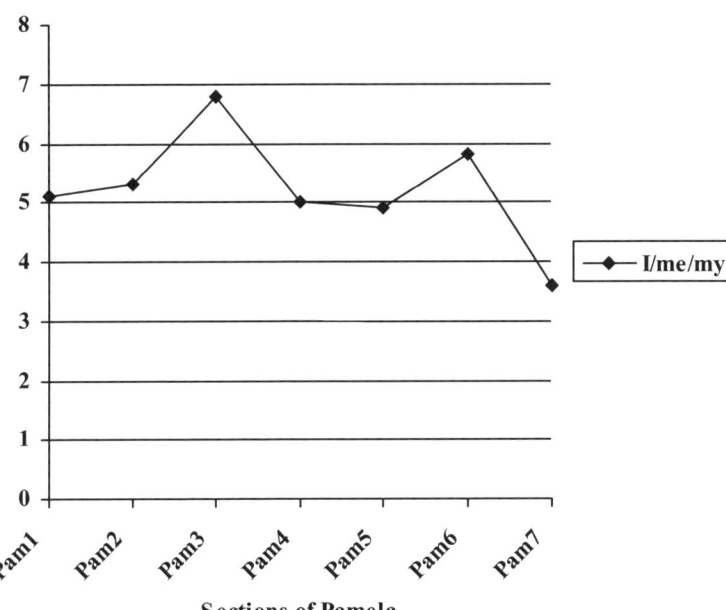

**Sections of Pamela**

What is particularly telling here is that Pamela does not simply return to the frequency of *if* that she used earlier, but in fact uses it much less frequently so that she is not simply retracing a line back to the original language but is using a different language.

There is certainly a lot more going on here. Her use of third person pronouns (particularly female third person pronouns) increases by the end of the novel, possibly showing more social engagement as she becomes mistress of the house. Her use of such pronouns is lowest when her language is closest to the male language of the novel. By the end of the novel, Pamela has moderated her language in several respects; perhaps it might even be said that she has found her own language that is not simply an imitation of male language.

Obviously, there is risk in relying on statistics. However, it does appear that there are some consistencies in the way in which male writers construct female voices or female narrators through their use of language. If this is true, it at least leaves open the possibility of shared cultural assumptions held by men about women. This seems borne out by other research I have done that suggests female writers do not seem to have these same assumptions about the language of women. They construct female characters that use language (or at least these items of vocabulary) in a way very similar to that used by male characters constructed by male writers. There is no evidence that female writers assume that men and women use language differently or, at least, that their vocabulary differs.

Perhaps more importantly, this brief look at Pamela suggests that within the commonalities and shared assumptions that may go into the construction of female characters, we can also see the construction of an individual character. These are statistics and numbers, but we can follow and explain these numbers in terms of this specific character and the circumstances that surround her. It is slightly more than midway through the novel when it becomes clear that Pamela will marry Mr. B- that Mrs. Jewkes says to her: 'You must alter your style, madam … O, returned I, this is a language I shall never forget…' (Richardson 2001: 303). Pamela does not forget her earlier language, but she does modify it. Through all that has occurred in the novel, she has fashioned her own voice.

## References

Eagleton, Terry. 2005. *The English Novel: An Introduction*. Oxford: Blackwell.

Gwilliam, Tassie. 1991. 'Pamela and the Duplicitous Body of Femininity' in *Representations* 34: 104-33.

Gwilliam, Tassie. 1993. *Samuel Richardson's Fictions of Gender*. Stanford, CA: Stanford University Press.

Hoover, David. 2003. 'Multivariate Analysis and the Study of Style Variation' in *Literary and Linguistic Computing* 18(4): 341-60.

Richardson, Samuel. 2001. *Pamela; or, Virtue Rewarded* (eds.) Thomas Keymer and Alice Wakely. Oxford: Oxford University Press.

Roulston, Chrisine. 1998. *Virtue, Gender, and the Authentic Self in Eighteenth-Century Fiction.* Gainesville, FL: University of Florida Press.

Stewart, Larry. 2003. 'Charles Brockden Brown: Quantitative Analysis and Literary Interpretation' in *Literary and Linguistic Computing* 18(2): 129-38.

Stewart, Larry. 2005. 'Empirical Analysis, Gender Assumptions, and the Language of Narration in Eighteenth-Century British Fiction' in *Empirical Studies of the Arts* 23: 65-77.

.

# Embedded Meaning of Free Verse Types - With an Example from the Introduction of T. S. Eliot's 'Ash-Wednesday' in Swedish

## Eva Lilja

### Abstract

Eliot's versification technique changes over time, but a freely used 4 beat line is its most significant device. Eliot takes up tendencies in ordinary speech, styling the phrases into something more salient. In many European countries, free verse was introduced in opposition to the taste of a conservative middle class. 'Ash-Wednesday' (1930) was translated into Swedish in 1938 by the modernist poet Erik Lindegren. The conservatism and religiosity of Eliot as well as his erudition made his authorship central to the Swedish middle class reader. On the other hand, as a leading modernist he fitted into the ideals of young *avant garde* poets of the time.

In 'Ash Wednesday', Lindegren transferred the verse rhythm in a way which comes closer to speech rhythm than the original. He thus underlined Eliot's so-called conversational style. In this way, Lindegren tried to make Eliot a bit more *avant garde* than he really was, thereby supporting the young Swedish modernists whose cause was thus helped by the perceived support of a highly ranked international author like Eliot.

Key words: T.S. Eliot, Erik Lindegren, Free verse, Verse rhythm, Four beat line, Translation, Modernism (history of)

## 1 Introduction

Types of versification have their extra significances. The high ranking of antique verse forms through history is well known. Today, the four beat line is regarded as a popular form, but in the Middle Ages it was the form of the court and the nobility (Lilja 2006: 209).

The introduction of free verse in the 20th century interplayed with the establishment of the modernist *avant garde*. In many European countries, free verse was introduced in opposition to the taste of a conservative middle class, which in the beginning interpreted the new verse form as a sign of bolshevism. The reception of Edith Södergran's poetry in Finland is a well-known example of this.

## 2 Three types of free verse

Early free verse may be classified according to the origin of its form elements. German free verse by Klopstock and Goethe emanated from Greek colon versification with its pregnant phrases (Hellmuth 1973: 252). Spondee and enjambment are other significant traits. The expressionists preferred this type of free verse, which has preserved some of the reputation of antique forms. Also Goethe's high reputation promoted this type of rhythm (Lilja 2002: 256).

German free verse by Heine had its form elements from the Middle Age four beat line, which comes close to common speech rhythm. The line should be end-stopped. For the last 500 years it has been regarded as a popular rhythm – thus it has been lowly ranked. The Anglo-American imagists preferred this type of free verse (Attridge 1988: 83, 95, Lilja 2002: 256).

Whitman's free verse emanated from Bible lyrics and the Psaltar. It is signified by its parallel intonation curves, end-stopped lines and about three phrases per line. The surrealists preferred this type of free verse, which mostly has been lowly ranked - this probably because of Whitman's own lack of education. Also folk poetry from different parts of the world is often signified by the long liner of the Whitman type (Lilja 2002: 257).

## 3 Transfer from French free verse into English free verse

Modernist Free verse was developed at France in the end of the nineteenth century. The French alexandrine was broken into pieces. A half line of the alexandrine contains 6 or 7 syllables – like a normal speech phrase. Many a French modernist poetry line sounds like alexandrine half lines (Scott 1990: 23).

Another road to French free verse was the prose poem. Poets like Baudelaire and Rimbaud used this form. Rimbaud's two poems in free verse, 'Marine' and 'Movement', might be apprehended as broken prose poems. Except from these, *Les Illuminations* in 1886, consists of prose poems only (Scott 1990: 182 and following). Rimbaud's two free verse poems share some devices with the Heine type of free verse. Line length, line endings and phrasing are about the same. The versification of Rimbaud happened to be similar to that of Heine - in spite of the lack of generic link (Lilja 2006: 266).

Laforgue imitated Rimbaud's versification patterns, which were borrowed by T.S. Eliot. This short French phrase became the main pattern for T.S. Eliot when he was looking for a rhythm of beauty without the beat. He turned away from meter, preferring segmental rhythm based on the speech phrase. Such a short phrase could then be stylised by the help of different equivalence categories. In this way, the versification of Laforgue came to influence the development of free verse in the Germanic languages – English, German, Dutch and Scandinavian literatures. Transferred to English, the phrase patterns happened to share devices with the Heine type of free verse – this is an observation by Annie Finch in her excellent *The Ghost of Meter* (1993: 87). This gives us a historical explanation why the Eliot's verse line often comes close to the Middle Age 4 beat line – but of course rules and rhymes are missing. To conclude:

- A phrase of a broken French alexandrine or a broken French prose poem makes a speech phrase with perhaps 6 - 7 syllables.
- Transferred into English with its stronger accent this will make a speech phrase with perhaps 2 stresses.
- Organised in pairs, such phrases will make a good 4 beat line.
- The Heine type of free verse uses mainly two stress phrases – in pairs or not.
- In this way, the Eliot versification establishes a connection between the Old English tradition and avant garde.

Though Eliot may have learned it from the French, when writing he often uses the Heine type of free verse, a verse type which in Sweden and England has preserved the indigenous image of the Middle Age four beat line. This upper class versification of the Middle Ages survived until modern times in children's rhyming and birthday poems. When it turned up again in the shape of modernistic free verse it must in a way have sounded familiar – in English and in Swedish. This may be part of an explanation why Eliot's verse form came to be the free verse norm in Sweden.

## 4 Swedish free verse – the Eliot influence

Around 1940 Eliot's poetry became widely recognised in Sweden, but French surrealism was also now introduced (Espmark 1977: 165). Surrealist imagery affected Swedish poetry deeply but the French long liner was never widely used. As for rhythm, Eliot's more traditional manner became the important influence. Eliot was awarded the Nobel Prize for Literature in 1948. There was a great Swedish interest in his writing from 1932, with the translation of 'The Waste Land', up to 1965 when he died. This meant that modernism during this period was connected to tradition, erudition and universalism as well as to *avant garde*.

Around 1950, the Heine type in its Eliot shape became established as the standard type of free Swedish versification - perhaps because of the connection to the Middle Age form, which had survived through the centuries in popular forms. To sum up:

- The extra significance of the four beat line was domestic and national - a popular form easy to recognise.
- Another reason for the break through of this form was of course the high reputation of Eliot.
- Still another reason is probably the similarity between this kind of versification phrase and the ordinary speech phrase.

When reading Swedish free verse, it is easy to recognise the (more or less) four beats of a line. But this is also the case when reading Swedish blank verse and alexandrine. Normally, four stresses are realised in the pentameter as well as in the alexandrine (Wåhlin 1999: 23).

## 5 Eliot's versification

Now, let us take a somewhat closer look at Eliot's versification. Of course, it has many roots – not only the French background discussed above. Eliot commented on the new free versification in an essay called 'Reflections on Vers libre' in *New Statesman* (1917). 'No verse is free', he says, a sentence which has received different interpretations for nearly a century., Eliot also comments on free versification in his essay about music in poetry. He promotes the idea of a tight relation between form and content, which should be unique for every single poem. This is the standard motivation for using free verse in early modernism. Discussing how to structure a poem, Eliot uses analogies from music. In *4 Quartets* (1943), Eliot was inspired by the structures of the sonata. His techniques of repetition refer to music as well - for example parallelisms and paronomasies. End stopped lines dominate and enjambments are exceptions.

Eliot's versification technique changes over time, of course. A freely used four beat line is its most significant device, but many old patterns are to be found. 'The Love Song of J Alfred Prufrock' (1917) uses a loosely handled pentameter. Parts of 'The Waste Land' (1922) have the four beat line and other parts pentameter. The very first page with its heavy enjambents comes close to antique versification. Pentameter makes a strong pattern in 'Ash-Wednesday' (1930). In 'Four Quartets' (1943) the four beat line is a dominating influence and so on (Cooper 1998: 43-66).

The rhythm of Eliot's phrases or half lines are partly investigated. Among others, Burns G. Cooper has analysed the phrase patterns of 'Four Quartets'. The list below shows the 14 most frequent stress patterns of the poem in order of frequency. The shortest phrase has three syllables and the longest one seven. All of them have two prominences. 85% of the half lines in '4 Quartets' have two prominences, 10% have three prominences and 4% have one prominence. Obviously two prominences must be looked upon as normal. A number of two prominences is typical also for ordinary English and Swedish speech phrases.

| | |
|---|---|
| oOoOo | ooOoOo |
| ooOoO | oOooOo |
| oOoO | ooOooOo |
| OooOo | oOoooOo |
| OooOo | oOooooOo |
| OoOo | OooO |
| ooOooO | ooOoooOo |

The longest half lines of 'Four Quartets' have eleven syllables and the shortest ones two. The spondee is the significant figure of free verse, because metered verse cannot accept it, but it is comparatively unusual in texts by Eliot, which means that it has a really strong effect when used.

## 6 Conversational style and speech rhythm

Eliot's so called conversational style has a special interest from a rhythmical point of view. Eliot himself points to ordinary speech, the language of conversation, as the most important field of studies for exploring the rhythm of free verse. In his writing he is cultivating tendencies of common English speech.

Some typical phrase patterns appear because of certain traits in English syntax like constructions with 'of', such as 'The Heart of Darkness' ( o O o O o ) - the most frequent phrase pattern in 'Four Quartets'. This little phrase is of course just as frequent in ordinary English speech. Eliot takes up such tendencies in speech, styling them into something more salient. Of course there are also such typical patterns in Swedish and in any other languages.

As already stated, the Middle Age four beat line comes close to a natural speech rhythm, and of course it is the same case with the Heine type of free verse. The opposite might be said about the free verse of Klopstock and Goethe with its antique origin. Some usual old Greek rhythmical figures turn out to be common in modern free verse, for example:

| | |
|---|---|
| OO | OoO |
| oO | oooO |
| Oo | OOoO |
| ooO | OoOO |
| Ooo | ooOO |
| OOO | OooO |
| oOO | OooOo |
| oOo | O ooo O |

Compared to the Eliot phrases, the Greek ones have a higher percentage of prominent positions, and those prominences stand often together. This gives a rhythm with qualities totally different from those of meter, a rhythm which was very much appreciated among early free verse writers.

To summarise, common form elements of free verse had extra significance due to some social factors – at least in Scaninavia:

- Spondee and enjambment gave an impression of solemnity because of their emanation from antique versification with its high reputation.
- A pair of phrases, each with two prominences, evoke familiar associations to children, peasants and talk.
- The long-liner had an air of avant garde in the first half of the Scandinavian 20th century.
- Traces of pentameter make vague associations to England and theatre.

Eliot used all those formal traits, but he favoured the talkative four beat line.

## 7 Ash-Wednesday

'Ash-Wednesday' (1930) was translated into Swedish in 1938 by the modernist poet Erik Lindegren for a literary journal, *Presens*. The translation was revised in 1942 for a collection of Eliot texts, and I use this revision. In the narrow-minded literary climate of Sweden in the Forties, a battle was going on between modernists and a nationalistic rhymed poetry. The middle class readers fought the free versification, calling it ugly and barbaric – and the fight was bitter.

In this situation Eliot had a special role. The conservatism and religiosity of Eliot as well as his erudition and his use of myths made his authorship central to the middle class reader. On the other hand, as a leading modernist he fitted into the ideals of young *avant garde* poets of the time. Both groups counted him as theirs. An *avant garde* author like Erik Lindegren translated the Eliot rhythm in a manner which comes closer to a speech rhythm than the Eliot original. Eliot's word music nearly disappears in the translation.

'Ash-Wednesday' consists of 6 poems. The example below is part of the first poem, verse groups 3 and 4 (the text and a rhythmical notation are to be found at the end of this article).

Every line starts with a capital in English, but the Swedish translation has lower-case letters, thus following national habits respectively. The English capital gives stability to the line. The Swedish way makes the style more informal and brings it closer to ordinary speech.

In his translation, Erik Lindegren underlines the rhythmical traits of spoken language, as in line number 14 where the severe epitrit 'Too much explain' (OO o O) becomes a loose combination like 'om jag alltför ofta förklarar' (oo O o O oo O o). There is one enjambment in English (line 5 'and') but the Swedish translation has eliminated it placing 'och' (that is 'and') in the beginning of line 6. Some more rhythmical peculiarities may be noticed:

- As to the pentameter lines, Lindegren is following the original scheme in line one but not in line eight which in Swedish is a four beat line. But the four beat lines are correctly translated in all the cases (line 2, 11, 18).

- The translation is signified by a lower percentage of prominences than what is the case in the English text, which improves an impression of speech.
- Eliot's text has a few offbeats of three syllables, in lines nine and 13, but in Lindegren's translation we find them in lines one, eight, nine, 12, 13, 15, and 18.
- A four syllable off beat is to be seen in line 17.
- Typical of the rhythm of 'Ash Wednesday' is a spondaic cadence, here in lines four, five, nine and, 16. Lindegren has transferred this device in lines four, six, 11, 13, 16 and 18. That makes two cases more than in the original. As already stated, the spondee is adopted from Old Greek stanzas.
- Gerard Manley Hopkin's so called 'sprung rhythm' was aiming at giving room for the spondee inside disyllabic rows. Here we have an example in line nine: 'Consequently I rejoice, having to construct something' (O o 0 ooo O / O ooo O O o).

**8 Conclusion**

Up to around 1950, there were mainly three types of free verse in the Germanic languages. Their different origins gave them different kinds of extra significance. Antique form elements added an old fashioned solemnity, the Bible forms arriving from the US seemed very *avant garde* and elements associated to the Nordic four beat line was felt homely and modern at the same time. This Old Nordic type of versification, which survived the centuries in a lower class context, reminded one of ordinary speech.

An odd detail in the history of free verse concerns the French symbolist tradition of versification. Transferred to English, this French free verse phrase happened to come close to the tradition from the old four beat line.

Eliot's versification became the most important pattern for Swedish free verse, especially after 1950. This is probably due to his preference for the free verse version emanating from the four beat line, the never forgotten Scandinavian Middle Ages verse rhythm.

In 'Ash Wednesday', Lindegren transferred the verse rhythm in a way which comes closer to speech rhythm than the original. He thus underlined Eliot's so called conversational style. In this way,

Lindegren tried to make Eliot a bit more *avant garde* than he really was, thus supporting the young Swedish modernists who were in need of some help from a highly regarded international author like Eliot.

## References

Attridge, Derek. 1982. *The Rhythms of English Poetry.* London: Longman

Cooper, G. Burns. 1998. *Mysterious Music. Rhythm and Free Verse.* Stanford, CA: Stanford University Press.

Eliot, T. S. 1917. 'Reflections on Vers libre' in *New Statesman* 14.

Eliot, T. S. 1969. 'Ash Wednesday' in *The Complete Poems and Plays of T. S. Eliot.* London: Faber and Faber.

Espmark, Kjell. 1977. *Själen i Bild: En Huvudlinje i Modern Svensk Poesi.* Stockholm: Norstedt.

Finch, Annie. 1993. *The Ghost of Meter. Culture and Prosody in American Free Verse.* Ann Arbor, MI: University of Michigan Press.

Hellmuth, Hans-Heinrich. 1973. *Metrische Erfindung und metrische Theorie beKlopstock.* München: Fink.

Lilja, Eva. 2002. 'Meter, Rhythm and Free Verse' in Küper, C. (ed.) *Meter, Rhythm and Performance.* Frankfurt am Main: Peter Lang: 253-62.

Lilja, Eva. 2006. *Svensk Metrik.* Stockholm: Norstedt.

Scott, Clive. 1990. *Vers libre. The Emergence of Free Verse in France.1886-1914.* Oxford: Clarendon Press.

Wåhlin, Kristian. 1999. *Studier i äldre svensk metrik. Valda problem 1300-1650. Efterlämnade skrifter.* Ed. by Eva Lilja & Mats Malm. Göteborg: Centre of Metrical Studies.

    …
Because I know that time is always time
2    And place is always and only place
And what is actual is actual only for one time
4    And only for one place
I rejoice that things are as they are and
6    I renounce the blessèd face
And renounce the voice
8    Because I cannot hope to turn again
Consequently I rejoice, having to construct something
10   Upon which to rejoice

And pray to God to have mercy upon us
12   And I pray that I may forget
These matters that with myself I too much discuss
14   Too much explain
Because I do not hope to turn again
16   Let these Words answer
For what is done, not to be done again
18   May the judgement not be too heavy upon us

                    (Ash-Wednesday I, verse group 3-4)

| | |
|---|---|
| o O o O / o O o O o O | pentameter |
| 2   o O o O o / o O o O | 4 beat line |
| o O o O o / o O o O o / o O O | spondee |
| 4   o O o / o O O | spondee |
| oo O o O / O oo O o⌣ | spondee |
| 6   oo O / o O o O | |
| oo O o O | |
| 8   o O o O o O / o O o O | pentameter |
| O o o ooo O / O ooo OO o | spondee |
| 10   oo O oo O | |

```
     o O o O / oo O oo O o          4 beat line
12   oo O / oo O o O
     O O o /  ooo O / o OO o O      2 spondees
14   O O o O
     o O o O o O / o O o O          pentameter
16   o O O O o                      spondee
     o O o O/O oo O o O             pentameter
18   oo O o / oo O O oo O o         4 beat line
```

...
för att jag vet att tid alltid är tid
2   och rum är alltid och endast rum
    och allt som är verkligt är verkligt blott för en tid
4   och blott i ett rum
    fröjdas jag över att allting är som det är
6   och försakar det heliga ansiktet
    och försakar rösten
8   för att jag inte kan hoppas på ändring mer
    fröjdas jag följaktligen och måste skapa något
10  att fröjdas över

    och ber till Gud att hysa misskund med oss
12  och ber att jag må glömma
    allt detta som jag alltför mycket resonerar
       med mig själv om
14  om jag alltför ofta förklarar
    för att jag inte hoppas att vända åter
16  låt dessa ord svara
    för vad som är gjort, som aldrig skall göras åter
    måtte domen inte falla för tung över oss

                    (Lindegren's translation of verse group 3-4)

ooo O / o O O oo O
2    o O o O o / o O o O
     o O oo O o / o O o O oo O
4    o O o O O
     O oo O o / o O o O oo O
6    oo O o / o O oo O 0 o
     oo O o O o
8    ooo O oo O o / o O o O
     O oo O ooo / o O o O o O o
10   o O o O o

     o O o O / ooo O 0 O o
12   o O ooo O o
     OO o / oo O˙o O ooo O o / oo OO
14   oo O o O oo O o
     ooo O o O o / ooo O o
16   o O o O O o
     oooo O / o O oo O o O o
18   O o O ooo O o / o O O oo

# Poetic Deviation and Cross-Cultural Cognition

## Mirjana Bonačić

### Abstract

The breaking of linguistic rules, particularly in poetry, is a feature of language use that is generally described as a device for creating new modes of meaning often giving rise to divergent interpretations. When it comes to translating, deviations in rules of form and in meaning are regarded as a major stumbling block to achieving equivalent meaning effects in translation. From a different angle, however, poetic translating can become a powerful method of understanding cognitive processes of making sense of deviant expressions. Since translation is a discourse involving different languages and different social contexts, it can help gain insight not only into expected cultural diversity but also into the complex question of cross-cultural cognitive convergence brought about by mutual comprehension.

The paper examines what kind of answer can be put forward when some recent cognitive linguistic insights into the nature of drawing meaning from text are applied to an account of a poem that is exemplary of deviant language (a poem by Cummings) and its translation into Croatian. The assumption is that such analysis may reveal how the conceptualisation of a poetic text world is effected through different languages and how this may lead to specific cross-cultural commonalities of meaning.

Keywords: poetic deviation; Cummings; poetic translation; cognitive stylistics; cross-cultural cognition; commonality of meaning.

## 1 Introduction

Translations can often provide valuable empirical evidence of different readings of a poetic text. Each reading of a poetic text is a kind of translation of its language into a particular conceptual representation of its multiple meaning potential and, on the other hand, each translation manifests not only a particular reading of the original but also how the translator, in the double role of reader and writer, interprets and then creates textual devices by which specific aesthetic and meaning effects come into being. So, the basic question in translation regarded as a process is not only *what* a text means but also *how* it means.

The analyst provides a description of the translator's cognitive and textual procedures that substantiates a specific relation between source text and target text. In analysis, therefore, lurks the ever-present question of how an analytic description refracts this relationship differently, depending on the adopted theoretical approach and tools of analysis or, in other words, how an account of the process of translation constitutes translational discourse itself. Where the analyst and the translator are the same person, the analysis can proceed from a double perspective, focusing simultaneously on meaning as developed in the mind of the reader while reading and on the textual production of meaning during translation.

In general, since translation is a mode of discourse involving different languages and different cultures, it engenders a relativist view of meaning by underscoring linguistic and cultural diversity without, however, precluding mutual comprehension in the encounter between cultures. In another paper (Bonačić 2005) I attempted to explain how different ways of language patterning during translation signal different mental conceptualisations of the original text and how divergent translations of a poetic text from English into two different Slavic languages reveal translation as a dialogic process which can be described in terms of translatability as the mode of a cross-cultural discourse.

In this paper, I will try to explore how an analysis of translatability at three levels of discourse, interpersonal, conceptual (ideational) and textual, can account for our ability to interpret a text that violates syntactic-semantic rules and how this ability can manifest itself interlinguistically as a cross-cultural cognitive convergence. I will examine how a simultaneous analysis of the mode of meaning of a poetic text and its translation can correlate specific linguistic data with the possibilities of interpretation when such data comprise various aspects of deviant language. I will examine the process of translating a poem that is exemplary of deviant language – a poem by E. E. Cummings. But first of all, I would like to take up some theoretical issues relating to poetic deviation.

## 2 Theoretical issues

In poetics, the breaking of linguistic rules is one of the features of literary language that is generally considered to be a paramount device for creating new modes of expression. In translation studies, however, deviations in rules of form and in meaning in the original text are, more often than not, regarded as a major stumbling block to achieving equivalent stylistic effects or even as presenting insoluble problems in translation. On the other hand, the question that interests linguists is how it is at all possible to process deviant or ungrammatical expressions.

Traditionally, it is considered impossible to modify a standard grammar in order to accommodate deviant sentences. From the standpoint of generative grammar, therefore, it was proposed that such poems as Cummings's might be regarded as a different language or dialect which required a separate grammar (Thorne 1970). But, as it was later argued from the perspective of literature as discourse (Widdowson 1975: 25-46), sentences which are ungrammatical are nevertheless interpretable in the context of a piece of literary writing without any need for the reader to construct a separate grammar. More recently, in cognitive linguistics many aspects of language use traditionally regarded as deviant, such as metaphor being deviant from ordinary 'literal' language, have been proved to be inherent patterns of human understanding (Lakoff & Johnson 1980). The view of metaphor as non-deviant but basic to language and thought has been extended to other instances of deviant language use. Thus, Margaret Freeman argues that Dickinson's deviant expressions, such as her ungrammatical -*self* anaphors, are perfectly grammatical if a special cognitive linguistic rule is proposed, namely that 'whenever a subject referent in one (originating) space projects a mental space (target) via a trigger or space-builder, its pronoun counterpart in the target space will take the corresponding -*self* anaphor form' (Freeman 1997: 11).

But, revealing as such principles of poetic composition may be, translation is more concerned with problems that may vary from poem to poem. The process of translation captures the process of conceptualisation in creative thinking, and the process is local. This means that the problem of specific instances of poetic deviation may be dealt with differently in the translational interpretation of different poems, irrespective of the general principle that renders them perfectly grammatical within the poetics of a particular poet. In poetic discourse, figurative effects of deviant expressions may play a crucial role in world creation in poems. Such meaning effects are context-specific and, in the process of translating and interpreting a poem, cannot be subsumed into or normalised by a general rule. Moreover, if we were to do away with the notion of deviation in rules of form, in meaning or in literary conventions, we would face the problem of how to account for the devices of de-familiarisation or dynamic re-conceptualisation which are a central feature of poetic discourse. The fact that such devices are also used in non-literary language does not warrant the abolishing of the notions of poetic deviation and ungrammaticality when dealing with the local problems of interpretation and poetic translation.

In fact, as cognitive linguistics equates meaning with cognitive processing (Langacker 1990), its focus of analysis is on cognitive constructs and dynamics, and its methods purport to extend to contextual aspects of language use, which 'means studying full discourse, language in context, inferences actually drawn by participants in an exchange' (Fauconnier 1999: 97). The basic claim is that 'it is only in rich contexts that we see the full force of creative on-line meaning construction' (Fauconnier 1999: 97). In particular, when uses of language that are traditionally viewed as deviant are treated as central, understanding the complex linguistic organisation involved leads to the study of local conceptual configurations or interconnected 'mental spaces'. However, the theory that enables us to account for such uses in cognitive linguistic terms should, in my opinion, be reinforced by a theory of discourse enabling us to account for stylistic effects of deviation in form and in meaning in particular cultural/social contexts of use or genres, such as poetic discourse.

I will now present a study of local conceptual configurations involved in my translation of Cummings' poem. Since an outside observer inevitably sees the translated text as a product rather than the process of meaning construction, my simultaneous analysis of the source and target text aims to provide an insight into 'the full force of creative on-line meaning construction' triggered by language use in the very process of translating the poem.

## 3 Stylistic analysis

### 3.1 The poem and its translation

What follows is a stylistic analysis of a cross-cultural, translational discourse from the double perspective of the translator as discourse participant and third person analyst.

The poem:

| 1  | yes is a pleasant country: |
|----|------|
| 2  | if's wintry |
| 3  | (my lovely) |
| 4  | let's open the year |
| 5  | both is the very weather |
| 6  | (not either) |
| 7  | my treasure, |
| 8  | when violets appear |
| 9  | love is a deeper season |
| 10 | than reason; |
| 11 | my sweet one |
| 12 | (and april's where we're) |

—e. e. cummings

A Croatian translation:

| 1 | 'jest' ugodno je mjesto:<br>[yes  pleasant is place] |
|---|------|
| 2 | 'ako' je zimsko<br>[if    is wintry] |
| 3 | (ljepoto moja)<br>[beauty my] |
| 4 | otvorimo          ljeto<br>[open (1st p. pl.) year/summer]<br>(let's open) |
| 5 | oboje baš je vrijeme<br>[both very is time/weather] |
| 6 | (a        nije ili)<br>[and/but isn't or] |
| 7 | zlaćana moja,<br>[golden my] |
| 8 | kad    ljubica živi<br>[when violet lives] |
| 9 | ljubav je dublje  doba<br>[love   is deeper season/period] |
| 10 | od      razuma;<br>[than reason] |
| 11 | medena moja<br>[honey  my] |
| 12 | (travanj je gdje  i     mi)<br>[April    is where also we] |

Translated by Mirjana Bonačić (2005)

The analysis aims to show how the translational decisions affect the construction of a poetic text world and how some of these factors may lead to specific cross-cultural commonalities of meaning. The reader of the paper, as observer, can critically relate the language data in question to a broader modality involving the translator/analyst's experiential assumptions, aesthetic judgements and attitudinal positioning.

The mode of meaning of both the original and translated text can be described at three coexistent and interrelated levels of discourse: interpersonal, conceptual, and textual. An important aspect of the interpersonal or social level of discourse is realised through our culturally conditioned and socially shared ability to identify a text as belonging to a specific genre. Within the broader framework of Western culture, as soon as we perceive some conspicuous features of Cummings' text, such as its distinctive arrangement in the form of verse, we expect it to be a poem and are ready to activate relevant ways of reading it. Thus, our internalised experience in poetic discourse guides us in the process of conceptualising the poem's meaning. The foremost among such ways of reading is perhaps the interpretative procedure whereby we apply our aesthetic perception to mark the distinctive manner of textual expression and to lend it a special significance of motivated choice thereby integrating the textual and conceptual levels of poetic discourse.

It is of interest to consider how an analytic description correlates linguistic data with the possibilities of interpretation and how such a description constitutes a specific discourse. I will digress to comment briefly on a different analytical approach to interpretative strategies which van Peer (1987) illustrates by using the same poem from Cummings. These strategies fall under two distinct models: top-down (the activation of particular schemata in our memory by textual elements which function as signals for such scripts) and bottom-up (from the linguistic elements of the text to a semantic macrostructure linked to a schematic superstructure). As van Peer rightly argues, the models are not mutually exclusive. In actual interpretation the top-down and bottom-up activities interact and 'the reader has to strike a *balance*: his stored scripts can only guide him insofar as they do not pass beyond the constraints imposed by the text itself' (van Peer 1987: 608). In his interpretation of Cummings the first activity yields a top-down sequence: poetry → modern poetry → two participants → two lovers → an invitation → to make love (van Peer 1987: 603). The second activity constructs out of parts of the text a cohesive whole in which 'springtime is the conventional season for courting and lovemaking' (van Peer 1987: 608). While confirming the broad configuration of my own interpretation, which can also be taken as evidence of the overlapping cross-cultural commonality of meaning, such an account of the poem's meaning normalises textual anomalies by subsuming them under conventional scripts too readily. Rather than the expressions 'my lovely' (3) and 'let's' (4), which van Peer first focuses on for their reference to the conventional script of love poetry (van Peer 1987: 603), it is the first two lines that grip the reader by their anomaly and effect of estrangement.

Aesthetic pleasure is afforded first by surprise and then by a gradual discovery of the coherent sequence of all deviations in the language of the poem. These deviant constructions trigger reasoning processes and meaning effects which can perhaps be made more explicit from the perspective of certain principles of conceptual integration and some basic concepts of cognitive grammar.

## 3.2 Deviant constructions

The textual level of analysis involves deviation in category rules which is conspicuously foregrounded in both the original and translated text. In the prominent position at the very beginning of the first two lines, where in the initial subject position in the sentences making up the lines and consisting of one subject-predicate unit we would normally expect a noun or a noun phrase, we find a reaction signal (English 'yes', Croatian *jest* 'yes') and a subordinating conjunction (English 'if', Croatian *ako* 'if'). These words do not have their expected, normal functions. The reaction signal is not a discursive response to a nonexistent previous question, and the conjunction does not function as a grammatical word. In both texts these words are used as full lexical words bearing half of the propositional content of the utterances. This gives rise to deviation in semantic restriction rules. Thus, in the combination of lexical items within the context of the first line, instead of a proper noun, such as the name of a concrete country or place, we get a linguistic item signalling a general attitude. The linguistic signal of consent, an abstract concept, is by predication identified with a concrete country or place. There is a profusion of such semantic anomalies in both texts. In the second line, the conjunction 'if', *ako*, normally introducing conditional clauses, acquires features that are typical of

winter: 'if's wintry', *'ako' je zimsko* 'if is wintry' (*ako* 'if' without
quotation marks would be taken for conjunction and yield the
irrelevant meaning 'if it is wintry' since Croatian does not use an
empty or prop subject in such expressions).

In the second stanza, the English pronoun 'both' and the Croatian dual
number *oboje* 'both' (5) do not have the discursive function of
anaphoric or deictic reference to some given entities. Their
independently stateable abstract meaning of community between two
entities is equated with the right or desirable 'weather', in Croatian
*vrijeme*, a polysemic word denoting 'time' and 'weather'. In the next
line (6), this quality is denied to the word 'either', normally an
adjective, pronoun or conjunction, and in Croatian, to the conjunction
*ili* 'or'. Finally, in the third stanza, the abstract concepts 'love', in
Croatian *ljubav*, and 'reason', in Croatian *razum*, are described as
'seasons', in Croatian *doba* 'season', and these are compared in terms
of their relative depth (9-10): 'love is a deeper season / than reason',
*ljubav je dublje doba / od razuma* 'love is a deeper season than
reason', as if a season could be deep or shallow.

How do we interpret all these syntactic and semantic anomalies? We
assign a discursive intention to all these absurdities and apparent
follies. This helps to explain why the poem is written like this and
what effects it has as a result. From the standpoint of a cognitive
linguistic approach, such unusual linguistic constructions motivate
particular imaginative projections which readers and writers perform
when they construe meanings by conceptual blending, the mental
mechanism that binds together and integrates multiple mental spaces
into complex ideas (Fauconnier & Turner 2003).

The reader will have performed the relevant conceptual blending by
now. Interpretation is much faster than analysis. However, analysis
can help us to understand and explain how we have done this. But
before I discuss the text at its conceptual level, I will briefly comment
on the notion of grammar as image.

Langacker's concept of figure-ground alignment may be considered
relevant to the description of the poem on the textual level (Langacker
1990). I would like to suggest that the linguistic construal of figure
and ground may be formed not only within individual sentences but
also on the level of the entire text. The figure-ground alignment within

individual sentences becomes a scene of moving images at textual level. The figures in the first two stanzas – the deviant subjects in the thematic position signifying abstract attitudinal positions – attract attention and are mapped sequentially as trajectors along the landmarks of concrete places in the transition from winter to spring. The relations within the lines are static, but there is a trajectory in the text as a guideline for interpretation – a dynamic transformation of strange, elusive signals in the first two stanzas to the clearly visible signs, full lexical items in the last stanza ('love', *ljubav*, 'reason', *razum*), almost as if filmed in close-up.

### 3.3 Conceptual blending and metaphorical coherence

In my view, the dynamic elaboration of the conceptual blending process can hardly be captured by depicting diagrams, such as those sometimes seen in cognitive stylistic analyses. Turner & Fauconnier (2003: 141) have also recently said that 'conceptual blending is a dynamic process that cannot be adequately represented by a static drawing'. And they usually describe the process at the level of single sentences or events. Here we are concerned with an entire poem. So, I will just give a brief account of the major aspects of the conceptual blending process involved in the mental representation of the poem's meaning effects. This process has multiple dimensions, spatial and temporal, horizontal within the spatial and temporal boundaries of individual lines, vertical in the sequential order of lines within the boundaries of the entire poem.

From the mental space of the speaking (lyric) voice in the poem's discursive world, which the reader constructs as soon as the text is identified as a poem, the space builders in the first two stanzas (1, 2, 5, 6), the deviant subjects 'yes', 'if', 'both', 'either', and in Croatian *jest* 'yes', *ako* 'if', *oboje* 'both', *ili* 'or', are motivated by the predicates within the respective lines to become partial discourse signals of abstract relations. Like some concrete fragments, they activate almost metonymically a sequence of fully conceptualised input mental spaces: 'yes', *jest* → consent, agreement; 'if', *ako* → condition, argument (hesitation may be implied); 'both', *oboje* → togetherness, a community of two entities; 'either', *ili* → separation, exclusion of one alternative. Sequentially in the text, they acquire features of either parallel or opposite abstract relations which are motivated on the interpersonal discourse level of argument and persuasion. In the last stanza (9, 10), we get explicit mention of 'love' and 'reason', in Croatian *ljubav* 'love' and *razum* 'reason', whereby the separate mental spaces of emotion and reason are activated directly (not metonymically).

The words that constitute the predicate part of the statements in the sequential order of the lines trigger two parallel sequences of input mental spaces in the domain of place and the domain of time, namely geographic places (l. 1: 'country', *mjesto* 'place'), and seasons and months (l. 4: 'year', *ljeto* 'year/summer'; l. 12: 'april', *travanj* 'April') with features of the typical weather (l. 2: 'wintry', *zimsko* 'wintry'; l. 5: 'the very weather', *baš...vrijeme* 'very...weather') and the typical thing and event, a herald of springtime (l. 8: 'when violets appear', *kad ljubica živi* 'when the violet lives'). Yet another sequence of input mental spaces is in the domain of sensations and senses, the sensation of pleasantness (l. 1: 'pleasant', *ugodno* 'pleasant') and the sense of coldness, a feature typical of winter (l. 2: 'wintry', *zimsko* 'wintry'). At last, the expressions 'let's open the year', in Croatian *otvorimo ljeto* 'let's open the year/summer' (4), and 'deeper season', in Croatian *dublje doba* 'deeper season/period' (9), invoke the concept of container. Time is conceived as a physical place which it is possible to open and enter and then, by implication, be in it: '(and april's where we're)', *(travanj je gdje i mi)* 'April is where also/and we' (12).

All these input spaces are elaborated in two main generic spaces that can respectively be defined as abstract structure of binary oppositions and as movement. These generic spaces determine selective mappings into the blend. Opposite elements are partly construed by inference: yes / no (if), spring / winter; warm / cold, pleasant / unpleasant, two (both) / one (either), love / reason. In the blend, these selected elements from the input spaces correlate and are integrated into complex blends, horizontally within the lines, and vertically in the sequence of the lines: yes (consent) → spring (pleasant, warm, the right season, violets, April) → two (both) → love (deeper), as contrasted to the other sequence: if (condition, possibility of refusal) → winter (wintry, cold, unpleasant) → one (either, single) → reason (less deep). The other generic space, the relation of movement, structures the poem's argument as movement or a journey (indicated by the arrow →).

The complex integration of the described multiple mental spaces and metaphorical mappings is motivated by some basic conceptual metaphors, such as those identified by Lakoff & Johnson (1980). First of all, metaphorical coherence is achieved by several conceptual metaphors representing the notion of love.

The metaphor LOVE IS WARMTH is conceptualised through the relation of the emotion of love to the sensation of pleasure and the physical sense of touch, which manifests the metonymic basis of the metaphor (l. 1: 'pleasant', *ugodno* 'pleasant'; l. 11: 'sweet', *medena* 'honey'). In both texts love is also indirectly associated with beauty and value (l. 3: 'lovely', *ljepoto* 'beauty'; l. 8: 'violets', *ljubica* 'violet'; l. 7: 'treasure', *zlaćana* 'golden'). These associations are foregrounded at the phonological textual level: in the English text between '<u>love</u>ly' and '<u>love</u>', in the Croatian text between *<u>lje</u>poto* 'beauty' and *<u>lje</u>to* 'year/summer' (which is the reason why the polysemic Croatian word *ljeto* has been chosen instead of the unambiguous *godina* 'year'), and between *<u>ljub</u>ica* 'violet' and *<u>ljub</u>av* 'love'.

The metaphor LOVE IS UNION AND COOPERATION is articulated in both texts. The notion of collaborative work is alluded to in l. 4: 'let's open', *otvorimo* 'let's open'; the notion of togetherness in l. 5: 'both', *oboje* 'both'; and the notion of union in l. 12: 'we're', *i mi* 'also/and we'. The basic metaphor LOVE IS A CONTAINER is implied through the coherence of the metaphorical mappings in lines 4, 9 and 12: love is a deeper season which can be opened and entered. Moreover, in the Croatian text the concept of container is foregrounded at the phonological textual level: in l. 1, the word *mjesto*, the 'place' of love, contains the entire word *jest*, the signal of consent (which is the reason why the word *mjesto* 'place', rather than *zemlja* 'country', has been chosen).

The metaphor LOVE IS A JOURNEY connects the last lines of the stanzas (4, 8 and 12) into a coherent statement: in the English text, 'let's open the year' / 'when violets appear' / '(and april's where we're)'; in the Croatian text, *otvorimo ljeto* / *kad ljubica živi* / *(travanj je gdje i mi)*. In both texts these lines have a similar rhythmic pattern (with the second stress falling on the fifth syllable rather than the fourth or, alternatively, with two unstressed syllables counted as one), distinct from the rest of the lines which are all governed by the same, regular iambic metre, with more or less frequent trochaic inversions at the beginning of the lines. In the original poem, the last lines (4, 8 and 12) also rhyme. In the Croatian text, only lines 8 and 12 are connected by an assonantal rhyme *živi / i mi* (with the stress falling on the conjunction *i*). Moreover, all the verbs in the poem are in the present tense as used to signify general truths. The only exceptions are line 4: 'let's open the year', *otvorimo ljeto* 'let's open the year/summer' – an invitation to initiate a journey through time, and the last line of the poem: '(and april's where we're)', *(travanj je gdje i mi)* 'April is where also we', in which the deictic reference is to the actual present or near-future time. This is a journey from wooing and persuasion to making love towards fulfilment. In both texts, the last line (12) ends before the sentence it contains is concluded, but there is a subdued hint of what can follow. It is left to the reader to make a guess.

The articulation of another metaphor follows a similar trajectory. ARGUMENT (PERSUASION) IS A JOURNEY: a journey from the persuasive reasons elaborated metaphorically throughout the poem to a convincing conclusion in the last line. Finally, the main principle underlying the described conceptual integration processes and metaphorical coherence is that all these metaphors constitute processes of embodied understanding and that there is a significant measure of the overlapping commonality of meaning in the interpretation of the two texts written in different languages and presupposing different cultures.

### 3.4 Deictic orientation and deictic shift

On the interpersonal level of poetic discourse, within the outward writer-text-reader interaction, which is governed by particular conventions of literary discourse and can also be considered a matter of social cognition, there is an inner discursive situation built by the convention of lyric voice and the rhetorical figure of apostrophe. In the poem, the speaking voice is the deictic centre. The inner interpersonal relation of 'I-you' is created in the poetic world by a series of vocative addresses occurring in the third line of each stanza: '(my lovely)', *(ljepoto moja)* 'my beauty/lovely' (3); 'my treasure', *zlaćana moja* 'my golden one' (7); 'my sweet one', *medena moja* 'my honey' (11). The possessive adjective 'my', in Croatian *moja* (explicitly feminine gender), signifies possession, while the form of address: 'lovely', 'treasure', 'sweet one', and in Croatian *ljepoto* 'beauty', *zlaćana* 'golden one', *medena* 'honey', signifies the transition from the sense of sight to the sense of touch. In the vein of critical discourse analysis, this could be interpreted as a transition from a more distant relationship – lover (woman) as an object of admiration, to the immediate proximity – lover (woman) as an object of possession, enjoyment and consumption (sweetness, honey, food).

The deictic shift occurs when the 'I-you' relationship changes into the inclusive expression 'let's open', *otvorimo* (1$^{st}$ p. pl. imperative) 'let's open', signifying an invitation to act together. In the last line of the poem, which brings a promise of fulfilment, it changes into 'we', *mi* 'we' (foregrounded in the Croatian verbless clause *gdje i mi* 'where also we'). The deictic orientation is also construed by the use of tense: from the present tense in all the assertions constituting a persuasive discourse of poetic argumentation to the present tense in the last line referring to the actual present or near-future moment of arrival to the destination.

### 3.5 Discursive function of punctuation

In both the original and translated text, the use of punctuation marks has a discursive function. The colon in l. 1 introduces a discourse of argumentation constructed by strange and deviant language. In the temporal span between the first and the last stanza this discourse becomes more explicit: 'yes', *jest* and 'both', *oboje* turn into 'love', *ljubav*, while 'if', *ako* and 'either', *ili* transform into 'reason', *razum*. This change is also marked by the use of brackets: from the subdued address in the brackets in l. 3, '(my lovely)', *(ljepoto moja)*, to the bold, outspoken address in l. 11, 'my sweet one', *medena moja*. This line is preceded by a semi-colon which indicates a pause after the aphorism 'love is a deeper season / than reason', *ljubav je dublje doba / od razuma* (9-10). This is a pause before the sudden fulfilment in the last two lines. After the semi-colon there is no need for further persuasion. The last, incomplete line is in brackets: '(april's where we're)', *(travanj je gdje i mi)*. It is an almost inaudible, vanishing whisper.

Brackets also appear in l. 6. This line contains the only negative statement in the poem: '(not either)', *(a nije ili)* 'and/but (it) isn't or'. The effect of conspicuous negation at the beginning of the expression is to foreground the negated item and at the same time to remove it from the construed world of the text, which is also signified by the use of brackets.

## 4 Conclusion

In conclusion, I would like to suggest that an account of language use in translation can reveal how figurative imagination constitutes the way we understand poems cross-culturally. In this particular case, in the simultaneous analysis of both the original and translated text, the same cognitive procedures and a significant degree of cross-cultural interpretative convergence have been evidenced. The aim of the paper has been to support the view that the theory called '*cognitive poetics* is a powerful tool for making explicit our reasoning processes and for illuminating the structure and content of literary texts' (Freeman 2000: 253). By relating the language of literary texts to the cognitive linguistic strategies that readers use to understand them, it can help us to explain how we interpret literary discourse at its conceptual and textual level. However, in my view and as I have tried to show in this paper, we still need the wider frame of adequate discourse theory to account for the interpersonal level of literary discourse which is relevant to the investigation of social and cross-cultural cognizance and can also answer such questions as how we acquire knowledge and understanding of particular genres or forms of discourse, such as poetic discourse.

## References

Barcelona, Antonio. (ed.). 2003. *Metaphor and Metonymy at the Crossroads: A Cognitive Perspective.* Berlin: Mouton de Gruyter.

Bonačić, Mirjana. 2005. 'The Translator's Craft as a Cross-Cultural Discourse' in Caldas-Coulthard, Carmen Rosa, and Michael Toolan (eds). *The Writer's Craft, the Culture's Technology* (PALA Papers 1). Amsterdam: Rodopi: 123-37.

Faucounnier, Gilles. 1999. 'Methods and Generalizations' in Janssen, Theo, and Gisela Redeker (eds). *Cognitive Linguistics: Foundations, Scope, and Methodology.* Berlin: Mouton de Gruyter: 95-127.

Faucounnier, Gilles, and Mark Turner. 2002. *Conceptual Blending and the Mind's Hidden Complexities.* New York: Basic Books.

Freeman, Margaret H. 1997. 'Grounded spaces: deictic -*self* anaphors in the poetry of Emily Dickinson' in *Language and Literature* 6(1): 7-28.

Freeman, Margaret H. 2003. 'Poetry and the scope of metaphor: Toward a cognitive theory of literature' in Barcelona (2003): 253-81.

Lakoff, George, and Mark Johnson. 1980. *Metaphors We Live By*. Chicago: The University of Chicago Press.

Langacker, Ronald W. 1990. *Concept, Image, and Symbol: The Cognitive Basis of Grammar*. Berlin: Mouton de Gruyter.

Thorne, James P. 1970. 'Stylistics and Generative Grammars' in Freeman, Donald C. (ed.) *Linguistics and Literary Style*. New York: Holt, Rinehart and Winston: 182-96.

Turner; Mark, and Gilles Fauconnier. 2003. 'Metaphor, metonymy, and binding' in Barcelona (2003): 133-45.

Van Peer, Willie. 1987. 'Top-Down and Bottom-Up: Interpretative Strategies in Reading E. E. Cummings' in *New Literary History* 18: 597-609.

Widdowson, Henry G. 1975. *Stylistics and the Teaching of Literature*. London: Longman.

# The Discourse of Silence:
# The Unspoken in Contemporary American Love Poetry

## Judith Munat

## Abstract

This is an investigation of one reader's intuitions regarding the representation of silence in poetic discourse (upon reading a collection of contemporary American love poetry). The aim of the study is to identify and analyze meaningful 'silences' (or absences) in the poems. After a discussion of the semiotics of silence, I consider the contours and functions of silence in interpersonal communication, and then focus on literary silence, describing its various possible representations on the printed page (at the levels of graphics, prosody, syntax, lexis and figurative language), with particular reference to the poems in the collection.

A reflection on some of the possible motivations underlying such silences in the discourse of desire is followed by more general considerations of the negative and positive values of silence. The ultimate objectives of the study are to determine how silence functions pragmatically in poetic discourse and to verify whether one reader's subjective intuitions can be supported by objective textual analysis.

> Within linguistics, silence has traditionally been ignored, [defined] negatively—as merely the absence of speech.(Saville Troike, 1985)
>
> silence […] merits to be fully treated in the study of linguistic communication.
>
> (Jaworski, 1997)

## 1 Introduction

This study has its origin in my reading of a collection of love poetry, *Isn't It Romantic:100 Love Poems by Younger American Poets* (Lauer 2004), in which I found surprisingly little talk of passion, love or desire, and even less that I would consider as 'romantic.' What I particularly noted as I read these poems was the difference between the language here and that of a group of 20th century (female) poets that I had previously studied for a paper presented at the University of Stirling (Munat 2004). In the more than 100 poems I examined in that earlier study there was a great deal of explicit sexual language, and I suppose I expected that these younger poets would employ equally direct language in speaking of love and desire as that used by poets of the previous generation, such as Olds or Shuttle or Peacock. Instead, I found the voices of these 'younger American poets' (both male and female) strangely muted by comparison. I consequently decided to identify what it was that I experienced as silence, or reticence, in reading this poetry. What are the concrete representations of this auditory silence – at the level of graphics, prosody, lexis, syntax and figurative language? And, above all, how are they to be interpreted?

## 2 Aims and methodological approach

Deborah Tannen (1985: xi) emphasizes that silence has traditionally been seen as the figure to be examined against the ground of talk. In the present study, instead, I shall be examining representations of silence as a meaningful figure against the ground of the written page, visible as concrete linguistic devices and meaningful as intentional communicative acts.

There have been numerous studies of silence in conversational exchange, but far fewer that consider the representation of silence in written text and, more specifically, its role and significance in poetry. Indeed, my first aim is that of identifying the devices by which such silences are represented on the page. If silence is normally perceived, as Tannen (1985: xv) states, when 'expected talk' is absent, we must seek those points in the text where verbal communication is suspended or restrained, where our expectations as reader/participant in the ongoing discourse are frustrated.

The second aim is that of interpreting the possible significance of these silences, which will necessitate *a priori* recognition of the type of silence: is it inadvertent and natural or a conscious choice? If so, is it self-imposed or the result of some external pressure? Is it to be attributed to a character trait of the speaker or is it an intentional speech act?

My third and final aim in this study is that of considering the possible meanings of these silences, especially in relation to the discourse of love, determining, for example, whether they are to be attributed to the intimacy between the speakers (where words become superfluous), or to emotions which impede communication. Only at this point can we begin to infer the reasons underlying these silences and attempt to reply to the central question at the basis of this study: what provokes such reticence in writing of love? Thus our attention will be focused on the pragmatic functions of silence in intimate discourse.

In outlining my approach I inadvertently reply to claims such as that made by Manning (1997:43), i.e., that corpus studies provide "more reliable, objective and informative description of a language" than studies based on "the observation, memory and intuition of individuals." Though recognizing the value of objective statistical data and of the wider linguistic patterns that emerge from extensive corpus studies, I strongly reject the implicature that individual observations and intuitions are unreliable, subjective and uninformative.

Mine is, in fact, a humanist approach to linguistic analysis, an approach that has been codified by Lipka (2003) as Observational Linguistics, an area of empirical linguistics (in opposition to Corpus Linguistics) stemming from anthropology and sociolinguistic research. In Lipka's view, participant observation allows a fruitful analysis of lexical and semiotic phenomena of language seen within its full linguistic, situational and cultural context.

Thus individual subjectivity and intuition play a primary role in this study, and are considered to be a fundamental 'tool' in linguistic research. The human mind, in fact, is capable of making connections and ferreting out meanings that would escape the most sophisticated of computers. A case in point is the study of textual representations of silence.

> Silence is a multifaceted linguistic construct, with a range of forms, serving different functions and whose meaning can be extended into the visual domain.
>
> (Jaworski, 1997)

## 3 Contours and functions of silence

### 3.1 The semiotics of silence

Considering silence as a semiotic sign, it may be placed in opposition to either linguistic (i.e, verbal) signs or non-verbal acoustic communication (such as music or noises of various sorts) (see Verschureren, 1985). And just as the verbal sign may be expressed in a variety of semiotic modalities (sign language, facial expressions, gestures of various sorts, graphemes, etc.), silence may have a variety of different realizations. It is important to emphasize that silence, as one type of semiotic sign, carries both verbal (linguistic) and cultural meanings.

According to Vainiomäki (2004), there are three semiotic aspects to silence: first, its role in producing communicative or cultural meanings; second, the spatio-temporal significations of silence in culture; third, the contours of silence (or where it begins and where it ends). We may thus deduce that silence carries with it a variety of meanings.

Silence in the broadest sense can be intended as the absence of sound or of verbal expression, but can only be identified and defined in contrast with non-silence[1]. If true silence even exists - and some, such as John Cage, have claimed that there is no such thing as total silence[2] - it can only be defined in relation to its polar opposite. In this opposition between silence and sound or between silence and speech (see Kurzon, 1998, for a full discussion), we must also consider intentionality and non-naturalness as distinguishing features of communicatively significant silence. An example of intentional silence, for example, would be John Cage's composition *4'33"*, where the pianist places his fingers on the keys but does not strike them; while a natural, non-intentional silence would be that of a sleeping person. The pianist's silence in the foregoing example is thus semiotically significant in that it is non-natural and intentional.

In his detailed discussion of the semiotics of silence, Kurzon (1998) attempts to establish the logical relations between silence, its contrary (speech or noise?) and its contradictory (non-silence?). He ultimately proposes Malandro's (1989) matrix of dyadic communication (as reproduced in Figure 1), that posits vocal and non-vocal verbal activity (speech and silence respectively) and vocal and non-vocal non-verbal activity (paralinguistics and body movements).

Sebeok (2001:16ff) specifies that human communication may be vocal (produced by the vocal cords as in speech or singing) or non-vocal (e.g., sign language, smoke signals, snapping one's fingers, clicking one's tongue). Non-vocal silence may be further characterized as verbal (sign language) or nonverbal (drums). With the exception of sign language or smoke signals, all of the foregoing are transmitted in the acoustic mode, which includes speech, music and a variety of sound effects. Nonverbal codes transmitted and perceived through the visual channel include works of art, scenery, dance, lighting, etc.

Human beings also communicate visually (but nonverbally) by body movements, facial expressions, eye gaze, gestures of various sorts, as well as through the clothes they wear.

|  | Verbal | Non-verbal |
|---|---|---|
| Vocal | **speech** | **paralinguistics and prosody**[3] |
| Non-vocal | **silence** | **gestures, proxemics, etc.** |

**Figure 1** Matrix of dyadic interactions from Malandro *et al*. 1989, based on

Saville-Troike's(1985) dimensions of code and channel.

Given that our primary concern here is with human verbal communication, I will not be considering numerous other channels, such as chemical, optical, tactile, electric, thermal, olfactory, etc.

> ...silence is meaningful.  The central problem of silence in discourse is to discover that meaning

(Kurzon 1998)

## 3.2 Silence as a marker of interaction

Sobkowiak (1997:43) theorizes a dichotomy between pragmatic and acoustic silence. The latter, being unintentional and natural, only exists as an ideal model and may be either the state of keeping silent or the absence of perceptible sound in the environment. Pragmatic silence, instead, is intentional and non-natural but referentially void and it retains the illocutionary force of a speech act: it may, for example, indicate a promise, a threat, an insult, a refusal, etc.[4]

Non-communicative silences, instead, are constituted by pauses and hesitations of an affective nature, connotative rather than denotative, and their norms of use will vary according to the speech community (Saville Troike 1985: 6). These silences are learned as part of speaker competence. A socially competent speaker must know, for example, whether speech is appropriate at meal-times, or in the presence of certain people, and how long a silence may last. Leech (1983: 141), in speaking of the 'polite and impolite implications of silence', suggests that it is a polite form of behaviour on the part of someone of low social status (e.g. a child), but may be seen as impolite when someone opts out of a conversation. Since silence is often interpreted as anti-social behaviour, this accounts for the many trivial conversational gambits and uninformative statements that are typical of phatic communion (e.g., 'What a lovely day!' when this is self-evident to the participants in the interaction).

Silence in interpersonal exchange may thus communicate a range of different meanings and is open to a variety of interpretations, depending on the frame in which it occurs: consider the silence of a child who has been asked a question by the teacher, or the silence of a lover who is asked to vow his or her fidelity, or the silence of a suspect when asked to explain his whereabouts at the time of a crime. Each of these silences will be interpreted in relation to the event or situation which 'frames' the silence.

Research in Conversation Analysis has focused on the functions, positions and duration of silence in conversation (see Sacks *et al.* 1974) and particular attention has been paid to its role in dialogue, where it serves to allow the speaker to gain conversational status, to manage interpersonal relations, or to maintain group identity. Socially significant silence is thus interactive (Ghita 1994: 387) and may occur either within a speaker's turn, at the moment of transition from one speaker to another, or occupy the space of an entire turn, and is principally used as part of an adjacency pair: when it is the first part, the preferred response is to break the silence. Its interpretation will ultimately depend, among other factors, upon its position in the on-going interaction.

Kurzon (1998:44) hypothesizes a variety of contexts or frames in which silence occurs and a range of possible interpretations, from that of resistance (here Melville's Bartleby immediately comes to mind), to shyness, fear, speech dysfluency, etc. It is the interlocutor's task to determine whether the silence is due to a personality trait, or whether it is volitional, thus communicating an intended speech act. Kurzon suggests the following range of possible modal interpretations of silence:

- unintentional (I cannot speak) – a psychological inhibition
- intentional and internal (I will not speak) – denial/rebellion

- intentional and external (I must not speak) - fear/secrecy

Jaworski (1997: 392) speaks of the 'distancing' function of silence, and, at the opposite end of the scale, silence which is a marker of intimacy between acquaintances. In the political or social sphere, he suggests that silence may signify, among other things, dominance, oppression or censorship (taboo, in fact, can be interpreted as a culturally imposed silence).

Ghita (1994: 380) considers the psycholinguistic function of silence in spoken interaction, where it serves to chunk speech into meaningful units, thus facilitating listener comprehension. But it may also be viewed in Gricean terms as a violation of the maxims of Quantity and Manner, leading to a variety of implicatures (see Grice 1989). The type of silence on which we will be focussing in the present study is volitional non-vocal verbal communication, employed as an alternative to speech.

> Silence is a presence
> it has a history
> a form
> Do not confuse it with any kind of absence
>
> (Adrienne Rich)

## 3.3 Representation of Silence in Literature

In our discussion of poetic silence I shall be considering poetry as interactive discourse, i.e., a dialogue between author and reader, or between the poetic persona and an addressee, who may be indicated in the text by deictic (pronominal) reference or may simply be identified with the reader. For silence to be meaningful in poetry, as in oral discourse, it must be intentional (i.e., intended to express a meaning).

Among the studies of silence in literature, Kallen (1997: 163), departing from research in the area of dialogue analysis, examines reported speech in the traditional ballad, investigating the uses that silence is put to. He identifies the choice 'to create or break silence' as a meaningful act within the ballad canon. And in her study of Pennac's *Malaussène*, Cant (2004: 175ff) observes that 'absence and silence [...] take on functions and values of their own' and even that 'silence is an active force [...] a weighty presence' becoming as identifiable as words[5]. And there is Loevlie's (2003) lengthy study of literary silences in Pascal, Rousseau and Beckett, which will be cited repeatedly in this chapter.

In the study of silence, data collection presents a considerable problem, as Jaworski points out (1997: 387), so the best we can hope to do is to identify the locus where silence occurs. Due to its elusive nature – it is neither a thing nor an object and therefore escapes empirical observation (Loevlie 2003: 9) – we can only attempt to comprehend its communicative function by examining the surrounding context. In other words, we study silence when it is broken (Jaworski 1997: 392).

## 4 Spatial representations of temporal silence

Kwiatkowska (1997) addresses the question of silence across modalities, in particular the translation of the spatial modality to the temporal level of expression, whereas we shall be looking at temporal expressions of silence translated in the spatial modality of writing. Thus the abstract domain of auditory perception is conceptualized through concrete spatial representations, a parallel to our cognitive predisposition to conceptualize abstract perceptions in concrete metaphorical associations (see Lakoff and Johnson 1980). Consequently, a blank page in the midst of printed text can be seen as a concrete representation of acoustic silence[6].

I seek here to identify the way in which the absence of verbal communication is represented on the page. While considering poetry to be a profoundly oral form of communication in that a large part of its meaning lies in prosodic features (even when read silently, our inner ear is nonetheless aware of the rhythm, meter, rhyme), it also has a strong visual element in the layout on the page, and not only. In this sense poetry can be considered as a multi-modal form of expression in which these two levels (the visual and auditory) are closely conjoined in generating meaning. Nonetheless, for purposes of analysis, I shall attempt to distinguish between these two levels in the following discussion.

### 4.1 Graphics and layout

In the layout of a poem, the background of the page, of whatever colour, including the margins, spaces between the lines and between stanzas, can be seen as an iconic representation of silence. This is more immediately perceptible than other formal features, such as caesurae and prosodic or metrical pauses (see discussion in Patten 1997: 371). Among the devices available to a poet for conveying unspoken meanings are graphic signals and symbols (typographic conventions), that can be interpreted as intentional silence - like the intentionality of the pianist's refusal to strike the keys in Cage's composition. It is this apparent intentionality that endows these devices with pragmatic meaning.

In the collection of poems being discussed, there is great variety in the stanzaic and line structure, varying from long lines and regular stanzas to solid prose paragraphs. But there are also numerous poems composed of short lines and brief stanzas that seem lost in the white space of the page and suggest hesitancy or inarticulateness. At times the stanzas are separated by multiple line spacing that seems to reflect gaps or interruptions in the discourse, and many have mid-line breaks, or incomplete utterances that are suddenly suspended. Still another spatial effect suggestive of silence is that of a long break in the midst of a poem, suggesting a breakdown in communication:

> No God's rain petals
>     Puddle, shallow
> Dreams and drifts
> As airy as lamb's eyes
> A breeze tosses
>     light sentencery
> for God loves me
> and hid me next to you
>
> (Ethan Paquin)

The shortest poem in the book is that of the opening page:

> Don't be mad,
> I'm in bed thinking
> of you at work.
>
> (Joshua Beckman)

placed in the middle of white space, creating the sensation of words spoken in isolation, in the absence of an interlocutor or, to cite Wolf (2005:122), white space as a correlative of silence[7].

> Enamored of silence, the poet's only recourse is to speak.
>
> (Octavio Paz 1973)

## 4.2 Prosodic silence

My view of poetry as a quintessentially oral experience is shared by Patten (1997). The reader is always sensitive to the prosodic features and thus to silences, perceived as interruptions in the flow of discourse. Among the prosodic features which may be interpreted as acoustic silence are elision or irregularities in the meter, sudden halts in the rhythm. The following excerpts from Lauer's collection of poetry will serve as illustration of such prosodic representations of silence:

> You are
> 　　　　walking up the stairs
> 　　　　　　of a clear glass building
> Designed
> for the repetition
> 　　　　of sensation
> When you reach the fourth floor,
> enter
>
> (Caroline Crumpacker)

Or another

> The purpose of the blanket
> is not to cover but to fall.
>
> You were made to
> Recognize, but poorly,
> Your lover.　　A puppet
> Crudely carved in your likeness
> beseeches your help….(etc.).
>
> (Elizabeth Robinson)

Here prosodic irregularities are accompanied by erratic line spacing and the isolation of single words within the lines, as well as by syntactic breaks. In fact, in the first example above, there seems to be no 'rhyme nor reason' (to use a common idiom) in the placement of the lines; the words land somewhat haphazardly on the page, giving the impression of sudden spurts of speech alternated with silence, represented by multiple spacing between the lines, thus creating rhythmic irregularities. The graphic layout functions as an image of interrupted speech, suggesting a sense of communicative inadequacy.

The following poem also presents irregularity in the lines and in the absence of a recognizable meter. Here a series of short simple sentences creates the effect of a halting meter, an apparent difficulty in expression:

> One day love
> is mere
> manipulation.

Someone needs something.

You sing them
Your song.

On another day love
Is purely
a possession.

You want something.

Someone paints
Your picture.   ....etc.

                                            (Graham Foust)

## 4.3 Syntactic silences

I have identified syntactic silences as those represented by ellipsis, minor (or syntactically incomplete) sentences, broken syntax, as in the following examples:

Poem before Dying. Poem
Shortly Before I Head to Dinner. Poem in Which
I Enter Drops of Dew Like a Man with Tiny Keys

                                            (James Shea)

Or the poem entitled 'It Was Raining in Delft', that reflects reticence and speech hesitations with incomplete clauses and the juxtaposition of noun phrases:

A cornerstone. Marble pilings. Curbstones and brick,
I saw rooftops. The sun after a rain showers.
Liz, there are children in clumsy jackets. Cobblestones
And the sun now in a curbside pool.
...
There are colonnades. Yellow wrappers in the square.
...
The green.  All the different windows.


ending with


Lead, zipper, sparrow, lintel, scarf, window, shade.

                                            (Peter Gizzi)

Here the poetic voice seems to have abandoned syntax as the poem
concludes with a list of objects, presumably those visible to the
speaker, with no indication of the logical relationship between them.
While on one hand this foregrounds the speaker's perception of the
way objects strike his vision in the sunlight following the rain (many
of the nouns in the list are, in fact, architectural details of the
buildings), on the other hand it communicates a sense of incoherence
as though the speaker were unable to fully express his perceptions.

Reticence and silence sometimes say more than words.

(Giuseppe Pontiggia)

## 4.4 Lexical silences

One case of lexical silence is the intentional omission of a word,
replaced by a blank line[8]; in the poem below (untitled) the names have
been omitted:

"Dear_____,"

and ends with:

"Yours, _____"

(Prageeta Sharma)

The absence of names might be read as the greatest silence of all, a
suppression of identity (in this case, both that of speaker and
addressee). But if we read the entire text we discover that the poet is
addressing her 'echo' ('we think together, we copy each other'). The
doubt remains, however, as to whether the 'echo' signifies the absence
of an interlocutor or whether it reflects the total identification with the
loved one, in which case this suppression of names may mirror the
loss of individual identity, the speaker's total fusion with the loved
one, making names (and speech) redundant.

Another type of lexical silence or reticence is represented by the
insistent repetition of the same lexeme; this could suggest an
unwillingness to utter any of the possible alternatives, or the inability
to find a word, as sometime happens in extreme emotional states. An
example is "The Sore Throat":

The throat is
sore for a
word. It is
sore with word-

desire, desire
for the word "she"
The word "she" : will
it appear?  Will

she appear?
(Is the word
"she" a she?)
She is a

word I always
without knowing,
had in my mind.
Once, to my shame,

I had no
idea
what to do
with the word

"she"; now it seems
like I don't know
any other
word.. It seems like…

(Aaron Kunin)

Here the monotony of repetition of 'word' and 'she' could be interpreted as an avoidance of other words that might have been used, or an inability to find appropriate alternative expressions. Lovelie (2003:76) sees repetition as that which the text cannot express—a relationship of frustration, of defeat, as the speaker strives to express the unsayable, but it might equally be seen as representing a breakdown in the poet's communicative powers.

## 4.5 Metaphors of silence

A useful distinction made by Loevlie (2003:30 ff.) is that between first-degree and second-degree silence. First-degree silence is that which is defined or described in the text, the explanation of silence, expressed through symbolic language (the signifier). Second-degree (or literary) silence is the signified that can not be expressed due to the inadequacy of language, but occurs as a dynamic arising from the text. This type of silence materializes in the reading of the text, emerging from the reader's construction of meaning[9].

Second-degree silence is the iconic (or non-symbolic) representation of silence, as in the excerpts examined above; this silence is mediated by language, though not immediately expressable in language, it is the unsayable that manifests itself through the experience of reading.

Below are some examples of first-degree silence in these poems, those in which silence is actually named through the use of symbolic language:

> You have the right to remain silent.
>
> (Ross Martin)
>
> But then I discovered arrogance and cruelty and silence
>
> (Anthony McCann)
>
> I love you in a language we've agreed to keep quiet about.
>
> (Lisa Lubasch)
>
> Out to where our sighs
> Were a kind of unanswerable question
>
> (Robert Casper)
>
> Why does the waiting
> scare you & me
> the silence that surrounds
> it, us, this life—
>
> (Kevin Young)

Metaphor, as one of the three realizations of an icon in Peirceian semiotics (along with image and diagram), falls within Loevlie's definition of second-degree silence[10]. The locus of a metaphor in a text may be identified, but the underlying associations can only be disambiguated or brought to the surface through the reader's active construction of meaning.

Metaphors functioning as icons of silence are many; a common primary or conventional metaphor for silence being that of death, but an exhaustive list of all possible creative or novel metaphors can obviously not be compiled as they are, practically speaking, unlimited. It is only the context of occurrence or the frame, together with the reader's active participation, that will permit the interpretation of such metaphorical associations

> I think of you when I am dead, the way rocks
> Think of earthworms and oak roots...
>
> (Reginald Shepherd)

Romance abides
in our ideas of death but upon our passing out of memory the
nonaffiliated eavesdroppers
shall swarm the cafes...

(Meredith Walters)

I've written love notes and I do not know
to whom. [...]   Useless notes,
empty and vaguely
sad.

(Kevin Prufer)

I have built the wall. I am convinced
everyone else has too.

(Chris Stroffolino)

I saw spaces between people,
mirrored pillars released from myself,
none is mine, no key
to the tuneless air

(Lori Shine)

The disambiguation of metaphor is a complex terrain and can not be adequately illustrated by extracting a few lines from longer poems, given that the support of longer stretches of text, or of the entire text, is necessary if we are to fully comprehend the web of cognitive associations. Thus the foregoing examples serve merely as an indication of potential sites of second-degree silence in these poems. The vehicles or source domains in the above metaphors are represented by 'empty notes', 'walls', 'space', all elements which denote or suggest, like the conventional metaphor of death, the impossibility of communication.

## 5 Other possible loci of silence

In addition to silence represented by the absence of speech, there are other, less prototypical silences which involve a holding back or avoidance of certain topics[11]. Jaworski (1992: 99) refers to these as silence which is dependent on speech, a failure to mention something. This type of silence, which is perhaps more appropriately to be referred to as reticence,  may even be located in an excess of irrelevant talk; it may be represented by the avoidance of particular words (taboo or euphemism), or in the monotonous repetition of the same word or thought (see section 3.4 above)[12].

What can we say of the reticence that underlies the impetuous flow of words in 'The Compass Room: East', a rush of words which, at least superficially, says nothing whatsoever of love or romance.

> Each book has a title and all chapters have numbers and each page has a number and each paragraph begins with a clear indentation, a pause or a clearing of a throat, and each sentence ends with a period and each word ends with a sound and each time we meet has the allure of progress away from something medieval such as violent unpaved roads and bawdy unplucked fowl running amok in the uncleared fields at the outer regions of fiefdoms. We congregate in dinners that are literate and referential, to books, to other people, to friends who favor not being there, knowing that we will speak about them lovingly yet with candor, sudden intonations of confession, unfounded opinions, half-truths, to oblige their spirits and to position ourselves nicely... (Thalia Field)

What, it is only natural to ask, is this speaker *not* saying? What topics are being avoided, suppressed, in this seemingly trival flow of speech? Loevlie (2003: 21) cites Steiner who considers an excess of speech to be 'a proliferation of words' that causes an emptiness at the core of language. According to Steiner, silence is sought by the poet to ward off the impoverishment of words. In a composition such as the one above, in order to penetrate the layers of trivia and arrive at possible deeper meanings, we must have recourse to inference[13]. On the surface level the poem says nothing of love, so we are forced to look for implicit subterranean meanings that are not overtly expressed. This is yet another type of absence in the expression of feelings.

## 6 Silence and desire

At the basis of this study lies the assumption that there is an indissoluble link between love, romanticism and desire. As I stated in an earlier study (Munat, 2004), love poetry may also deal with love for children, for home, for parents and friends. But the poetry being discussed here is an expression of romantic love (as stated explicitly in the title of the collection) and we may thus legitimately assume that desire and sexuality are 'natural' components of such love.

Deignan (1997:24) cautions that it is necessary to distinguish between language (and, therefore, silence) used in the *description* of desire, and language used in the *expression* of desire. While the former is 'public' language (of the type that might be encountered in a textbook or editorial comment), the latter is intimate language, the private language adopted between lovers. Poetic discourse falls along the continuum somewhere between these public and private discourses since, on one hand, poetry is an expression of intimate feelings, but it is also presented for public consumption, placed in the public view. We may draw a parallel between this distinction and that made earlier (see section 3.5) between first-degree and second-degree silence: the former is silence *described* in symbolic language, while the latter, as part of the intimate *expression* of desire, emerges from the text, it is perceived in the reading. In the discussion of these poems, it is primarily this intimate or private sphere of expression that we have been examining as the locus of silent communication.

In their study of language and sexuality, Cameron & Kulick (2003:11 ff.) point out that sexual behaviour is culturally determined and is thus semiotically coded. If sexuality shapes and is shaped by what is said, it is also shaped by what is not said. The authors, in fact, speak of 'the structuring significance of the not-said, of silence.' Harvey and Shalom (1997) see sexual desire as an area of human experience that exceeds the capacity of language to represent it. Thus many of the silences that we have evidenced may result from the unexpressability of desire, what Green & Kahn (1991:26ff) call the 'forbidden subtext of the mind', hidden desires that cannot be articulated. Ghita (1994:386) also states that silence 'can express what cannot be verbalized', what is beyond words.

Silence may also be placed in relation to gender, but I have made no attempt in this study to distinguish male from female voices. While the two are fairly evenly balanced in the volume, the examples I have cited in this study represent the work of 12 male poets and seven females. But this hardly constitutes a serious statistical observation, as I have randomly sought examples that serve as illustration of types of silence, and many others have not been considered. This is not intended to be a systematic, line-by-line study of every poem in the volume, which might well be a suggestion for further research. Only then will it be possible to make some serious gender-related observations.

If it is true, as Harvey & Shalom (1997:1) state, that 'human beings need to give form in language to their desires for one another', we have seen that, at times, silence replaces words as the vehicle of communication: this may happen when desire is overwhelming, provoking a strong emotion that impedes speech, or when it is experienced as a negative emotion, e.g., as cause for suffering due to the absence or departure of the loved one. Abandonment, unfulfilled desire are at the roots of negative silence which can be placed in opposition to the positive silence, the unsayable, of shared desire that requires no expression.

## 7 Positive and Negative Values of Silence

Representations of silence, as we have seen, occur at many levels in poetic discourse and their interpretation will depend on the linguistic co-text as well as on the text world which is constructed in any single poem (in this case, the text world replaces the wider social context of actual speech events). While I have selected some of the poems in which silence, or reticence, is felt to be a tangible presence, I have made no attempt at in-depth analysis of the single compositions. My principal aim in this study is to illustrate how silence may pervade a text, weaving through it, alternating with explicit verbal expression. All of these manifestations of silence, however, are not to be read as negative silences. If silence, at times, signifies a lack of rapport, a breakdown in communication, other silences may be seen as positive.

Among the positive interpretations of silence, Tannen (1985:94) suggests that it is evidence of the perfect rapport between intimates who do not need to exchange words or engage in verbal interaction in order to achieve understanding. This type of silence represents an intimate communion that goes beyond words.

Dauenhauer (1980:55) also sees positive aspects of silence residing in an abstinence or unwillingness to employ a determinate expression in a given situation, in the desire to avoid negative connotations.

Whether a silence is interpreted as a negative or positive presence depends on whether the participants (including the reader) experience it as reticence or omission or as comfortable amity. When nothing is said, but some meaning is intended, the interpretation will be determined by the intimacy and shared views between the speakers. The ambiguity of silence derives in part from underlying cultural expectations, but also from our particular perspective with regard to the on-going interaction: for example, whether we view it through the eyes of the speaker or the addressee.

In the final analysis, silence may be a failure of language or it may be evidence that speech is sometimes superfluous between intimates, in moments when verbal communication would be redundant. Thoughts left unspoken because they are mutually shared or words unspoken for fear or opposition are instances of silence with drastically different underlying motivations, and disambiguation must rely on the wider context.

## 8 Conclusions

Having looked only at brief excerpts from a less than a quarter of the poems in this volume, I do not presume to have represented all of the poetry or all of the poets in the collection. There are other poems that overtly express passion and love, and I do not want to make any sweeping statements about the volume in its entirety. I also recognize that these poems reflect the choice of the editors and are not necessarily representative of everything that is being published (or written) by the generation of 'young American poets'[14]. What I *have* attempted to do is examine how silence is represented in poetry and how one reader perceived such silence, drawing provisional conclusions regarding possible functional motivations underlying these silences.

The major difficulty encountered in exploring the functions of silence is the dominant negative view of silence as a void, whereas it must also be considered as a more positive reality: in Adrienne Rich's words, it is a presence. Silence, as we have seen, may carry with it a variety of meanings and cultural connotations, both positive and negative, which vary across different communities of speakers and different speech situations.

By investigating the means available to the poet for constructing meanings which go beyond the printed word - the 'unsayable' - I hope to have opened a door to further research that will lead to deeper understanding of the pragmatics of silence and the study of how texts mean.

## Endnotes

[1]Johannesen (1974:26), in fact, says that 'silence takes on meaning only in a surrounding context of verbal and nonverbal symbols.'

[2]According to Cage (1961:191), 'There is no such thing as silence. Something is always happening that makes a sound.' These natural sounds in the environment, however, are not meaningful in terms of their communicative value.

[3]Paralinguistics is intended here to include meaningfully contrastive vocal or voice-related sounds, distinct from non-vocal gestures, facial expressions, etc. (see definition in Crystal 1971)

[4]By 'communicative' silence I intend a silence which is deliberately produced in what is perceived by both parties as a communicative situation. Jensen (1973: 249) speaks of silence as having a linking function, binding people together, or serving to sever relationships.

[5]Cant (2004: 176) specifically refers to ellipses that represent gaps in speech.

[6]Lippard (1981: 61) speaks of the white page in Mallarmé's poetry. Other poets that have used blank space as symbolic representations of silence include Kamienska (discussed by Jaworski 1993), who wished to express her dissatisfaction with words by including blank pages in one of her poetry collections, thus taking refuge in silence.

[7]Wolf (2005: 122), in discussing a concrete poem entitled *Silence* (*Schweigen*) by Gomringer, speaks of 'white space as a correlative of the silence that surrounds the poem'.

[8]Visual blanks on the printed page are described as 'iconic silences in literary performance' or the 'iconicity of absence' (see Wolf 2005:122).

[9]This is in accord with Kamuf's (2000) view of reading as outlined in her paper 'The End of Reading' that Andrea Macrae at Nottingham has kindly brought to my attention; Kamuf sees reading as a personal and silent act, allowing the reader to reflect and construct his or her own meanings, diametrically opposed to the model of reading as information-extraction.

[10]For a discussion of metaphor as icon and the examination of the web of inter-related metaphorical meanings created across an entire text, see Munat (2005).

[11]One frequently-cited case of such a negative silence (see Loevlie 2003: 17) is the refusal to speak of the Holocaust, due to denial or shame and Jaworski (1993: 110) sees the maintaining of silence over certain issues as a major political tool for control.

[12]Artistic repetition, according to Jaworski (1993: 105) may also bring the audience to 'a higher, meditative-like level of consciousness, reflection, and understanding.'

[13]As Jaworski (1997: 382) points out (quoting Tyler), inference itself is a form of silence in that an inference depends on what is left unsaid.

[14]From a rapid glance at the biographical notes, the age of the poets in the volume stretches from 25 to 44 (at the time of publication), thus born between 1960 and 1979.

## References

Cage, J. 1961. *Silence.* Cambridge, MA: MIT Press.

Cameron, D., and D. Kulick, 2003. *Language and Sexuality.* Cambridge: Cambridge University Press.

Cant, S. 2004 'Come des pages pleines de silence: image, word, absence and silence in Pennac's *Monsieur Malaussène*' in English, A. and Silvester, R. (eds). *Reading Images and Seeing Words.* Amsterdam: Rodopi: 171-79.

Crystal, David. 1971. 'Paralinguistics' in Minnis, N. (ed.). *Linguistics at Large.* London: Gollanez: 162-74.

Dauenhauer, B. P. 1980. *Silence, The Phenomenon and Its Ontological Significance.* Bloomington, IN: Indiana University Press.

Deignan, A. 1997. 'Metaphors of Desire' in Harvey, K. and Shalom, C. (eds). *Language and Desire.* London: Routledge: 21-42.

Ghita, A. 1997. 'Pragmatic Aspects of Silence' in Pietri. E. (ed.). *Dialoganalyse 5,* Arbeitstagung Paris, 1994, Tubingen: Niemeyer.

Green, G. and C. Kahn, (eds). 1991. *Making a Difference: Feminist Literary Criticism.* London: Routledge.

Grice, Paul. 1989. *Studies in the Way of Words.* Cambridge, MA: Harvard University Press.

Harvey, K., and C. Shalom. (eds). 1997. *Language and Desire: Encoding Sex, Romance and Intimacy.* London: Routledge.

Jaworski, Adam. 1997. 'White and white: Metacommunicative and metaphorical silences' in Jaworski (1997): 381-401.

Jaworski, Adam. 1993. *The Power of Silence.* Newbury Pk, CA:Sage

Jaworski, Adam (ed.). 1997. *Silence: Interdisciplinary Perspectives.* Berlin: Mouton de Gruyter

Jensen, J. V. 1973. 'Communicative Functions of Silence' in *Etc.: A Review of General Semantics* 30(3): 249-57.

Johannesen, R. 1974. 'The Functions of Silence: A Plea for Communication Research' in *Western Speech* 38: 25-35.

Kamuf, P. 2000. 'The End of Reading', Paper presented at the Book/Ends conference, University at Albany (October 2000).

Kurzon, D. 1998. *Discourse of Silence.* Amsterdam: John Benjamins.

Lakoff, G. and Mark Johnson. 1980. *Metaphors we Live By.* Chicago, IL: University of Chicago Press.

Lauer, B. F., and A. Kelley. (eds). 2004. *Isn't It Romantic: 100 Love Poems by Younger American Poets.* Amherst, MA: Verse Press.

Leech, Geoffrey. 1983. *Principles of Pragmatics.* London: Longman.

Lipka, L. 2003 'Observational Linguistics and Semiotics' in Hladky, J. (ed.). *Language and Function: To the memory of Jan Firbas.* Amsterdam: John Benjamins: 211-22.

Lippard, L. R. 1981. 'The Silent Art' in *Art in America* 55: 58-63.

Loevlie, E. 2003. *Literary Silences in Pascal, Rousseau and Beckett.* Oxford: Oxford University Press.

Malandro, L. A., L. L. Barker, and D. A. Barker. 1989. *Nonverbal Communication*. New York: Mc Graw Hill.

Manning, E. 1997. 'Kissing and Cuddling: The Reciprocity of Romantic and Sexual Activity' in Harvey, K. and C. Shalom. (eds). *Language and Desire*. London: Routledge: 43-59.

Munat, Judith. 2004. 'The Caged Bird: The Expression of Sexuality in Twentieth-century Women's Poetry", Paper presented at the Poetry and Sexuality Conference, University of Stirling, Stirling, UK (July 1, 2004).

Munat, Judith. 2005. 'Iconic Functions of Phraseological Units and Metaphor' in Maeder, C., Fischer, O. and Herlofsky, W. (eds.). *Outside-In – Inside-Out*. Amsterdam: John Benjamins: 389-410.

Patten, K. 1997. 'Teaching 'Discovering Silence'' in Jaworski (1997) 369-78.

Paz, O. 1973. *Alternating Current*. New York: Viking.

Sacks, Harvey., Schegloff, Emanuel. A. and Jefferson, Gail. 1974. 'A Simplest Systematics for the Organization of Turn-taking in Conversation' in *Language* 50: 696-735.

Saville-Troike, Muriel. 1985. 'The Place of Silence in an Integrated Theory of Communication' in Tannen, D. and Muriel Saville-Troike. (1985): 3-18.

Sebeok, T. 2001. 'Nonverbal Communication' in Cobley, P. (ed.) *The Routledge Companion to Semiotics and Linguistics*. London: Routledge: 14-27.

Sobkowiak. W. 1997. "Silence and Markedness Theory" in Jaworski (1997): 39-61.

Tannen, D. 1985. 'Silence: Anything But' in Tannen, D. and Muriel Saville-Troike, (1985): 93-111.

Tannen, D. and Muriel Saville-Troike. (eds). 1985. *Perspectives on Silence*. Norwood, NJ: Ablex.

Vainiomäki, T. 2004. 'Silence as a Cultural Sign' *Semiotica* 150-1/4: 347-61.

Verschueren, Jef. 1985. 'What People Say They Do with Words: Prolegomena to an Empirical-Conceptual Approach to Linguistic Action.' Norwood, NJ: Ablex.

Wolf, W. 2005. 'Non-supplemented Blanks in Works of Literature as Forms of Iconicity of Absence' in Maeder, C., O. Fischer, and J.

Herlofsky (eds). *Outside-In – Inside-Out*. Amsterdam: John Benjamins: 113-32.

# Top or Flop: Characteristics of Bestsellers

## Sabine Albers

### Abstract

Ignored by literary science, loathed by critics and loved by readers – bestselling novels seem to evoke powerful emotions. But what exactly is it that makes a bestseller a bestseller? Which elements of social cognition lead to a novel becoming one? Does there perhaps exist a schema that a bestseller activates – and that therefore causes people to buy the book? If this is the case it should be possible to discover the prototypical attributes which constitute that schema. This project investigates the hypothesis that identification plays a key role in that respect; that there is a connection between the potential for identification a novel possesses and its selling numbers. The more a reader can identify with the protagonist of a novel the better it sells. The aim was to develop a method to measure the potential of identification and then compare it to the selling numbers of each novel. This paper discusses the methods of measurement developed and how they were applied in an experiment to test the above-mentioned hypothesis.

Keywords: Identification, Identification measurement, Bestseller, Novel, Selling numbers, Schema activation

## 1 Introduction

What do a thriller like *The Da Vinci Code* by Dan Brown and a historical novel like *Outlander* by Diana Gabaldon have in common? Both sold more than one million copies and dominated the world's bestseller rankings for months; both provoked a flood of secondary literature commenting on the background of the story plus several forums on the internet discussing them and both are considered to be low culture by literary critics. But if the quality of those novels is so low, why do they achieve sales numbers a Nobel prize winner like Günter Grass could only dream about? Perhaps the average reader is simply stupid, unable to recognize real quality and going for a cheap thrill instead. But even if this is the case, the question remains 'What constitutes that thrill?' Do bestselling novels have anything in common besides their selling numbers? What makes a bestseller a bestseller?

Consider the following:

(i) A boy who cares for his siblings because his father is an unemployed alcoholic witnesses his mother's death during childbirth.
(ii) A famous doctor travels to the capital to start a new job at court. He is welcomed very warmly.

The first example contains in condensed form the content of the opening scene of the novel *The Physician* by Noah Gordon, which was one of the best selling books of the last decade. In most people it evokes interest, pity and caring, even some kind of identification with the protagonist. On the other hand, boredom and indifference may be typical reactions to the second example, which presents the content of the opening scene of a novel called *Imhotep* by Pierre Montlaur. It did not see a third edition. These – so far completely unscientific – impressions pose the central question of this project: Is there a scientific way to determine whether there is a connection between the potential of identification a novel possesses and its selling numbers? Does there, perhaps, exist a schema that a bestseller activates – and that makes people want to buy the book?

To test this hypothesis the aim of this study was to develop a method to measure the potential for identification a novel possesses, and then to compare it to its selling numbers. The methods developed to fulfil this aim, and how they were applied in an experiment, will be demonstrated in the following.

## 2 Definition of Identification

To measure identification one has to know what it is. Therefore the first thing needed is a definition of identification. Research on the process of identification concentrates roughly on three areas: (1) trigger mechanisms (2) course (3) consequences. Work on trigger mechanisms has been carried out by researchers like Zillman & Cantor (1976), Many & Wiseman (1992), Tan (1994) and Andringa et al. (1997). For example, Zillman & Cantor found that empathy is not in all cases responsible for reactions to a protagonist's emotions. Tan showed that an important prerequisite for emotional identification with a protagonist, is an understanding of what a specific event means to that character. Andringa et al. discovered that the narrator's perspective in film has no special influence on the process of identification.

The course of the identification process was studied by Keith Oatley (1994). His theory of identification in literary fiction was inspired by Aristotle's concept of mimesis and will be elaborated later on. Another angle takes Zillman (1994) who discards the idea of identification altogether and introduces the concept of empathy instead.

The consequences of the process of identification were studied by Hakemulder (2000) in his 'Moral Laboratory'. His results confirmed that narratives influence people's ideas and emotions much more strongly than essay-like texts dealing with facts. Identification with a literary character can therefore strengthen a person's understanding of people in foreign cultures. Moreover, the process of identification during reading changes the reader's image of self. Questions like 'What would I do in this situation?' lead to heightened self reflexion, that causes – if not changes in behavioural patterns – at least a clearer picture of oneself.

So, there are a number of theories of identification to be found in literary studies and psychology. The present study uses the one by Keith Oatley (1994). Oatley proposes four different features that must be fulfilled for identification with a situation or a character to occur. First and most essentially the reader has to adopt the goals of the protagonist. Second, there must be speech acts addressed to the reader. For example, in the phrase 'He was as nice to me as a fox is to a chicken' the first part gives information about the story, the rest invites the reader to think about how a fox might behave towards a chicken. Third, the text must give the reader a chance to produce a constructive integration of the disparate elements. This means that readers create an image of the characters and their world from hints and clues in the text, which in itself consists merely of ink marks on a sheet of paper. The last feature necessary for identification is the creation of an imaginary world, which is achieved by giving details, e.g. telling the reader the colours of a bird, a dress etc.

Even a cursory glance at these four features shows that the last three of them are present in almost every published novel. They seem in fact to be a prerequisite to getting published. A writer who can't create a convincing imaginary world will probably not get published. That leaves the first – and according to Oatley most important – feature: Getting the reader to adopt a protagonist's goals. But how does one do that? The research literature does not offer any answers to that question. Therefore one has to look elsewhere, namely to the literature on creative writing. There one finds practical instructions on how a writer can get a reader to identify with a protagonist's goals, namely by creating: (1) an emotionally touching opening scene. (2) a protagonist with a so-called 'noble goal', a goal, the reader can support (Frey 1993:134).

These two elements can therefore be considered attributes of a schema that, when activated, leads to identification. Taking all this into account, the present study will test the following hypothesis: *The more emotionally touching the opening scene of a novel and the more 'noble' the goal of the protagonist is the higher the potential for identification a novel possesses.*

## 3 Identification Measurement

To measure how 'touching' an opening scene or how 'noble' a protagonist's goal is, the use of a questionnaire seems appropriate. Since one cannot very well expect informants to read hundreds of pages of text, one needs a shortened version of the content and goal of the book one wants to investigate. Such shortened versions were produced by using the qualitative content analysis developed by Mayring in 1993. Reduction, explication and structuring generated a condensed version of the content of an opening scene and of the goal of a novel's protagonist. For example, for the novel *The Physician* one gets the lines 'A boy who cares for his siblings because his father is an unemployed alcoholic witnesses his mother's death during childbirth' as content and 'To prevent his siblings from starving and to give them and himself the best possible future' as the goal of the protagonist.

Using these descriptions the novels to be investigated were rated by means of a questionnaire, which consisted of two questions: 'How much does this situation touch you emotionally?' and 'How much would you support this goal?' For the first question the condensed versions of the opening scenes were used. Each opening scene was rated separately on Likert scales ranging from 'extremely' to 'none' corresponding to -2 to +2. The result was a value for the emotionality f the opening scene of each novel, which is one of the two characteristics needed to identify with the protagonist of a novel according to Frey (1993: 134) (cf. paragraph 1).

The second question produced a value for the 'nobility' of the protagonist's goal – the second important prerequisite for identification with the protagonist of a novel – by having informants rate the condensed versions of the protagonist's goals, again by the use of the Likert scales mentioned before. The original questionnaire can be found in appendix I.

The mean responses given by informants for 'emotionality' and 'goal' were then compared to the selling numbers of each novel. But before that one had to decide which books to use.

## 4 Definition of Bestseller and Worstseller

This study defined 'Bestseller' (Top) as a novel which has been N° 1 on the bestseller ranking of at least two countries. On the other hand, a 'Worstseller' (Flop) is a novel which wasn't listed on any bestseller ranking and got less than three editions. The bestseller group consisted of the novels *The Physician* by Noah Gordon, *Pillars of the Earth* by Ken Follet, *Ramses* by Christian Jacq and *Child of the Morning* by Pauline Gedge. The Flops were represented by *Imhotep* by Pierre Montlaure, *Inanna* by Thomas Mielke, *L'Affaire Toutankhamon* by Christian Jacq and *The Hippopotamus Marsh* by Pauline Gedge.

In order to control for thematic matter, the corpus contains historical novels only. Moreover, two of the authors – Christian Jacq and Pauline Gedge – have each written one of the Tops and one of the Flops. This was done for a purpose. Historical novels were chosen because they are timeless, so one didn't have to worry about a bestseller becoming a bestseller because the author hit on some hot topic. And by using Tops and Flops by the same writer the effect advertising might have had on the number of copies sold was excluded. In the case of Jacq and Gedge their bestselling novel was a surprise bestseller that got very little advertising, whereas the Flop got huge amounts of advertising.

## 5 Experiment

The eight novels were rated by a questionnaire. 25 informants - 15 females, 10 males, aged between 30 and 58, all avid readers with no professional literary background – whose mother tongue is German, answered the questionnaire described in paragraph 2. The results are as follows:

(extremely = +2, very = +1, a little = 0, hardly = -1, none = -2)

| | Novel | Mean for Emotionality | Mean for Goal | Standard Deviation |
|---|---|---|---|---|
| **Top** | The Physician | +1.4 | +1.5 | 0.59/0.68 |
| | Pillars of the Earth | +1.3 | +0.9 | 0.57/0.81 |
| | Ramses | +0.4 | +0.4 | 0.99/1.27 |
| | Child of the Morning | +0.3 | +0.3 | 1.25/1.21 |
| **Flop** | Imhotep | -1.0 | -1.3 | 0.91/0.80 |
| | Hippopotamus Marsh | -1.1 | -1.2 | 0.62/1.18 |
| | Inanna | -0.2 | +0.3 | 0.87/0.98 |
| | L'Affaire Toutankhamon | +0.1 | -0.8 | 1.11/0.97 |

The results were checked for significance via inferential statistics, in this case by an ANOVA, producing the following results:

Question 1 (Emotionality)     $p = 3.38^{-28} \Rightarrow p < .001$

Question 2 (Goal)     $p = 7.23^{-26} \Rightarrow p < .001$.

In both cases the result has $p < 0.001$, meaning that the differences between mean responses to the novels are highly significant. In other words, the differences observed here are not tied to the sample of informants, but may be generalized for the larger population. So we can be relatively certain that the numbers allocated to the novels in the table above are reliable. That allowed the values for emotionality and goal to be used as coordinates which gave each novel an exact place in a coordinate system. On the vertical axis are the means for 'Emotionality', the horizontal axis contains the means for 'Goal'. The ellipses mark the range of variances.

Visualized like this, one can see that the bestsellers concentrate all in the upper right quadrant. They received positive marks on 'Emotionality' as well as on 'Goal'. It is interesting that two of the flops (*Inanna* and *L'Affaire Toutankhamon*) were both rated positively on one of the two criteria. But apparently neither an emotionally touching opening scene nor a 'noble' goal are by themselves sufficient to allow identification with a character. A combination of both seems to be necessary.

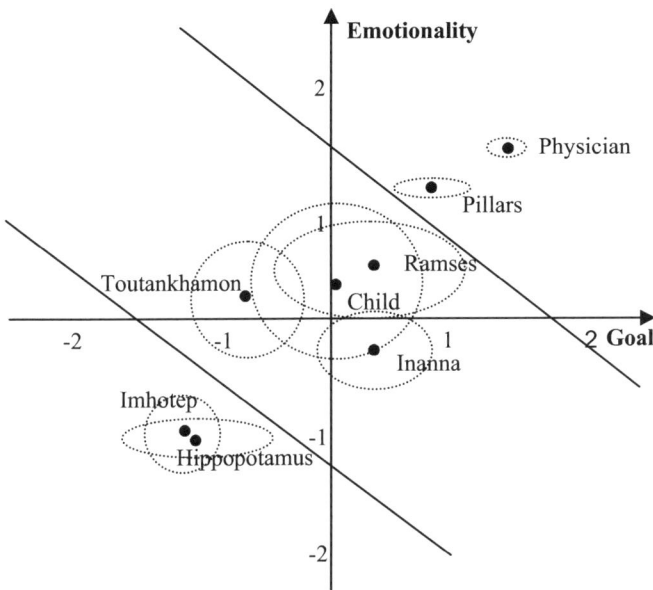

Another interesting result emerges when we study the standard deviations in some more detail. (The standard deviation is a measure for dispersion; it indicates how much unanimity – or lack of unanimity – there was in the informants responses: a high standard deviation means most answers are far away from the mean, indicating lack of unanimity.) For *The Physician*, *Pillars of the Earth*, *Imhotep* and *The Hippopotamus Marsh* standard deviations are low, whereas around the center they were mostly over 1.0, which is quite a lot, considering that the scale ranges from -2 to +2. So while one can be reasonably sure about the placement of those books at the margins of the coordinate system there is an area around the centre where giving reliable statements is difficult.

## 6 Conclusions and Outlook

(1) A method of identification measurement was developed that seems to be of use.

(2) A schema seems to exist that causes people to identify themselves with another person. It is strong enough to work even in fictional situations with fictional characters.

(3) Bestsellers activate that schema. There seems to be a connection between identification and bestsellers.

(4) An emotionally touching opening scene and a 'noble' goal of the protagonist are elements of the schema. Bestsellers seem to be characterized by a combination of both.

At least two questions arise from these results. Although the test subjects had no problems answering the questionnaire, it would be interesting to know what exactly it is that makes a scene touching or a goal worthy of support. If it is indeed true that emotionality and a protagonist with a noble goal produce a gripping story, additional information could be valuable to writers as well as publishing companies – and of course to literary scholars.

Connected to that is the question of whether identification needs only those two elements, emotionality and a noble goal. Considering the complexity of the topic it seems highly probable that there are more such elements that play a role in identification. Finding out what further elements of social cognition constitute the schema, whose activation apparently makes people buy a novel, is one direction in which future research should head.

## References

Follet, K. 1990. *Die Säulen der Erde*. Bergisch-Gladbach.

Frey, J. 1993. *Wie man einen verdammt guten Roman schreibt*. Köln

Gedge, P. 1981. *Die Herrin vom Nil*. Hamburg.

Gedge, P. 1998. *Der fremde Pharao*. Hamburg.

Hakemulder, J. 2000. *The Moral Laboratory. Experiments Examining the Effects of Reading Literature on Social Perception and Moral Self-Concept*. Utrecht.

Gordon, N. 1996. *Der Medicus*. München.

Jaqc, C. 1993. *Im Bann des Pharao*. München.

Jaqc, C. 1997. *Ramses. Der Sohn des Lichts*. Hamburg.

Many, J., and D. Wiseman. 1992. 'The Effect of Teaching Approach on Third-Grade Students' Response to Literature' in *Journal of Reading Behaviour* 24(3): 265-87.

Mayring, P. 1993. *Qualitative Inhaltsanalyse*. Weinheim.

Mielke, T. 1992. *Inanna*. Hamburg.

Montlaur, P. 1990. *Imhotep*. Hamburg.

Oatley, K. 1994. A taxonomy of the emotions of literary response and a theory of identification in fictional narrative' in *Poetics* 23: 53-74.

Tan, E. 1994. 'Film induced affect as a witness emotion' in *Poetics* 23: 7-32.

Zillman, D., and J. Cantor. 1977. 'Affective Responses to the Emotions of a Protagonist' in *Journal of Experimental Social Psychology* 13: 155-65.

## Appendix I (Original Questionnaire)

**1. Im Folgenden finden Sie acht Situationsbeschreibungen. Wie stark sind Sie emotional berührt?**

Ein offenbar unschuldiger Mann wird öffentlich hingerichtet. Seine Geliebte, die mit seinem Kind schwanger ist, muss zusehen.

Nicht    Kaum    Etwas    Sehr    Extrem

Ein berühmter Arzt reist in die Residenzstadt, um eine Stelle im Palast anzutreten. Er wird freundlich empfangen und mit allen Ehren aufgenommen.

Nicht    Kaum    Etwas    Sehr    Extrem

Eine Frau trifft sich mit ihrem Geliebten. Sie unterhalten sich über ihre beruflichen Zukunftsaussichten, die bei beiden hervorragend sind. Er teilt ihr mit, dass er beruflich eine Weile fort muss, woraufhin sie ihm den Laufpass gibt.

Nicht    Kaum    Etwas    Sehr    Extrem

Ein Junge, der sich um seine Geschwister kümmert, weil der Vater ein arbeitsloser Säufer ist, wird Zeuge, wie seine Mutter bei der Geburt eines Kindes stirbt.

Nicht    Kaum    Etwas    Sehr    Extrem

Ein Fürst zieht sich auf das Dach seines Palastes zurück, um seine Gedanken zu ordnen. Während er die Aussicht genießt, kommt ihm der Gedanke, dass er als König besser für das Land sorgen könnte.
Nicht    Kaum    Etwas    Sehr    Extrem


Ein Junge wird von seinem königlichen Vater gezwungen, gegen einen wilden Stier zu kämpfen.
Nicht    Kaum    Etwas    Sehr    Extrem


Eine Königin in der Nacht vor ihrem gewaltsamen Tod. Sie weiß, dass die Mörder kommen, hat Angst und fühlt sich einsam. Sie beschließt, dem Tod erhobenen Kopfes entgegen zu treten.
Nicht    Kaum    Etwas    Sehr    Extrem


Ein steinreicher, gelangweilter Lord auf Weltreise. Als sein Schiffskoch krank wird, operiert er ihm souverän den Blinddarm heraus, obwohl er so etwas noch nie getan hat.
Nicht    Kaum    Etwas    Sehr    Extrem


**2. Welche der folgenden Ziele würden Sie wie stark unterstützen?**
Die eigenen Geschwister vor dem Verhungern bewahren und ihnen eine Zukunft geben.
Nicht    Kaum    Etwas    Sehr    Extrem


Die Wünsche des Königs perfekt erfüllen.
Nicht    Kaum    Etwas    Sehr    Extrem


Seinem Volk ein guter König sein.
Nicht    Kaum    Etwas    Sehr    Extrem


Das eigene Leben mit allen Mitteln – auch auf Kosten anderer – retten.
Nicht    Kaum    Etwas    Sehr    Extrem

Ein wundervolles Gebäude bauen, um den Menschen einen Ort der Ruhe zu schaffen und gleichzeitig der eigenen Familie ein gutes Leben zu bieten.
Nicht   Kaum   Etwas   Sehr   Extrem


Einen fremden König stürzen, um selber König zu werden.
Nicht   Kaum   Etwas   Sehr   Extrem


Für das Volk eine gute Königin sein.
Nicht   Kaum   Etwas   Sehr   Extrem


Einen gewaltigen Schatz finden, um Ruhm zu erwerben.
Nicht   Kaum   Etwas   Sehr   Extrem


## Appendix II (Statistics)

| Novel | Emotionality | | | Goal | | |
|---|---|---|---|---|---|---|
| | Mean | Standard Deviation | Variance | Mean | Variance | Standard Deviation |
| Phy. | +1.4 | 0.59 | 0.36 | +1.5 | 0.47 | 0.68 |
| Pill. | +1.3 | 0.57 | 0.33 | +0.9 | 0.66 | 0.81 |
| Ram. | +0.4 | 0.99 | 1.00 | +0.4 | 1.61 | 1.27 |
| Child. | +0.3 | 1.25 | 1.58 | +0.1 | 1.46 | 1.21 |
| Imhot. | -1.0 | 0.91 | 0.84 | -1.3 | 0.64 | 0.80 |
| Inann. | -1.1 | 0.87 | 0.87 | +0.3 | 0.96 | 0.98 |
| L'Aff. Tout. | -0.2 | 1.11 | 1.25 | -0.8 | 0.93 | 0.97 |
| Hippo. Marsh | +0.1 | 0.62 | 0.58 | -1.2 | 1.39 | 1.18 |

# 'A Tale of Two Cities': Lexical Bundles as Indicators of Linguistic Choices and Socio-cultural Traces[1]

## Tania Shepherd, Sonia Zyngier and Vander Viana

## Abstract

This study focuses on the frequency and nature of the lexical choices in two corpora made up of 195 creative writing texts produced by Brazilian public school pupils, living in two markedly different places: a violent inner-city area, and a semi-rural setting near a small market town. To this end, the research adopts a frequency and distribution approach for the extraction and comparison of sequences of words in each of the corpora.

Initially, the discussion focuses on the methodological difficulties encountered when dealing with texts produced by language users with orthographic and punctuation problems. Subsequently, the concept of 'lexical bundles' is applied to the data in question, i.e., the most frequent sequences of words are extracted, and classified according to Biber, Conrad & Cortes' (2004) framework. Finally, results are presented which highlight the large number of lexical patterns in the texts from the semi-rural group, in contrast with a large degree of lexical variability in the texts written by the inner-city pupils. It is suggested that these differences may be attributed to the sociological profile of each individual group.

Key words: lexical bundles; children's writing; discourse analysis; linguistic choices; socio-cultural traces

## 1 Introduction

> It was the best of times, it was the worst of times, it was the age of wisdom, it was the age of foolishness, it was the epoch of belief, it was the epoch of incredulity, it was the season of Light, it was the season of Darkness, it was the spring of hope, it was the winter of despair, we had everything before us, wc had nothing before us, we were all going direct to Heaven, we were all going direct the other way – in short, the period was so far like the present period, that some of its noisiest authorities insisted on its being received, for good or for evil, in the superlative degree of comparison only.

Thus opens Charles Dickens' *A Tale of Two Cities*, referring to the year 1775. Why does it ring, in certain ways, so familiar? More than ever, the world is divided into the haves and have-nots. For instance, at the time this paper was being written (March 14, 2005) the cover of

*Time Magazine* read: 'How to end poverty: eight million people die each year because they are too poor to stay alive'. On page 31, the caption under photos of homeless children sleeping in a train station in Jakarta read: 'In a world of plenty, 1 billion people are so poor, their lives are in danger.'

Can linguistics help transform this reality? One possible contribution would be an attempt to understand how changes in life quality may be expressed in language. To this end, researchers of the REDES[2] group investigated how violence impregnates the daily lives of people in Rio de Janeiro using newspaper articles as data (Zyngier, Fialho & Menezes 2004). Their argument was that language reflected everyday violence in subtle ways. The focus was on language *not intended* to deal with violence centrally or even tangentially to determine whether indices of violence appeared in conceptual metaphors of daily newspaper sections which reported on sports, politics and economy. They found that 40% of the metaphors in the sections studied mirrored violence. A subsequent research decision was made to extend the investigation to include compositions written by Brazilian school children. The two groups selected attended an inner-city and a rural public sector school: two quite distinct settings. The inner-city school was located in a slum area between two highways in the city of Rio de Janeiro. The rural school was in a market town of 15,000 inhabitants, in the State of Minas Gerais. The two groups of children (totalling 195) were asked to write a composition of about 20 lines on any one free-choice topic.

The compositions were collected, labelled in terms of place, sex and age of the child and subsequently typed to be probed by the software program WordSmith Tools (Scott 1999). A list of the most frequent words was extracted from each of the corpora, and grouped in terms of semantic fields. The categories reflected in these semantic fields enabled the researchers to establish which topics each one of the two groups of children considered worthy of mention, despite the fact that the writing task had been on free-choice topics. Among the topics formed by the various semantic fields was family life, the children's relation with their immediate context, and the manner they dealt with many different issues, including that of violence (Jordão et al. 2005).

Using the same corpus made up of free-choice topic compositions, the present study increases the span of word range in an effort to investigate n-grams, that is, recurrent strings of a pre-established number of words extracted electronically from the corpus. In this way, we hope to probe beyond the actual description of what the children talk about and focus on *how* they write about these topics.

This chapter assumes that texts result from patterned language and that words in any text do not occur at random, as posited by Sinclair (1991: 109-110). The chapter also assumes that, at its simplest form, 'the idiom principle' is seen to be operational when two words are chosen together. However, the tendency for words to co-occur may involve more than two words. The research incorporates the belief that much of our everyday language consists of building blocks which are derived from the idiom principle, which, in turn, occasionally switch to unexpected units from the open-choice principle. In addition, following Teliya *et al.* (1998: 55), it is believed here that multiword units illustrate the correlation between language and culture, or rather, that an analysis of cultural data may be obtained from lexical units, either of words or of word-combinations. It is hypothesized that the inner-city and rural school children investigated will produce their own formulaic patterns repeatedly, and that the language they use may be embedding visions which echo the scene Dickens described over 100 years ago.

As the paper focuses on both multiwords and children's writing, the section below explores, of necessity, existing investigations of unbroken sequence of words which repeat themselves in any one corpus. The section also focuses, albeit briefly, on research into children's writing by means of Corpus Linguistics methods.

## 2 Research into Children's Writing and Corpus Linguistics

The present study investigates lexical associations in children's writing from the perspective of Corpus Linguistics. It focuses on sequences made up of a specific number of words, which tend to occur with a certain frequency within specific digital corpora, namely, lexical bundles (Biber, Conrad & Cortes 2004).

Children's writing has been the target of investigation from the perspective of Corpus Linguistics in several previous studies. Berber Sardinha & Shimazumi (1996), for example, carried out a study whose aim was to characterize the writing of young learners in the UK as represented in a sample of the APU (Assessment of Performance Unit) archive, by contrasting it with a reference corpus made up of adult writing. Despite the fact that the APU archive consisted of compositions written by two age group students (11 and 15 year olds), a decision was made to digitize only those compositions written by the older group. It was presumed that this latter group would exhibit a higher level of complexity and thus allow for a fairer comparison with the reference corpus, which was made of Guardian newspaper texts. The study focused on the extraction and comparison of isolated words because these were seen to reflect what the texts are about. It also focused on lexical phrases because these are believed to indicate how texts have been organized, as well as the level of affect and informality texts may display. In terms of lexical phrases, the analysis concentrated on bigrams (or pairs of words) and trigrams (or triplets). However, no reason was given for these choices, nor did the writers provide any specific way of dealing with the sequences found, apart from listing them. The comparison of the two corpora was made by means of keyword analysis, which illuminated important aspects of the learners' writing. It was found, for instance, that the learners' writing was permeated with personal stance (*I* being the main keyword to articulate stance) and that it tended to provide explanations (*because* was also a major keyword). The main key themes were seen to be related to the immediate environment of the adolescents (family, school, and children). The key themes of either The Guardian or the APU corpora were not necessarily transparent in the individual frequency wordlist, but only became apparent through keyword extraction.

Sampson (2003) has also looked at children's use of oral and written language with the help of Corpus Linguistics. His corpus was British, was compiled in the 1960s and, unlike that of the present study, consisted of open-ended compositions written by children from suburban and semi-rural schools. The investigation used parsing as a methodology and concentrated on type and complexity of phrases and clauses. The final objective was to compare child writing to adult speech and published writing. Although Sampson (2003) coined a category which he termed 'wordiness' to describe the pervasive verbosity in children's writing, he was not interested in studying the lexical items in the data per se. Rather, his research aimed at identifying the presence or absence of the syntactic categories he had developed for his parser.

Although the study of children's writing has not yielded a significant number of works which focus on lexis from the perspective of Corpus Linguistics, the literature encompassing investigation of relatively fixed lexical groupings, as well as of pre-fabricated expressions in English language, is extensive (cf. Stubbs 2001). However, the terminology used to refer to these multiword sequences displays very little consensus. In terms of research focusing on English as a first language, they include 'formulae', 'routines', 'phrasal lexemes' (Moon 1998), 'collocational frameworks' (Renouf & Sinclair 1991) and 'n-grams' (Sinclair 2004). In terms of English as a second or foreign language, there are 'prefabricated patterns' (Granger 1998b) and 'phrasicon' (De Cock et al. 1998) among others. In addition to the lack of consensus in terms of nomenclature, there is also little agreement about which sequences of multiwords ought to be analysed, or the number of tokens each sequence ought to include (two words or more) and how to analyse the sequences (form, function, or both).

Despite the apparent discrepancy in analytical targets, the studies cited above display one point in common, namely the underlying belief that some of the lexical choices made by any language user, in either writing or speech, may encompass two or more words behaving as a single lexical item with a specific meaning. Despite the fact that the authors cited above do not openly acknowledge it, their studies may be said to have incorporated the 'idiom principle' concept (Sinclair 1991: 109). According to Sinclair, language users operate under two principles 'idiom principle' and 'the principle of open choice'. The 'idiom principle' has to do with choosing blocks of items heard or read previously. As an alternative to the idiom principle, users resort to the 'principle of open choice', or rather, they choose words which are less predictable in order to complete their messages.

As Hunston (2002: 143) argues, it is impossible to prove or refute the existence of either principle in the making of messages. However, by scanning an electronic corpus, it may be demonstrated that multiword sequences do exist, and that, in certain types of corpora, certain sequences are more likely to appear than in others, i.e., that they may be corpus specific.

A further evidence of these multiword sequences and their corpus specificity has been provided by two recent studies (Biber 2004 and Biber, Conrad & Cortes 2004). These authors used data made up of four sub-corpora as a basis for the extraction of four-word sequences, which they call "lexical bundles"[3]. Four distinct sub-corpora for each one of the textual registers, seen to underpin academic life, were compiled. The oral end of the academic genre spectrum was exemplified by conversation (at the office, in study groups and service encounters, and at the library, for example) as well as the expository class. Data from academic textbooks and academic prose were selected to represent the written end of the spectrum. The data base stemmed from a variety of academic fields and from various geographic areas of the United States. Both choices were strategic ploys to ensure that the resulting four sub-corpora did not contain region or topic biases. The number of multiword items was randomly established at four. Contractions such as *don't* were counted as one item. Four-word sequences were extracted from each sub-corpus based on the criteria of frequency and distribution. The extracted sequences were then analysed both in terms of distribution, function and structure. In terms of quantity of lexical bundles per sub-corpus, it was found that the oral registers, especially those from lessons, contain almost twice as many bundles as those of the written genres (Biber, Conrad & Cortes 2004: 379).

These studies also developed a classification system for the lexical bundles extracted, which covered both the structure and function of the various bundles. In terms of structure, three major groups were found in the data, namely Type 1, containing bundles with fragments of verbal phrases; Type 2 which consists of dependent clauses fragments or the dependent clause itself and finally Type 3 which were either (fragments of) noun phrases or prepositional phrases (Biber, Conrad & Cortes 2004: 382). Finally, and most importantly, the extracted bundles were seen to convey notably distinct functions, namely stance, reference or discursive organization, each of which displayed further sub-divisions, mirroring the range, the size and the nature of the data studied. Below is a description of each individual function, as well as an attempt to plot function and sub-function diagrammatically.

The so-called stance bundle was seen to form two categories, namely epistemic bundles and attitudinal / modality bundles, the latter group entailing further subdivisions into desire, obligation, intention and ability. Stance was also seen to be expressed in either personal or impersonal terms, as shown in Table 1, below.

| | | Epistemic | Personal |
|---|---|---|---|
| | | | Impersonal |
| Stance expressions | Attitudinal / Modality | Desire | Personal |
| | | Obligation / Directive | Personal |
| | | | Impersonal |
| | | Intention / Prediction | Personal |
| | | | Impersonal |
| | | Ability | Personal |
| | | | Impersonal |

**Table 1** Biber et al.'s stance category and subdivisions

Reference bundles were the second of the functional categories. Their function was to generally identify either an entity as a whole or a specific attribute of an entity, seen as particularly important. Reference was found to be either clear, focused identification or imprecise. Two further groupings of referential bundles were found in the data, namely those which included some specification of attributes of an entity and those which presented reference to time / place / text.

| | | Identification / Focus |
|---|---|---|
| | | Imprecision |
| Referential expressions | Specification of attributes | Quantity specification |
| | | Tangible framing attributes |
| | | Intangible framing attributes |
| | Time / Place / Text reference | Place reference |
| | | Time reference |
| | | Text deixis |
| | | Multi-functional reference |

**Table 2** Biber et al.'s reference categories and subdivisions

The third functional category, i.e., discourse bundles, was that which was seen to organize the discourse, by either introducing / focusing on a topic or elaborating / clarifying it.

| Discourse organizers | Topic introduction / Focus |
|---|---|
| | Topic elaboration / Clarification |

**Table 3** Biber et al.'s discourse category and subdivisions

Finally, there is a fourth group of bundles, which were typical of, and circumscribed to, the conversation sub-corpus under investigation. These were labelled special conversational functions, and included markers of politeness as well as expressions signalling questions and reporting.

By juxtaposing the results of various categories of bundles which pertained to the four registers, it was relatively straightforward to highlight which type and function of bundle was more pervasive in which register. The absence of a particular type of bundle in a register, however, did not mean that the function was absent in the register altogether. Rather, this indicated that the function may have been realized by means which were too varied and too individualized to form bundles.

The section below explains how the framework developed by Biber, Conrad & Cortes (2004) was used to extract and classify the lexical bundles found in the data of the present research.

## 3 Methodology

As stated in Section 1, the present study focuses on a corpus of children's writing, itself divided into two different sub-corpora: one consisting of compositions written by children from a rural area (henceforth corpus A) and another written by inner-city children (henceforth corpus B) in Brazil. At the time the data was collected, neither group of children, whose ages ranged from 12 to 14, had full command of the spelling or punctuation of Brazilian Portuguese, a fact which presented methodological difficulties in so far as the two corpora had to be digitized.

Once the compositions were collected and labelled so as to show indications of place, as well as sex and age of the child, they were made into computer text files to be probed by WordSmith Tools (Scott 1999). A total number of tokens was calculated for each group, the inner-city children having produced 12,205 and the Minas children, 14,662 tokens. In terms of corpus size, both corpora were small (viz. Berber Sardinha 2004: 26). As far possible, the compositions were typed *verbatim*, i.e., errors in syntax were preserved, but misspellings were all corrected so as to enable the software to pick up lexical sequences. The children's restricted knowledge of punctuation rules also created problems both during the digitization and the analytical phase. The decision to preserve the children's original punctuation meant that the software picked up 'false' sequences of words, as in 'bicycle I like' from 'I like to ride a bicycle I like'. As a result, such sequences, created by lack of punctuation, had to be eliminated from the final bundle list.

The first choice for lexical bundle length was three words. However, it soon became clear that this threshold was too low, as the number of sections of overlapping bundles was considerably higher, as for example in the bundle formed by the name of one the cities, '*Rio de Janeiro*', itself a three-word bundle, which overlapped with the fragment of a prepositional group '*no Rio de*' [in Rio de]. In order to reduce these numerous overlapping cases, the researchers decided to work with a four-word unit as proposed by Biber, Conrad & Cortes (2004).

Biber, Conrad & Cortes (2004) used two criteria to decide on what really constituted a bundle. The first was frequency: a bundle had to appear a minimum number of times in every million of words. The second criterion was dispersion: a group of words had to appear in a minimum number of different text files making up the corpus. As the present corpus was small, the frequency criterion per se had to be discarded. However, dispersion was retained, in an effort to eliminate any idiosyncratic and repetitive use of the same sequence by any child writer. Thus it was established that for four-word sequences to be considered bundles they had to appear in at least three different compositions per corpus. Following the extraction of lexical bundles, an attempt was made to classify the same by using Biber, Conrad & Cortes' (2004) structural and functional categories.

In terms of Type 1 bundles the two sub-corpora presented only examples of lexical bundles either incorporating or beginning with a verb phrase without the personal pronoun (which in Portuguese is dispensable), as in '*nasci no dia #*' [(I) was born on the] or lexical bundles beginning with a subject pronoun followed by a verb phrase, as in '*Eu estudei na escola*' [I studied at school].

Type 2 bundles included no more than the sub-category with dependent clauses fragments as in '*que eu mais gosto*' [which I like more]. No Type 2 bundles starting with subordinators were found in the corpus.

In contrast, the last of the categories, Type 3 bundles which consist of noun or prepositional phrases, was quite frequent. This category appeared mainly in the format of a noun phrase and prepositional phrase fragments, as in '*o nome do meu*' [the name of my], and as a prepositional phrase with embedded modifiers as in '*na casa da Geiza*' [in Geiza's house].

As far as Biber, Conrad & Cortes' (2004) functional categories are concerned, three were consistently encountered with various degrees of frequency and distribution, depending upon the corpus examined. These are stance, representing attitudes or assessments; discourse organizers, concerned with the relationships between prior and coming discourse; and referential, establishing direct reference to concrete or abstract entities.

In terms of stance, there were only examples of the desire subtype as in '*Eu gosto muito de*' [I like very much], with or without the personal pronoun. There were no instances of either obligation, intention or ability. The only instance of a discourse organizing bundle in both sub-corpora served the function of topic introduction and was exemplified by '*era uma vez uma*' [once upon a time there was a/an], signalling the beginning of a narrative. However, the compositions were rich in referential bundles of the identification / focus type as well as time / place / text reference. The examples of identification / focus may be seen in '*minha matéria preferida é*' [my preferred subject is], '*que eu mais gosto*' [which I like most], '*o brasil é um*' [Brazil is a/an]. There were also numerous examples of time / place bundles as in '*nasci no dia #*' [(I) was born on the #], '*hoje em dia a*' [nowadays the] or in '*moro na cidade de*' [(I) live in the city of] and '*na casa da Geiza*' [in Geiza's house]. There were no examples of the other two referential sub-categories of imprecision or specification. However, two extra functional labels had to be created to account for bundles such as '*com os meus colegas*' [with my colleagues] and '*com a minha tia*' [with my aunt] as well as expressions like '*do meu pai é*' [of my father is], which indicated, respectively 'circumstance' and 'possession'.

An unexpected problem was caused by multiword place names, as for example the often mentioned name of a school ('*Escola Municipal Augusta Maria de Souza*'). It appeared as a bundle in a multitude of ways, sometimes abbreviated as '*E. M. Augusta Maria*', '*E. Municipal Augusta Maria*', or even '*Augusta Maria de Souza*'. In an effort to solve the problem of this identification reference, i.e., in order to prevent the various bundles referring to the same entity from being counted as separate bundles, it was decided to consider as a bundle only the core of the noun group '*Augusta Maria de Souza*'.

## 4 Analysis

Once the frequency lists of lexical bundles in each of the two corpora were compiled, analysed and plotted into graphics, two very different pictures emerged, as shown below[4].

**Graph 1** Distribution of bundles in each of the corpora

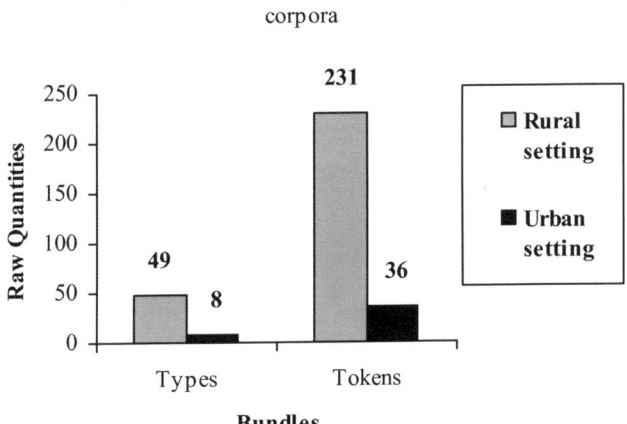

Graph 1 demonstrates, in absolute terms, how the two corpora differ in terms not only of the total number of individual bundles (231 in corpus A and 36 in corpus B), but also in terms of how many different bundles are used within the total number of bundles. Despite this numerical difference, both the inner-city and the rural group have a similar ratio of type/token in terms of bundles, 22.22% and 21.21% respectively.

In terms of structure, the picture which emerges is also one of differences. The three structural groups posited by Biber, Conrad & Cortes (2004), namely Type 1, which incorporates verb phrase fragments, Type 2 whose onset are dependent clause fragments, and Type 3 which contains noun / prepositional phrase fragments are all found in both corpora, albeit with markedly different distributions. In corpus A, almost one in every two lexical bundles consists of verb phrase fragments. In addition, 29.01% are clause fragments. The presence of these two organizational groups means that the compositions written by the rural children resort to repeated clausal patterns.

**Graph 2** Distribution of structural groups in corpus A

In corpus B, the distribution of structural groups is quite different, with type 3 bundles being the most common.

**Graph 3** Distribution of structural groups in corpus B

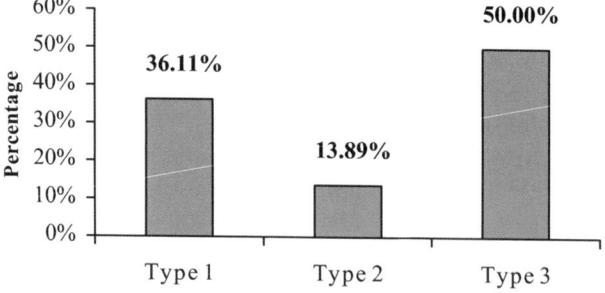

If one considers that types 1 and 2 convey the idea of the various processes (in the Hallidayan sense) which are being used in the text, it becomes apparent that the rural school children prefer to depict their world in terms of patterned verbs and clauses. In contrast, the adoption of bundles on the part of inner-city children is equally distributed between broached topics and the processes which are used to depict them.

In terms of function, corpus A is seen to prioritize reference to the detriment of stance and discourse organizers.

**Graph 4** Functional classification of lexical bundles in corpus A

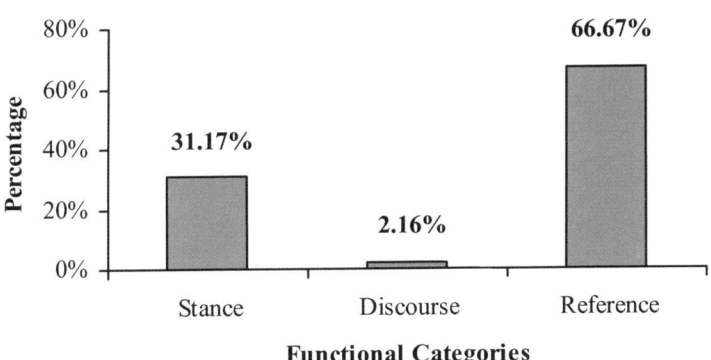

In corpus B, however, there are no more than two types of functional bundles: discourse and reference, the latter being present in almost 89% of the corpus.

**Graph 5** Functional classification of lexical bundles in
corpus B

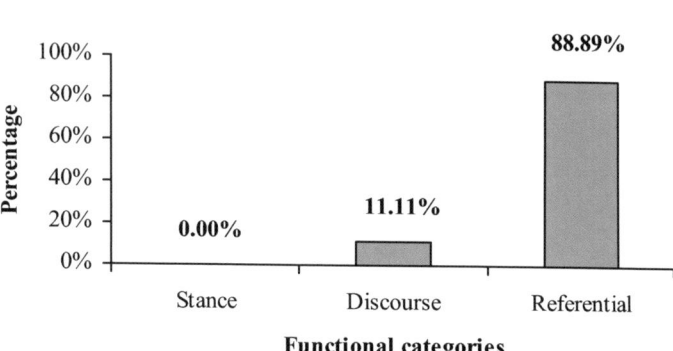

31.17% of the bundles in corpus A represent instances of stance. The main difference between the two corpora is the absence of stance bundles in corpus B. This absence in the inner-city compositions should not be interpreted as a total lack of stance. Rather, it reflects the fact that the children have preferred to express stance in individual ways. There is also another point worth noting, namely that there is one type of stance being verbalized in corpus A: that of desire. In other words, the group of children from the rural area use similar chunks of lexis to express stance, and the only type of stance they express is that of desire as in *'eu gosto de jogar'* [I like to play]. There is no thread of communal expression of either obligation, intention or ability.

Corpus A and corpus B are similar in terms of discourse bundles. Although corpus B has 11.11% of discourse bundles and corpus A only 2.16%, a closer examination of the nature of the bundles reveals that there is in fact no more than one discourse bundle in both corpora, namely *'era uma vez um'* [once upon a time there was a/an], a frozen item used to introduce story telling.

Undoubtedly, reference bundles are the most frequent categories in both corpora totalling 66.67% in corpus A and 88.89% in corpus B. The reference bundles in corpus A include identification / focus

(66.88%), place (16.23%), possession (7.79%), circumstance (5.20%) and time (3.90%), with substantial emphasis on identification.

Corpus B, which encompasses the inner-city compositions, contains no more than four types of reference bundles: identification / focus (43.75%), place (31.25%), time (15.63%) and circumstance (9.37%). An equally important weight is given by the children to identifying things and to establishing a place reference.

The overall distribution of reference bundles in both corpora suggests that the rural school children actually prefer to identify the various topics they discuss in terms of patterns, four times as much as they focus on place. The figure in the inner-city children's compositions is only 1.4 to 1. Reference to place is patterned as often as reference to topic.

In summary, corpus A displays a tendency to use more patterned bundles, and may be described as relying more heavily on the principle of idiom. Among the bundles used, there is a preference for identification by means of clauses and verb phrases. In addition, these children from the rural setting are not reluctant to show what they like/dislike. In contrast, corpus B does not pattern likes/dislikes, but gives equal weight to things and places, suggesting lack of a strong sense of place.

## 5 Conclusion

A bundle is an artificial construct that computers can extract from corpora and not a linguistically coherent notion, though it may point to the existence of linguistically important combinations and functions. This paper analysed texts written by children from two radically distinct environments. The choice of these settings aimed at verifying how, when given the chance, children depict the world in which they live through language, more specifically, through repeated strings or individualized lexical choices. The differences found both in the number and the types of bundles produced by the children in each group may be interpreted in two ways. The first interpretation would be related to the interface between the choice of bundles and the activity of processing. According to Wray (2002: 74), the use of ready-made multi-word strings could be explained in terms of reducing text processing effort, which, in turn, is seen as easing the task of communication. As Kuiper (1996: 3 cited in Wray 2002) also argues 'when a speaker uses a formula, he or she needs only to retrieve from the dictionary instead of building it up from its constituent parts'. The second possible interpretation is that the same speech community may possess, even when given the chance to express themselves freely, similar sets of repeated strings (as occurred with the children from the rural setting). This finding seems to support Wray's point that (2002: 74), 'an individual's inventory of holistically stored sequences is heavily influenced by the current patterns of usage in the speech community'. However, following Halliday (1985 et seq.), this relationship is dialectic, or rather, the speech community's repertoire of patterns may also feed into the community members' inventory. Individuals select for their usage the sequences which they have stored as chunks.

How do these two possible interpretations explain the differences in the writing of the two groups of children selected as participants for the present research? It may be suggested that ease of processing is the least plausible of explanations for the presence or absence of lexical bundles. The children from the rural setting may be posited as representing the world in terms of repeated strings or patterns. These, in turn, help them express a strong sense of stance and focus on similar topics of mutual interest, mirroring sequences which they may have heard, and incorporated as their own, from their community. They seem to feel in tune with their setting, reflecting the way their group sees and feels the world. In contrast, the inner-city children mirror either a lack of desire to sound 'like the others', or what is more intriguing, a desire to sound like a speech community which neither manifests stance or whose language is fragmented and may represent the isolation of the individual in the slum setting.

This paper began with Dickens' claim that, for good or for evil, the society at that time could only be defined in terms of sharp contrast and divisions. The preliminary analysis of the data described above suggests that Dickens' vision of a divided society still holds true for the two groups of children from present-day Brazilian society investigated.

## Endnotes

[1] We dedicate this paper to John Sinclair (*in memoriam*), who introduced us to the notion of lexical bundles. We would also like to thank Suzana Jordão for collecting the data and David Shepherd for his valuable comments on the text.

[2]REDES stands for 'Research and Development in Empirical Studies'. See http://lwww.letras.ufrj.br/redes

[3]'Lexical bundles', 'clusters' (Scott 1999) and 'n-grams' are different labels for the same linguistic evidence, namely, that lexical items tend to occur in chunks.

[4]Following Biber et al.'s (2004) methodology, this study did not resort to extracting and analysing keywords. It must be stressed that the extraction of keywords would considerably decrease the number of analytical units, resulting in less robust and less illuminating evidence. In addition, as Berber Sardinha (personal communication, 2007) has pointed out, if the focus is not genre or register analysis, 'then the case for keywords is not very strong. In fact, since the aim here is to investigate stance and opinion, you would not want to discard any data, which is what keyword does.'

## References

Berber Sardinha, Tony. 2004. *Lingüística de Corpus*. São Paulo: Manole.

Berber Sardinha, Tony, and Marilisa Shimazumi. 1996. 'Approaching the Assessment of Performance Unit Archive of Schoolchildren's Writing From the Point of View of Corpus Linguistics'. Paper presented at the 2nd Teaching and Language Corpora (TALC) conference (Aug. 9-12, 1996). Online at: http://www2.lael.pucsp.br/~tony/1998apu_talc.pdf (consulted 14.03.2005).

Biber, Douglas, Susan Conrad and Viviana Cortes. 2004. 'If You Look at…: Lexical Bundles in University Teaching and Textbooks' in *Applied Linguistics* 25(3): 371-405.

Biber, Douglas. 2004. 'Lexical Bundles in Academic Speech and Writing' in Lewandowska-Tomaszczyk (2004): 165-78.

Biber, Douglas, et al. 1999. *Longman Grammar of Spoken and Written English.* London: Longman.

De Cock, Sylvie, et al. 1998. 'An Automated Approach to the Phrasicon of EFL Learners' in Granger (1998c): 67-79.

Cowie, Anthony Paul (ed.). 1998. *Phraseology: Theory, Analysis and Applications*. Oxford: Oxford University Press.

Granger, Sylviane. 1998a. 'The Computer Learner Corpus: A Versatile New Source of Data for SLA Research' in Granger (1998c): 3-18.

Granger, Sylviane. 1998b. 'Prefabricated Patterns in Advanced EFL Writing: Collocations and Formulae' in Cowie (1998): 145-160.

Granger, Sylviane (ed.). 1998c. *Learner English on Computer.* London: Longman.

Halliday, Michael. 1985. *An Introduction to Functional Grammar.* London: Edward Arnold.

Hunston, Susan. 2002. *Corpora in Applied Linguistics.* Cambridge: Cambridge University Press.

Jordão, Suzana, et al. 2005. 'Violência no Imaginário da Criança. in Zyngier, Sonia, Vander Viana and Fabiana Fausto (eds). *Venturas & Denventuras: Coletânea dos Trabalhos do V ECEL.* Rio de Janeiro: Editora da Faculdade de Letras da UFRJ: 172-88.

Lewandowska-Tomaszczyk, Barbara (ed.). 2004. *Practical Applications in Language and Computers.* Frankfurt: Peter Lang.

McEnery, Tony, and Andrew Wilson. 1996. *Corpus Linguistics.* Edinburgh: Edinburgh University Press.

Moon, Rosamund. 1998. 'Frequencies and Forms of Phrasal Lexemes in English' in Cowie (1998): 79-100.

Renouf, Antoinette, and John Sinclair. 1991. 'Collocational Frameworks in English' in Aijmer, Karin, and Bengt Altenberg (eds). *English Corpus Linguistics.* London: Longman: 128-43.

Sampson, Geoffrey. 2003. 'The Structure of Children's Writing: Moving From Spoken to Adult Written Norms' in Granger, Sylviane, and Stephanie Petch-Tyson (eds). *Extending the Scope of Corpus-Based Research.* Amsterdam: Rodopi: 177-93.

Scott, Mike. 1999. *WordSmith Tools.* Oxford: Oxford University Press.

Sinclair, John. 1991. *Corpus, Concordance, Collocation.* Oxford: Oxford University Press.

Sinclair, John. 2004. 'Preface' in Lewandowska-Tomaszczyk (2004): 7-11.

Stubbs, Michael. 2001. *Words and Phrases.* Oxford: Blackwell.

Teliya, Veronika, et al. 1998. 'Phraseology as a Language of Culture: Its Role in the Representation of a Collective Mentality' in Cowie (1998): 55-75.

Wray, Alison. 2002. *Formulaic Language and the Lexicon.* Cambridge: Cambridge University Press.

Zyngier, Sonia, and Tania Shepherd. 2003. 'What is Literature Really?: A Corpus-driven Study of Students' Texts' in *Style* 37(1): 15-26.

Zyngier, Sonia, and Tania Shepherd. 2002. 'Hidden Concepts of Literature in a Pedagogical Setting: A Corpus-based Approach' in Csábi, Szilvia, and Judit Zerkowitz (ed.). *Textual Secrets: The Message of the Medium*. Budapest: Eötvös Loránd University: 220-235.

Zyngier, Sonia, Olivia Fialho and Danielle Menezes. 2004. 'Invisible Wars: violence in daily papers' Paper presented at the 9th conference of the International Society for the Empirical Study of Literature and Media (IGEL) (Aug. 3-7, 2004). Online at: http://www.arts.ualberta.ca/igel/igel2004/Proceedings/Zyngier.pdf (consulted 14.03.2005).

# Naughty or Nice? Empirical Studies of Literature in the Classroom[1]

## Sonia Zyngier

## Abstract

Since its beginning in the late 19th century, literary education has lacked theories that systematize teaching and methodologies that validate practice. Consequently, much work in the area has relied on argument rather than on real data. What is needed in literary education are ways in which scholars develop descriptions of methods that will help them arrive at evidence-based conclusions. However, this is easier said than done. Trying to cope with the problems of dealing with hypotheses, statistics and numbers in general, Humanities students tend to see the experience as both frightening and fascinating. In order to find out the difficulties students of literature encounter when learning to do empirical research, a questionnaire was distributed to 14 participants from different countries who attended the IGEL[2] Summer Institute in 2004. Participants were asked how they became interested in empirical studies, what their literary biography was, what they considered the main problems of empirical work to be, and how they thought it related to literary education. Respondents agreed that there is a need to teach students how to deal with real, palpable knowledge by means of well-structured and objective data. This article presents the main problems participants raised in empirical work.

Keywords: literary education; empirical studies; stylistics; methodology; research teaching.

## 1 Introduction

The area of literary education has been diverse, multiple and complex. Methodologies and approaches to the teaching of literature have been published (cf. Clark & Zyngier, 2003 and the special issue of *CAUCE*, 'Reading Beyond Text: Processes and Skills', edited by John McRae, 2001) and yet no major theoretical paradigm has been developed. This paper looks at the present situation and offers a new perspective which joins teaching and research. It also brings out the pitfalls this perspective may produce. Ultimately, it is expected that the experience of literature in the classroom becomes a much more stimulating and conscious activity by all the participants involved.

Mostly a product of the last quarter of the 19th century, academic literary studies flourished under the assumption that 'literature could or should be taught – rather than simply enjoyed or absorbed as part of the normal upbringing of gentlefolk' (Graff 1987: 1-2). Since its institutionalization, it has given jobs to many practitioners who in some regions have described what they do but who have reflected little on theories which underpin their practice. In Brazil, for instance, there are many pre-service centres for language teachers but practically none for future teachers of literature. The assumption is that teaching literature comes naturally and what the future professional needs is just knowledge of the content to be taught. In addition, educational theories are not always put to the test. As an example, there have been a variety of studies in favour of critical pedagogy but very little empirical research on their effects. Questions relating to how far they actually promote autonomy and/or pleasure, or what actually results from this autonomy are still to be developed.

Added to the lack of evidence-based theories of teaching literature, most literary scholars have not assimilated work developed by stylisticians. They do not, for example, describe models in which to carry out their investigations, and which would help them verify the validity of their statements. Many literary scholars remain on the level of producing subjective grand narratives on textual interpretation. As a consequence, work in the area has relied more on argument than on palpable data. Compared to literary scholars, stylisticians, who use linguistic and cognitive evidence to understand literary discourse, are still too few (cf. Brumfit and Carter, 1986; Short, 1989; Verdonk, 2002; Stockwell, 2002; Short & Archer, 2003; Simpson, 2004; Watson & Zyngier, 2006).

An explanation for this situation can be offered: from its early days, literary theory has adhered to the hermeneutic tradition from biblical times. In his famous REDE lecture first published in 1959, Snow (1998) argued that in fact we have lived in two completely different working cultures: the world of scientists and that of the humanists. Snow sustained that a third culture should be developed, where this duality would collapse. His lecture found a harsh critic in F.R. Leavis, as reviewed by Kimball (1994). But perhaps the time is ripe now, as empirical studies find a way into the Humanities (van Peer et al., 2007).

Still, in many places today, the student of literature is introduced to canonical works he or she has to read and respond to, without any further information or training on how to do it. For linguistics and language studies, the development of a third culture became possible when the interpretative model proposed by the founder of 20th century anthropology (Malinowski 1923; and ethnographers like Erikson 1992, among others) were adopted for the study of language acquisition. At that time, there was some consideration of whether this model could illuminate literary studies. However, one of the problems of ethnographic approaches is precisely their reliance on subjective interpretations and their exploratory rather than explanatory nature.

Aware of this situation, I have come to realize that the teaching of literature will never evolve if it remains linked to the hermeneutic tradition of textual interpretation. Knowledge of literary tradition and major works is just not enough. Literary scholars also need to observe how students respond to texts, how they react emotionally, how they process the information, how effective the educational models they adopt are. For this to occur, empirical work needs to be developed on a larger scale. It is time literary scholars moved away from the interpretative and hermeneutic paradigms which have shaped their work, and tried to back their arguments with real data and more verifiable methods. What is needed in literary education is research that describes the objectives, methods, results, and arrives at evidence-based conclusions. It is true that research on how literary texts are processed and received has been growing (Andringa 1990; Miall 1996; van Peer & Chatman 2001; Fialho 2005; Watson & Zyngier 2006; among others) but bridges still have to be established between research and practice.

## 2 Problems

In this context, five universities joined in a collaborative project to develop new methods of teaching and doing empirical research cross-culturally. These universities were located in Alberta, Kiev, Munich, Rio de Janeiro, and Utrecht. Here was a concrete move towards a change. Lecturers were now senior researchers supervising projects both undergraduate and postgraduate students developed cross-culturally. As the Research and Development in Empirical Studies (REDES) Project began in September 2002, participants soon realized that doing empirical research was easier said than done. Trying to cope with the problems of dealing with hypotheses, statistics and numbers in general, Humanities students have been finding the experience both frightening and fascinating. In addition, many problems emerged as participants tried to collaborate through the Internet (Mendes 2005).

## 3 Materials and methods

To find out what goes on when students try to do empirical work, I developed a questionnaire and asked 14 participants who attended the IGEL[2] Summer Institute at the University of Alberta in August 2004 to indicate what their motivation for studying literature had been, what they considered the main problems in the teaching of literature, what kind of texts they liked to read and why, and how they saw the development of empirical research in literary studies. I also wanted to know how these participants became interested in empirical studies and what they thought the main problems in doing empirical work were. I also tried to find out what fascinated them, and whether they thought empirical research could bring any benefit to their students. The Summer Institute provided a perfect setting, since the participants came from different countries (Australia, Brazil, Canada, Denmark, Finland, Germany, Hungary, Spain, and Sweden) and from two main areas: humanities and social sciences.

The questionnaire contained open and closed questions. Some parts of the closed questions were adapted from a questionnaire used elsewhere to verify reading habits (cf. Fialho and Zyngier 2003). The statements on empirical work participants were asked to grade were collected from studies published earlier in three proceedings from previous IGEL conferences.

The open questions were categorized and yielded quite interesting results. I will present here the problems they raised in the teaching of literature and carrying out empirical research within the area of literary studies. The answers to this question centred on *what, how,* and *who,* that is, on the object of study, the methodology and the people involved (students and teachers).

## 4 Results

As the respondents were nine postgraduate students and five well-seasoned researchers, their age and experience varied. They represented nine different countries, as specified above, and confirmed that teaching literature in their contexts tended to concentrate on master interpretations of canonical works. They also complained that literature was being taught as pieces of information, as data sources or as something idiosyncratic and that, instead of the experience of literature, teachers looked for authorial intention. They also pointed out that new methods had to be thought of because, to them, teaching had become an anachronism.

In terms of teaching methodology, participants complained that no real relation was made between literature, life and culture. They also criticized the fact that the process of reading was not addressed in the classroom. Some participants with a background in psychology also pointed out that they had not been introduced formally to a technique in psychological interpretation.

As for the teaching contexts, respondents stated that classes were mostly carried out as lectures where students were not heard or could not exchange views freely. Students seemed to lack focus and concentration. When meetings took place in seminar formats, students often felt they were under time constraint and constant stress. Participants said that all in all there was little time to read all the material needed for the courses. They tended to agree that students lacked reading skills and knowledge of the areas of philosophy, history, and linguistics.

The respondents also criticized literature teachers for not really motivating students. They said that most literature teachers they had met at University tended to offer subjective and personal responses and impose their tastes, personal interests and ideology. They pointed out that literature professionals limited themselves to certain approaches and that they lacked methodology, theory and knowledge of linguistics.

Faced with this picture, participants suggested that students need hands-on experience, under good, constant and effective supervision. They also need a common set of readings that will help them build knowledge of literary tradition and of a scientific and philosophical background. Statistics and how to use SPSS, concordances, and new technology in general were also suggested as necessary. In terms of methodology, students would benefit from networking and collaborating in team projects and cooperating with experts in different fields. Participants believed that in the appropriate setting, students would develop focus, honesty, and perseverance. They also pointed out that institutional support was needed in terms of more courses, summer schools, a change of curriculum, and more institutional financing.

Once these problems had been raised, participants seemed to think that empirical studies could be a solution to many of them. Their first contacts with empirical studies had been at the University (nine), at conferences or from colleagues (three), doing research in reception theory (two).

Respondents complained, however, that if and when empirical work is introduced to students it comes at a very late point in their academic life and that undergraduate level of contact with researchers is minimal. However, when asked about the source of their interest in it, their responses varied. This lack of consensus is a matter to be investigated. It may indicate either the richness of the area or a source of many problems.

Four major reasons for engaging with empirical studies were identified in their responses. They were mostly on the epistemological, methodological, and contextual levels. Even if some of them are not inherent to empirical studies, I report here what participants brought up. To them, empirical studies:

a. expand scientific knowledge, structure reality and look for relevant answers.
b. provide a framework that enables them to deal with creativity and science and to look at data objectively.
c. help the understanding of reception, reading and language use. Besides, they can be an effective way to show students how to carry out research.
d. deal with individual and cultural differences. If students work collaboratively and interculturally, they will have to learn how to cope with researchers in other areas, in other countries, and from other perspectives.

In short, participants claimed that one just cannot do without empirical studies. To them, empirical work has methodological rigor. It is accountable, reliable, generalizable, impartial, objective and systematic. It provides real evidence, assessment of causality, validation of theories, links between theory and practice, a common language, and goes against subjectivism. In addition, empirical studies may use statistics to help researchers understand the world. By being applicable to many disciplines, empirical studies can be innovative in interdisciplinary and intercultural contexts. This is where the potential for future work in literary education can be found. Together with knowledge about literature and its tradition, more emphasis should be given to how literature is experienced by real readers, how it affects them, how students react to literary devices, how contemporary readers respond to earlier texts, etc. Pedagogical stylistics (Zyngier, 2006) has already begun to work on sensitizing students to the making of texts. Now we need students to learn how to become researchers who can investigate how literature is experienced.

It must be pointed out that these respondents had already carried out empirical work, albeit on different levels. They were either in the very early stages or had already had full experience of how to do research. What this study emphasizes is that literature cannot be taught in lecture halls as it has been for so many decades now. It will only survive as a discipline if the students′ epistemological curiosity is raised so that they find out by themselves the what, the how, and the why of literature.

Having pointed out the problems in the teaching of literature and how participants thought empirical studies could be of great help, I list below the main problems they see in the area. When asked to rate a series of statements on a scale of one to five (1 being the lowest and 5 the highest), respondents rated more highly the following problems:

a.  You never know whether respondents are being honest (Average 3.1).

b.  Participants do not answer questionnaires properly (Average 3.0).

c.  I find it difficult to measure aspects of the cultural world (Average 2.9).

d.  After collecting the data, I realise the questionnaire or experiment had many problems (Average 2.8).

e.  Statistics is a completely different area and I can't understand it (Average 2.7).

f.  I think that empirical methods fail in offering absolute certainties (Average 2.7).

g.  Objectivity and impartiality are unattainable ideals (Average 2.7).

h.  I do not know where my data will lead me to (Average 2.5).

i.  Interpreting data can never be objective anyway (Average 2.5).

This list will be discussed together with other issues raised in the next section.

## 5 Discussion

The problems listed above can actually be clustered into four main categories:

a. *Methodological problems* (one, two, and four), which can be somehow remedied. If researchers make respondents feel they are responsible for the results of the research, there will be a better chance that they will collaborate in an honest way. They also need to be informed on the level of their participation. In addition to that, pilot studies are highly recommended before the real investigation is launched in order to evaluate and improve the instrument or the design.

b. *Uncertainty* (one, five, and eight), which is indeed a problem to students when not accounted for. To a certain degree, uncertainty can indeed be one of the strengths of research. If the researcher knows beforehand where the data will lead to, what the results will be, where the answer lies, there is no reason for carrying out the investigation. Students should be aware that the focus is on the navigation itself, on the process of investigation, and not on the shore, on the point of arrival, which is always provisional anyway.

c. *Estrangement* (five), a feeling researchers experience when going into areas with which they are not familiar. This aspect also raises a lot of concern with students, who feel they are never prepared enough. Instead of a problem, it would be much better to consider it a challenge. Learning how to make connections between areas and disciplines can be very productive and senior researchers should show this to the students.

d. *Imprecision* (three, six and nine): Here, again, participants raised the problem of objectivity/subjectivity. However, empirical studies are not imprecise if we understand them as a means to look at patterns that are repeated and/or can be controlled. In literary studies, empirical work loses much of its imprecision if directed to the description and the explanation of patterns of textual production or reception.

The results of the questionnaire showed that to participants, empirical work provides *real*, *causal*, *reliable*, and *transmissible data*. To them, the world is real and there is a need to arrive at palpable knowledge by means of solid, well-structured and objective data analysis. They indicated a rejection of subjectivism and of empty rhetoric so as to arrive at a foundation of knowledge.

## 6 Conclusion

In summary, are empirical studies of literature naughty or nice? Can they be of help to the student of literature or are they a means of confounding them even further? Much is still to be done before we can answer these questions. This paper is only of an exploratory nature. It has collected responses from 9 beginning and 5 experienced researchers from a wide variety of contexts so as to trigger a process of self-reflection. I am well aware that many of the issues raised here need to be fleshed out. More data is also needed before any generalization can be drawn. What this initial probe has found out is that there are definitely difficulties in the teaching of literature, in the carrying out of empirical research, and in how to find a balance between both. Further work can concentrate on the problems participants pointed out, categorizing them under four different dimensions: cognitive (level of knowledge, etc.), emotional (excitement, motivation, etc.), social (relevance of the work), personal growth (what they learn as students and researchers). Based on data collected from professionals and novices in literary studies and empirical research, this paper has suggested that empirical work can help promote the experience of literature in the educational setting once many of its impediments are removed. As Bortolussi & Dixon (2003: 22) have shown, 'it is possible to put some of the sound and rigorous empirical methods of the sciences at the service of literary studies'. This paper is in line with those who have tried to go against what Short (2001: 341) has called 'the fashion-statement approach to the description and understanding of literary works', which I have translated as the grand narratives rather than evidence-based statements. Short (2001: 342) warns us that

> ...within literary criticism this kind of careful, painstaking work is done less and less. Instead, the bandwagon rolls on to the next new fashion, and

conveniently literature is never subjected to the forms of careful academic
inquiry we see in other subjects. Instead, its status as a mystical, magical,
unknowable beautiful beast is protected.

This 'beautiful beast' has been finding its ways into the classroom for
decades. I believe that if we are to stimulate students to become
independent researchers who contribute with relevant knowledge,
there is no other viable alternative than to promote an environment
where students can carry out empirical studies of literature.

## Endnotes

[1] I would like to thank Don Kuiken, who organized the IGEL Summer Institute and
helped me with the questionnaires, the 14 participants who answered them, and
Milena Mendes and Olívia Fialho, who helped me with the analysis. My thanks also
go to Willie van Peer for reading an earlier version of this manuscript and for
providing illuminating criticism.

[2] Internationale Gesellschaft für Empirische Literaturwissenschaft.

## References

Andringa, Els. 1990. 'Verbal Data on Literary Understanding: a
    Proposal for Protocol Analysis on Two Levels' in *Poetics* 19: 231-
    57.

Bortolussi, Marisa, and Peter Dixon. 2003. *Psychonarratology:
    Foundations for the Empirical Study of Literary Response.*
    Cambridge: Cambridge University Press.

Brumfit, Christopher, and Ronald A. Carter. 1986. *Literature and
    Language Teaching.* Oxford: Oxford University Press

Clark, Urszula, and Sonia Zyngier. 2003'Towards a pedagogical
    stylistics'. *Language and Literature12* (4): 339-351.

Erickson, Frederick. 1992. 'Ethnographic Microanalysis of
    Interaction' in LeCompte, Margaret D., Judith Preissle Goetz and
    Wendy L. Millroy (eds). *The Handbook of Qualitative Research in
    Education.* New York: Academic Press: 201-25.

Fialho, Olivia. 2005. '*Pelos Caminhos da Literatura: Estudo
    Empírico Sobre Refamiliarização e Afeto*'. Unpublished M.A.
    dissertation, Universidade Federal do Rio de Janeiro.

Fialho, Olivia, and Sonia Zyngier. 2003. 'Reading Preferences: a
    Comparative Study' in Zyngier, Sonia, Milena Pereira Mendes and
    Patrícia Pinheiro (eds). *Pontes & Transgressões: Estudos
    Empíricos de Processos Culturais.* Rio de Janeiro: Universidade
    Federal do Rio de Janeiro: 56-66.

Graff, Gerald. 1987. *Professing Literature: an Institutional History*. Chicago: Chicago University Press.

Kimball, Roger. 1994. '"The two cultures" today' in *The New Criterion online*. Online at: http://www.newcriterion.com/archive/ 12/feb94/cultures.htm (consulted 02.12.2005).

Malinowski, Bronislaw. 1923. 'The Problem of Meaning in Primitive Languages' in Ogden, Charles Kay, and Ivor Armstrong Richards (eds). *The Meaning of Meaning*. London: Paul Trench and Trubner, 1923: 296-336.

Mendes, Milena Pereira. 2005. 'Redes in Action: creating new researchers'. Paper presented at the 25th PALA conference, University of Huddersfield, England (July 18-23, 2005).

Miall, David. 1996. 'Empowering the Reader: Literary Response and Classroom Learning' in Kreuz, Roger, and Sue MacNealy (eds). *Empirical Approaches to Literature and Aesthetics*. Norwood, NJ: Ablex: 463-78.

Short, Mick. (ed.) 1989. *Reading, Analysing and Teaching Literature*. Essex: Longman.

Short, Mick. 2001. 'Epilogue' in Van Peer, Willie, and Seymour Chatman (eds.) *New Perspectives on Narrative Perspective*. Albany: State University of New York Press, 2001: 339-355.

Short, Mick, and Dawn Archer. 2003 'Designing a worldwide web based stylistics course and investigating its effectiveness'. In *Style 37* (1): 27-64.

Simpson, Paul. 2004. *Stylistics. A resource book for students*. London & New York: Routledge.

Snow, Charles Percy. 1998. *The Two Cultures* (ed. Stephen Collini). Cambridge: Cambridge University Press.

Stockwell, Peter. 2002. *Cognitive Poetics: an Introduction.*London and New York: Routledge.

Van Peer, Willie, and Seymour Chatman (eds). 2001. *New Perspectives on Narrative Perspective*. Albany, NY: SUNY Press.

Van Peer, Willie; Frank Hakemulder, and Sonia Zyngier. 2007. *Muses and Measures.Empirical Research Methods for the Humanities*. Cambridge: Cambridge Scholars Publishing.

Verdonk, Peter. 2002. *Stylistics*. Oxford: Oxford University Press.

Watson, Greg, and Sonia Zyngier. 2006. *Literature and Stylistics for Language Learners*. London: Palgrave/Macmillan.

Zyngier, Sonia. 2006. 'Stylistics: Pedagogical Applications'. In: Keith Brown, (Editor-in-Chief) *Encyclopedia of Language & Linguistics, Second Edition, 12*, pp. 226- 232. Oxford: Elsevier: 226-232.

Zyngier, Sonia, and Tania Maria Granja Shepherd. 2003. 'What is Literature Really? a Corpus-driven Study of Students' Texts' in *Style* 37(1): 15-26.

## Appendix

*This questionnaire has been designed to find out what your interests in empirical studies are and your difficulties in dealing with this methodology. We hope the results of this research will turn into suggestions for the teaching of literature and cultural studies. The data will be treated statistically and anonymity will be kept. So, please be as frank as possible. Before you start, we would like to thank you for your cooperation.*

1.   How did you first get to know empirical studies?

2.   What is your interest in doing empirical research?

3.   Why do you think empirical studies are necessary?

4.   Based on your previous experience with literature teachers, make a list of the main problems you find in Literature teaching. Please rate these problems on a scale from 1 to 5 most serious problem (5) to the least serious problem (1).

5.   Tick number in the following box which corresponds to your opinion on the reasons that made you study Literature:
(*does not hold true at all* = 1 to *holds true fully* = 5; please always make a cross)

| | |
|---|---|
| I am interested in the history of literature. | 1 2 3 4 5 |
| I am interested in literature in general. | 1 2 3 4 5 |
| I wanted to increase my communicative abilities. | 1 2 3 4 5 |
| I wanted to get a rounded education. | 1 2 3 4 5 |
| I saw friends, teachers, parents as role models. | 1 2 3 4 5 |
| I could not get a place in the discipline I wanted to study first. | 1 2 3 4 5 |
| I am interested in writing. | 1 2 3 4 5 |
| I was interested in going beyond the meaning of texts. | 1 2 3 4 5 |

| | |
|---|---|
| I was interested in the literary processing of psychological, philosophical or political questions. | 1 2 3 4 5 |
| I am fond of reading. | 1 2 3 4 5 |
| I like to deal with language structures and grammar. | 1 2 3 4 5 |
| I knew I would have a good job prospects outside university. | 1 2 3 4 5 |
| Other reasons:................................................................... | 1 2 3 4 5 |

6.    Please fill in three different sorts of texts which you like to read most frequently

(a) ......................................................................................................
(b) ......................................................................................................
(c) ......................................................................................................

*For each text type you mentioned in 6 above, please rate why you like reading it.*

6a.  I like reading ................................... (please fill in the text type),

(*does not hold true at all* = 1 to *holds true fully* = 5; please always make a cross)

| | |
|---|---|
| To gain insight in thoughts and actions of other people. | 1 2 3 4 5 |
| To relax. | 1 2 3 4 5 |
| Because I can identify with the description. | 1 2 3 4 5 |
| Because it is important for my all-round education. | 1 2 3 4 5 |
| Because I get help for my personal problems. | 1 2 3 4 5 |
| Because I like to be captivated by texts. | 1 2 3 4 5 |
| Because the described things could have happened in reality. | 1 2 3 4 5 |
| Because I get new ideas and suggestions. | 1 2 3 4 5 |
| To entertain myself. | 1 2 3 4 5 |
| Because I can deal with problems in my mind without having direct consequences for myself. | 1 2 3 4 5 |
| Because I can use my imagination. | 1 2 3 4 5 |
| Because I am fond of the style of language [linguistic forms of expression]. | 1 2 3 4 5 |
| Because I can get new information. | 1 2 3 4 5 |
| Because it adds to my personal development. | 1 2 3 4 5 |

| Because this reading has nothing to do with reality. | 1 2 3 4 5 |
|---|---|
| Because I want to be able to join in the conversation about this reading. | 1 2 3 4 5 |
| Because I am challenged intellectually. | 1 2 3 4 5 |
| In order to deal with questions concerning the conception of the world. | 1 2 3 4 5 |
| Further reasons: | 1 2 3 4 5 |

6b. I like reading (please fill in the text type),

(*does not hold true at all* = 1 to *holds true fully* = 5; please always make a cross)

| To gain insight in thoughts and actions of other people. | 1 2 3 4 5 |
|---|---|
| To relax. | 1 2 3 4 5 |
| Because I can identify with the description. | 1 2 3 4 5 |
| Because it is important for my all-round education. | 1 2 3 4 5 |
| Because I get help for my personal problems. | 1 2 3 4 5 |
| Because I like to be captivated by texts. | 1 2 3 4 5 |
| Because the described things could have happened in reality. | 1 2 3 4 5 |
| Because I get new ideas and suggestions. | 1 2 3 4 5 |
| To entertain myself. | 1 2 3 4 5 |
| Because I can deal with problems in my mind without having direct consequences for myself. | 1 2 3 4 5 |
| Because I can use my imagination. | 1 2 3 4 5 |
| Because I am fond of the style of language [linguistic forms of expression]. | 1 2 3 4 5 |
| Because I can get new information. | 1 2 3 4 5 |
| Because it adds to my personal development. | 1 2 3 4 5 |
| Because they have nothing to do with reality. | 1 2 3 4 5 |
| Because I want to be able to join in the conversation. | 1 2 3 4 5 |
| Because I am challenged intellectually. | 1 2 3 4 5 |
| In order to deal with questions concerning the conception of the world. | 1 2 3 4 5 |
| Further reasons: ............................................................. | 1 2 3 4 5 |

6c. I like reading (please fill in the text type),

(*does not hold true at all* = 1 to *holds true fully* = 5; please always make a cross)

| | |
|---|---|
| To gain insight in thoughts and actions of other people. | 1 2 3 4 5 |
| To relax. | 1 2 3 4 5 |
| Because I can identify with the description. | 1 2 3 4 5 |
| Because it is important for my all-round education. | 1 2 3 4 5 |
| Because I get help for my personal problems. | 1 2 3 4 5 |
| Because I like to be captivated by texts. | 1 2 3 4 5 |
| Because the described things could have happened in reality. | 1 2 3 4 5 |
| Because I get new ideas and suggestions. | 1 2 3 4 5 |
| To entertain myself. | 1 2 3 4 5 |
| Because I can deal with problems in my mind without having direct consequences for myself. | 1 2 3 4 5 |
| Because I can use my imagination. | 1 2 3 4 5 |
| Because I am fond of the style of language [linguistic forms of expression]. | 1 2 3 4 5 |
| Because I can get new information. | 1 2 3 4 5 |
| Because it adds to my personal development. | 1 2 3 4 5 |
| Because they have nothing to do with reality. | 1 2 3 4 5 |
| Because I want to be able to join in the conversation. | 1 2 3 4 5 |
| Because I am challenged intellectually. | 1 2 3 4 5 |
| In order to deal with questions concerning the conception of the world. | 1 2 3 4 5 |
| Further reasons: ............................................. | 1 2 3 4 5 |

7.   We are trying to find out the main problems Humanities students and scholars find in when doing empirical research. Please rate the following statements according to whether you agree or not with them (*does not hold true at all* = 1 to *holds true fully* = 5; please always make a cross)

| | |
|---|---|
| I have problems in finding labs and instruments. | 1 2 3 4 5 |
| I can never find enough participants. | 1 2 3 4 5 |
| You never know whether respondents are being honest. | 1 2 3 4 5 |
| Participants do not answer questionnaires properly. | 1 2 3 4 5 |
| After collecting the data, I realise the questionnaire or experiment had many problems. | 1 2 3 4 5 |

| I do not know where my data will lead me to. | 1 2 3 4 5 |
|---|---|
| I hate numbers. | 1 2 3 4 5 |
| I feel I have to create my own categories each time I conduct a study. | 1 2 3 4 5 |
| It is hard to find a theoretical framework for my study. | 1 2 3 4 5 |
| Statistics is a completely different area and I can't understand it. | 1 2 3 4 5 |
| I find that empirical studies deal with culture superficially, without doing justice to its richness and depth. | 1 2 3 4 5 |
| I find it difficult to measure aspects of the cultural world. | 1 2 3 4 5 |
| I cannot see how I could develop historical studies since empirical studies are concerned only with present-day people. | 1 2 3 4 5 |
| Empirical studies are a-theoretical. | 1 2 3 4 5 |
| I feel that if I manipulate situations, I am not dealing with real settings. | 1 2 3 4 5 |
| I don't think empirical studies can describe Humanistic disciplines, which are subjective in nature. | 1 2 3 4 5 |
| I think that empirical methods fail in offering absolute certainties. | 1 2 3 4 5 |
| Interpreting data can never be objective anyway. | 1 2 3 4 5 |
| Objectivity and impartiality are unattainable ideals. | 1 2 3 4 5 |
| It is difficult to measure attitudes of readers. | 1 2 3 4 5 |
| You cannot borrow methods from natural sciences to study human culture. | 1 2 3 4 5 |
| Much empirical work simply confirms what everyone knew all the time. | 1 2 3 4 5 |
| Empirical studies negate the uniqueness of each individual and thereby cannot account for the endless variation between people. | 1 2 3 4 5 |
| You cannot generalize when it comes to people's behaviour. | 1 2 3 4 5 |
| Sometimes I see that there are too many variables involved in my study so I cannot show the real effects of exposure. | 1 2 3 4 5 |
| I don't think I could replicate my study. | 1 2 3 4 5 |

| Sometimes I feel I am just generating numbers and not explaining anything. | 1 2 3 4 5 |
|---|---|
| Further reasons: | 1 2 3 4 5 |

8.  Please list the main strengths you find in empirical studies:

9.  Indicate three theoretical books that have made a difference in your academic development.

10. Please indicate what is most needed for students of empirical studies.

THANK YOU FOR YOUR COOPERATION. THE RESULTS WILL BE POSTED ON THE REDES FORUM.

## Bibliography

Achugar, Mariana. 2004. 'The Events and Actors of 11 September 2001 as Seen from Uruguay: Analysis of Daily Newspaper Editorials' in *Discourse and Society* 15 (2–3): 291-320.

Alderson, J. Charles. and Short, Mick. 1989. 'Reading Literature' in Short, M. (ed.) *Reading, Analysing and Teaching Literature.* London: Longman: 72-119.

Allan, Stuart, (ed.). 2005. *Journalism: Critical Issues.* Milton Keynes: Open University Press.

Allan, Stuart. 2004. *News Culture.* Milton Keynes: Open University Press.

Andringa, Els. 1990. 'Verbal Data on Literary Understanding: a Proposal for Protocol Analysis on Two Levels' in *Poetics* 19: 231-57.

Attridge, Derek. 1982. *The Rhythms of English Poetry.* London: Longman

Barcelona, Antonio. (ed.). 2003. *Metaphor and Metonymy at the Crossroads: A Cognitive Perspective.* Berlin: Mouton de Gruyter.

Berber Sardinha, Tony, and Marilisa Shimazumi. 1996. 'Approaching the Assessment of Performance Unit Archive of Schoolchildren's Writing From the Point of View of Corpus Linguistics'. Paper presented at the 2nd Teaching and Language Corpora (TALC) conference (Aug. 9-12, 1996). Online at: http://www2.lael.pucsp.br /~tony/1998apu_talc.pdf (consulted 14.03.2005).

Berber Sardinha, Tony. 2004. *Lingüística de Corpus.* São Paulo: Manole.

Biber, Douglas, et al. 1999. *Longman Grammar of Spoken and Written English.* London: Longman.

Biber, Douglas, Susan Conrad and Viviana Cortes. 2004. 'If You Look at…: Lexical Bundles in University Teaching and Textbooks' in *Applied Linguistics* 25(3): 371-405.

Biber, Douglas. 2004. 'Lexical Bundles in Academic Speech and Writing' in Lewandowska-Tomaszczyk (2004): 165-78.

Bishop, Hywel, and Adam Jaworski. 2003. 'We Beat 'em: Nationalism and the Hegemony of Homogeneity in the British

Press Reportage of Germany versus England during Euro 2000' in *Discourse & Society* 14(3): 243-71.

Black, M. 1962. *Models and Metaphors* Ithaca. NY: Cornell University Press.

Bonačić, Mirjana. 2005. 'The Translator's Craft as a Cross-Cultural Discourse' in Caldas-Coulthard, Carmen Rosa, and Michael Toolan (eds). *The Writer's Craft, the Culture's Technology* (PALA Papers 1). Amsterdam: Rodopi: 123-37.

Booker, Christopher. 2004. *The Seven Basic Plots: Why We Tell Stories.* London: Continuum.

Bortolussi, Marisa, and Peter Dixon. 2003. *Psychonarratology: Foundations for the Empirical Study of Literary Response.* Cambridge: Cambridge University Press.

Brain, J. 1986. *Room at the Top-* Harmondsworth: Penguin Books.

Brandt, Line. 2006. 'Dramatization in the Semiotic Base Space: A Semiotic Approach to Fictive Interaction as a Representational Strategy in Communicative Meaning Construction' in Oakley, Todd and Anders Hougaard (eds). *Mental Spaces Approaches to Discourse and Interaction.* Amsterdam: John Benjamins.

Brandt, Per Aage. 1983. *Sandheden, saetningen och döden – Semiotiske aspekter af kulturanalysen.*Copenhagen: Basilisk.

Brandt, Per Aage. 1989. 'Genese og diegese – Et problem i den almene narratologi' in *Religionsvidenskabeligt tidsskrift* 14: 75-85.

Brandt, Per Aage. 2004. *Spaces, Domains and Meaning. Essays in Cognitive Semiotics.* Bern: Peter Lang.

Brandt, Per Aage. 2007. 'Kognitiv semiotic,' in Thellefsen, Torkild and Sörensen, Bent (eds). *Livstegn. Encyklopaedi semiotik.dk*: Copenhagen: Haase and Söns Forlag: 122-24.

Brandt, Line, and Per Aage Brandt. 2005a. 'Conceptual Metaphor and Imagery'. Online at: www.hum.au.dk/semiotics/ (consulted February 2006).

Brandt, Line, and Per Aage Brandt. 2005b. 'Making sense of a blend: A Cognitive-Semiotic Approach to Metaphor' in *Annual Review of Cognitive Linguistics* 3: 216-49.

Brown, Penelope, and Stephen Levinson. 1978. 'Universals in Language Usage: Politeness Phenomena' in Goody, D. (ed.)

*Questions and Politeness*. Cambridge: Cambridge University Press: 56-289.

Brown, Penelope, and Stephen Levinson. 1987. *Politeness*. Cambridge: Cambridge University Press.

Brumfit, Christopher, and Ronald A. Carter. 1986. *Literature and Language Teaching*. Oxford: Oxford University Press

Bruner, J. 1991. *Acts of Meaning*. Cambridge, MA: Harvard University Press.

Bruner, J. 1997 'Labov and Waletzky Thirty Years On' in *Journal of Narrative and Life History* 7(1-4): 61-8.

Burke, K. 1945. *A Grammar of Motives*. New York: Prentice Hall.

Cage, J. 1961. *Silence*. Cambridge, MA: MIT Press.

Cameron, Deborah. 1998. 'Performing Gender identity: Young Men's Talk and the Construction of Heterosexual Masculinity' in J. Coates (ed.) *Language and Gender: A Reader*. Oxford: Blackwell: 270-83.

Cameron, D., and D. Kulick, 2003. *Language and Sexuality*. Cambridge: Cambridge University Press.

Cant, S. 2004 'Come des pages pleines de silence: image, word, absence and silence in Pennac's *Monsieur Malaussène*' in English, A. and Silvester, R. (eds). *Reading Images and Seeing Words*. Amsterdam: Rodopi: 171-79.

Carr, Adrian, and Lisa A. Zanetti. 1999. 'Metatheorizing the Dialectic of Self and Other' in *American Behavioural Scientist* 43(2): 324-45.

Carston, Robyn. 1997. 'Enrichment and Loosening: Complementary Processes and Deriving the Proposition Expressed' in *Linguistische Berichte* 8: 103-27.

Carston, Robyn. 2002. *Thoughts and Utterances: The Pragmatics of Explicit Communications*. Oxford: Blackwell.

Chafe, Wallace. 1987. 'Cognitive Constraints on Information Flow' in Tomlin, Russell. (ed.) *Coherence and Grounding Discourse*. Amsterdam: John Benjamins: 21-51.

Chapman, Tony. 1999. 'Stage Sets for Ideal Lives: Images of home in contemporary show homes' in Chapman, Tony and Jenny Hockey (eds) *Ideal Homes? Social Change and Domestic Life*. London: Routledge: 44-58.

Cheshire, Jenny and Peter Trudgill. (eds) 1998. *The Sociolinguistics Reader. Vol. 2: Gender and Discourse.* Arnold: London.

Chibnall, Steve. 1977. *Law-and-Order News.* London: Tavistock.

Christie, Agatha. 1978. *The Man in the Brown Suit.* Frogman: Triad Panther.

Clark, Urszula, and Sonia Zyngier. 2003'Towards a pedagogical stylistics'. *Language and Literature12* (4): 339-351.

Coates, Jennifer. (ed.). 1988. *Language and Gender: A Reader.* Oxford: Blackwell.

Coates, Jennifer. 1995. 'The Role of Narrative in the Talk of Women Friends', paper presented at the University of Technology, Sydney.

Coates, Jennifer. 1996. *Women Talk: Conversation between Women Friends.* Blackwell: Oxford.

Coates, Jennifer. 1997. 'One-at-a-time: the Organisation of Men's Talk' in Johnson, S. and U. Meinhof (eds), *Language and Masculinity.* Oxford: Blackwell: 107-29.

Coates, Jennifer. 2004. *Women, Men and Language* (3$^{rd}$ ed.). Harlow: Longman.

Coe, Kevin, et al. 2004. 'No Shades of Gray: The Binary Discourse of George W. Bush and an Echoing Press' in *Journal of Communication* 54(2): 234-52.

Cook, Guy. 1994. *Discourse and Literature.* Oxford: Oxford University Press.

Cooper, G. Burns. 1998. *Mysterious Music. Rhythm and Free Verse.* Stanford, CA: Stanford University Press.

Cowie, Anthony Paul (ed.). 1998. *Phraseology: Theory, Analysis and Applications.* Oxford: Oxford University Press.

Cruse, Alan. 1986. *Lexical Semantics.* Cambridge: Cambridge University Press.

Crystal, David. 1971. 'Paralinguistics' in Minnis, N. (ed.). *Linguistics at Large.* London: Gollanez: 162-74.

Dauenhauer, B. P. 1980. *Silence, The Phenomenon and Its Ontological Significance.* Bloomington, IN: Indiana University Press.

De Cock, Sylvie, et al. 1998. 'An Automated Approach to the Phrasicon of EFL Learners' in Granger (1998c): 67-79.

De Galleani, J. 1989. 'Silent Game' in Blackman, Roy and Laskey, Michael (eds). *Smiths Knoll* 3.

Deignan, A. 1997. 'Metaphors of Desire' in Harvey, K. and Shalom, C. (eds). *Language and Desire*. London: Routledge: 21-42.

Delin, Judy. 2000. *The Language of Everyday Life: An Introduction*. London: Sage.

Eagleton, Terry. 2002. 'Review of *I. A. Richards' Selected Works 1919-1938* ed. John Constable (London: Routledge, 2001)' in *London Review of Books* 24(8): 13-5.

Eagleton, Terry. 2005. *The English Novel: An Introduction*. Oxford: Blackwell.

Edwards, John. 2004. 'After the Fall' in *Discourse and Society* 15 (2-3): 155-84.

Edwards, John, and J. R. Martin. 2004. Introduction: Approaches to Tragedy' in *Discourse and Society* 15 (2–3): 147-54.

Eggins, S. and D. Slade. 1997. *Analysing Casual Conversation*. London: Cassell.

Eliot, T. S. 1917. 'Reflections on Vers libre' in *New Statesman* 14.

Eliot, T. S. 1969. 'Ash Wednesday' in *The Complete Poems and Plays of T. S. Eliot*. London: Faber and Faber.

Emmott, Catherine. 1997. *Narrative Comprehension*. Oxford: Oxford University Press.

Erickson, Frederick. 1992. 'Ethnographic Microanalysis of Interaction' in LeCompte, Margaret D., Judith Preissle Goetz and Wendy L. Millroy (eds). *The Handbook of Qualitative Research in Education*. New York: Academic Press: 201-25.

Espmark, Kjell. 1977. *Själen i Bild: En Huvudlinje i Modern Svensk Poesi*. Stockholm: Norstedt.

Fairclough, Norman. 1989. *Language and Power*. London: Longman

Fairclough, Norman. 1995. *Media Discourse*. London: Edward Arnold

Faucounnier, Gilles. 1999. 'Methods and Generalizations' in Janssen, Theo, and Gisela Redeker (eds). *Cognitive Linguistics: Foundations, Scope, and Methodology*. Berlin: Mouton de Gruyter: 95-127.

Fauconnier, Gilles, and Mark Turner. 1998. 'Conceptual Integration Networks' in *Cognitive Science* 22(2): 133-87.

Fauconnier, Gilles, and Mark Turner. 2000. 'Conceptual Integration Networks'. Online at: http://markturner.org/cin.web/cin.html (consulted February 2006).

Fauconnier, Gilles, and Mark Turner. 2003 *The Way We Think. Conceptual Blending and the Mind's Hidden Complexities.* New York: Basic Books.

Fialho, Olivia. 2005. '*Pelos Caminhos da Literatura: Estudo Empírico Sobre Refamiliarização e Afeto*'. Unpublished M.A. dissertation, Universidade Federal do Rio de Janeiro.

Fialho, Olivia, and Sonia Zyngier. 2003. 'Reading Preferences: a Comparative Study' in Zyngier, Sonia, Milena Pereira Mendes and Patrícia Pinheiro (eds). *Pontes & Transgressões: Estudos Empíricos de Processos Culturais.* Rio de Janeiro: Universidade Federal do Rio de Janeiro: 56-66.

Fillmore, Charles J. 1985. 'Frames and semantics of understanding' in *Quaderni di Semantica* 6(2): 222-54.

Finch, Annie. 1993. *The Ghost of Meter. Culture and Prosody in American Free Verse.* Ann Arbor, MI: University of Michigan Press.

Fish, Stanley. 1980. *Is There a Text in this Class? The Authority of Interpretive Communities.* Harvard: Harvard University Press.

Fitzgerald, F. Scott. 1979. *Selected Short Stories.* Moscow: Progress Publishers.

Follet, K. 1990. *Die Säulen der Erde.* Bergisch-Gladbach.

Forster, E. M. [1910] 1941. *Howards End.* London: Penguin.

Fowler, Roger. 1991. *Language in the News: Discourse and Ideology in the Press.* London: Routledge.

Freeman, Donald C. 1993 '"According to my Bond": *King Lear* and Recognition' in *Language and Literature* 2(1): 1-18.

Freeman, Margaret H. 1997. 'Grounded spaces: deictic -*self* anaphors in the poetry of Emily Dickinson' in *Language and Literature* 6(1): 7-28.

Freeman, Margaret H. 2003. 'Poetry and the scope of metaphor: Toward a cognitive theory of literature' in Barcelona (2003): 253-81.

Frey, J. 1993. *Wie man einen verdammt guten Roman schreibt.* Köln

Fulton, Helen, et al. 2005. *Narrative and Media.* Cambridge: Cambridge University Press.

Gavins, Joanna, and Gerard Steen. 2003. *Cognitive Poetics in Practice.* London: Routledge.

Gedge, P. 1981. *Die Herrin vom Nil.* Hamburg.

Gedge, P. 1998. *Der fremde Pharao.* Hamburg.

Genette, Gerard. 1972. *Figures III.* Seuil: Paris (tr. 1980 *Narrative discourse*, Basil Blackwell).

Gentner, Dedre, and Donald R. Gentner. 1983. 'Flowing waters or Teeming Crowds: Mental Models of Electricity' in Gentner, Dedre and Albert L. Stevens (eds). *Mental Model.* Hillsdale, NJ: Lawrence Erlbaum Associates: 99-129.

Ghita, A. 1997. 'Pragmatic Aspects of Silence' in Pietri. E. (ed.). *Dialoganalyse 5,* Arbeitstagung Paris, 1994, Tubingen: Niemeyer.

Gibbs, Raymond. 1984. 'Literal Meaning and Psychological Theory' in *Cognitive Science* 8: 275-304.

Gibbs, Raymond. 1994. *The Poetics of Mind: Figurative Thought, Language, and Understanding.* Cambridge: Cambridge University Press.

Giddens, Anthony. 1991. *Modernity and Self Identity: Self and Society in the Late Modern Age.* Oxford: Polity.

Giora, Rachel. 1997. 'Understanding Figurative and Literal Language: The Graded Salience Hypothesis' in *Cognitive Linguistics* 7: 183-206.

Giora, Rachel. 1999. 'On the Priority of Salient Meanings: Studies of Literal and Figurative Language' in *Journal of Pragmatics* 31: 919-29.

Giora, Rachel. 2003. *On Our Mind.* Oxford: Oxford University Press.

Giora, Rachel, and Noga Balaban. 2001. 'Lexical Access in Text Production: On the Role of Salience in Metpahor Resonance' in Sanders, T., J. Schilperoord, and W. Spooren (eds). *Text Representation.* Amsterdam: John Benjamins: 111-24.

Giora, Rachel, and Ofer Fein. 1999. 'On Understanding Familiar and Less-Familiar Figurative Language' in *Journal of Pragmatics* 31: 1601-618.

Goffman, Erving. 1967. *Interaction Ritual.* Chicago:AldinePublishing.

Gordon, N. 1996. *Der Medicus.* München.

Graff, Gerald. 1987. *Professing Literature: an Institutional History.* Chicago: Chicago University Press.

Graham, Phil., Thomas Keenan and A. Dowd. 2004. 'A Call to Arms at the End of History: A Discourse-historical Analysis of George W. Bush's Declaration of War on Terror' in *Discourse and Society* 15 (2-3): 199-221.

Granger, Sylviane. 1998a. 'The Computer Learner Corpus: A Versatile New Source of Data for SLA Research' in Granger (1998c): 3-18.

Granger, Sylviane. 1998b. 'Prefabricated Patterns in Advanced EFL Writing: Collocations and Formulae' in Cowie (1998): 145-160.

Granger, Sylviane (ed.). 1998c. *Learner English on Computer.* London: Longman.

Green, G. and C. Kahn, (eds). 1991. *Making a Difference: Feminist Literary Criticism.* London: Routledge.

Grice, Paul. 1989. *Studies in the Way of Words.* Cambridge, MA: Harvard University Press.

Gwilliam, Tassie. 1991. 'Pamela and the Duplicitous Body of Femininity' in *Representations* 34: 104-33.

Gwilliam, Tassie. 1993. *Samuel Richardson's Fictions of Gender.* Stanford, CA: Stanford University Press.

Hakemulder, J. 2000. *The Moral Laboratory. Experiments Examining the Effects of Reading Literature on Social Perception and Moral Self-Concept.* Utrecht.

Halliday, Michael. 1985. *An Introduction to Functional Grammar.* London: Edward Arnold.

Hamilton, Craig. 2002. 'Conceptual Integration in Christine de Pizan's *City of Ladies,*' in Semino, Elena and Culpeper, Jonathan (eds). *Cognitive Stylistics. Language and Cognition in Text Analysis.* Amsterdam: John Benjamins: 1-22.

Hartley, John. 1982. *Understanding News.* London: Routledge.

Harvey, K., and C. Shalom. (eds). 1997. *Language and Desire: Encoding Sex, Romance and Intimacy.* London: Routledge.

Hejinian, Lyn. 2000. *The Language of Inquiry.* Berkeley: University of California Press.

Hellmuth, Hans-Heinrich. 1973. *Metrische Erfindung und metrische Theorie beKlopstock.* München: Fink.

Helm, J. (ed.) 1967. *Essays on the Verbal and Visual Arts*. Seattle, Washington: University of Washington Press.

Hidalgo Downing, Laura. 2000. *Negation, Text Worlds and Discourse: The Pragmatics of Fiction*. Stamford, CT: Ablex Publishing Co.

Hogan, Patrick Colm. 2003. *Cognitive Science, Literature and the Arts: A Guide for Humanists*. New York: Routledge.

Hoover, David. 2003. 'Multivariate Analysis and the Study of Style Variation' in *Literary and Linguistic Computing* 18(4): 341-60.

Hunston, Susan. 2002. *Corpora in Applied Linguistics*. Cambridge: Cambridge University Press.

Jaqc, C. 1993. *Im Bann des Pharao*. München.

Jaqc, C. 1997. *Ramses. Der Sohn des Lichts*. Hamburg.

Jaworski, Adam (ed.). 1997. *Silence: Interdisciplinary Perspectives*. Berlin: Mouton de Gruyter

Jaworski, Adam. 1993. *The Power of Silence*. Newbury Pk, CA:Sage

Jaworski, Adam. 1997. 'White and white: Metacommunicative and metaphorical silences' in Jaworski (1997): 381-401.

Jeffries, Lesley. 1998. *Meaning in English: An Introduction to Language Study*. Basingstoke: Palgrave.

Jeffries, Lesley. 2000. 'Don't throw out the baby with the bathwater: in defence of theoretical eclecticism in stylistics' in *PALA Occasional Papers* 12.

Jeffries, Lesley. 2002. 'Meaning Negotiated: An Investigation into Reader and Author Meaning' in Csábi, Szilvia. and Zerkowitz, Judit. (eds.). *Textual Secrets: The Message of the Medium*. Budapest: Eötvös Loránd University: 247-61.

Jensen, J. V. 1973. 'Communicative Functions of Silence' in *Etc.: A Review of General Semantics* 30(3): 249-57.

Johannesen, R. 1974. 'The Functions of Silence: A Plea for Communication Research' in *Western Speech* 38: 25-35.

Johnson, Mark. 1987. *The Body in the Mind*. Chicago: University of Chicago Press.

Johnstone, B. 1993. 'Community and Contest: Midwestern Men and Women Creating their Worlds in Conversational Storytelling' in D. Tannen (ed.) *Gender and Conversational Interaction*. New York: Oxford University Press: 62-8.

Jones, Steven. 2002. *Antonymy: A Corpus-based perspective.* London: Routledge.

Jordão, Suzana, et al. 2005. 'Violência no Imaginário da Criança. in Zyngier, Sonia, Vander Viana and Fabiana Fausto (eds). *Venturas & Denventuras: Coletânea dos Trabalhos do V ECEL.* Rio de Janeiro: Editora da Faculdade de Letras da UFRJ: 172-88.

Kamuf, P. 2000. 'The End of Reading', Paper presented at the Book/Ends conference, University at Albany (October 2000).

Kimball, Roger. 1994. '"The two cultures" today' in *The New Criterion online.* Online at: http://www.newcriterion.com/archive/12/feb94/cultures.htm (consulted 02.12.2005).

Kittay, E. 1987. *Metaphor: Its Cognitive Force and Linguistic Structure.* Oxford: Clarendon Press.

Kövecses, Zoltan. 1986. *Metaphors of Anger, Pride and Love.* Amsterdam: John Benjamins.

Kövecses, Zoltan. 2000. *Metaphor and Emotion Language.* Cambridge: Cambridge University Press.

Kövecses, Zoltan. 2002. *Metaphor: A Practical Introduction.* Oxford: Oxford University Press.

Kreidler, Charles. W. 1998. *Introducing English Semantics.* London: Routledge.

Kress, Gunther and Theo van Leeuwen. 1996. *Reading Images: The Grammar of Visual Design.* London: Routledge.

Kress, Gunther, and Theo van Leeuwen. 2001. *Multimodal Discourse: The Modes and Media of Contemporary Communication.* London: Arnold.

Kurzon, D. 1998. *Discourse of Silence.* Amsterdam: John Benjamins.

Labov, William. 1972. *Language in the Inner City: Studies in the Black English Vernacular.* Philadelphia: University of Pennsylvania Press.

Labov, William, and J. Waletzky. 1967. 'Narrative Analysis: Oral Versions of Personal Experience' in J. Helm (ed.) *Essays on the Verbal and Visual Arts*

Lakoff, George. 1987. *Women Fire and Dangerous Things What Categories Reveal about the Mind.* Chicago: University of Chicago Press

Lakoff, George. 1990. *Women, Fire, and Dangerous Things, What Categories Reveal About the Mind.* Chicago: University of Chicago Press.

Lakoff, G. and Mark Johnson. 1980. *Metaphors we Live By.* Chicago, IL: University of Chicago Press.

Lakoff, George, and Mark Turner. 1989. *More than Cool Reason.* Chicago: University of Chicago Press.

Lambrou, Marina. 2003. 'Collaborative Oral Narratives of General Experience: When an Interview becomes a Conversation' in *Language and Literature* 12(2): 153-74.

Lambrou, Marina. 2003. *Story Patterns in Personal narratives: a Variationist Critique of Labov and Waletzky's Narrative Schema Model,* paper presented at the Poetics and Linguistics Association (PALA) at the University of Birmingham.

Lambrou, Marina. 2005. *Story Patterns in Oral Narratives: A Variationist Critique of Labov and Waletzky's Model of Narrative Schemas.* Unpublished PhD Thesis: Middlesex University.

Langacker, Ronald W. 1990. *Concept, Image, and Symbol: The Cognitive Basis of Grammar.* Berlin: Mouton de Gruyter.

Lauer, B. F., and A. Kelley. (eds). 2004. *Isn't It Romantic: 100 Love Poems by Younger American Poets.* Amherst, MA: Verse Press.

Lazar, Annita, and Michelle M. Lazar. 2004. 'The Discourse of the New World Order: 'Out-casting' the Double Face of Threat' in *Discourse and Society* 15 (2-3): 223-42.

Leech, Geoffrey. 1983. *Principles of Pragmatics.* London: Longman.

Lehrer, Adrienne, and Eva Feder Kittay (eds). 1992. *Frames, Fields, and Contrasts: New Essays in Semantic and Lexical Organisation.* Hillsdale, NJ: Lawrence Erlbaum Associates.

Lehrer, Adrienne, and Keith Lehrer. 1982. 'Antonymy' in *Linguistics and Philosophy* 5: 483-501.

Leudar, Ivan., Victoria Marsland and Jiri Nekvapil. 'On Membership Categorization': 'Us', 'Them' and 'Doing Violence' in Political Discourse' in *Discourse and Society* 15 (2-3): 243-66.

Lewandowska-Tomaszczyk, Barbara (ed.). 2004. *Practical Applications in Language and Computers.* Frankfurt: Peter Lang.

Lilja, Eva. 2002. 'Meter, Rhythm and Free Verse' in Küper, C. (ed.) *Meter, Rhythm and Performance*. Frankfurt am Main: Peter Lang: 253-62.

Lilja, Eva. 2006. *Svensk Metrik*. Stockholm: Norstedt.

Lipka, L. 2003 'Observational Linguistics and Semiotics' in Hladky, J. (ed.). *Language and Function: To the memory of Jan Firbas*. Amsterdam: John Benjamins: 211-22.

Lippard, L. R. 1981. 'The Silent Art' in *Art in America* 55: 58-63.

Löbner, Sebastian. 2002. *Understanding Semantics*. London: Arnold.

Loevlie, E. 2003. *Literary Silences in Pascal, Rousseau and Beckett*. Oxford: Oxford University Press.

Lyons, John. 1977. *Semantics*. Cambridge: Cambridge University Press.

Machin, David, and Theo van Leeuwen. 2005. 'Language Style and Lifestyle: The Case of a Global Magazine' in *Media, Culture & Society* 27(4): 577-600.

Malandro, L. A., L. L. Barker, and D. A. Barker. 1989. *Nonverbal Communication*. New York: Mc Graw Hill.

Malinowski, Bronislaw. 1923. 'The Problem of Meaning in Primitive Languages' in Ogden, Charles Kay, and Ivor Armstrong Richards (eds). *The Meaning of Meaning*. London: Paul Trench and Trubner, 1923: 296-336.

Manning, E. 1997. 'Kissing and Cuddling: The Reciprocity of Romantic and Sexual Activity' in Harvey, K. and C. Shalom. (eds). *Language and Desire*. London: Routledge: 43-59.

Many, J., and D. Wiseman. 1992. 'The Effect of Teaching Approach on Third-Grade Students' Response to Literature' in *Journal of Reading Behaviour* 24(3): 265-87.

Martin, J. R. 2004. 'Mourning: How we get Aligned' in *Discourse and Society* (15) 2-3: 321-44.

Mayring, P. 1993. *Qualitative Inhaltsanalyse*. Weinheim.

McEnery, Tony, and Andrew Wilson. 1996. *Corpus Linguistics*. Edinburgh: Edinburgh University Press.

Medhurst, Martin J. 2000. 'Text and Context in the 1952 Presidential Campaign: Eisenhower's "I shall go to Korea" speech' in *Presidential Studies Quarterly* 30: 464-84.

Mendes, Milena Pereira. 2005. 'Redes in Action: creating new researchers'. Paper presented at the 25th PALA conference, University of Huddersfield, England (July 18-23, 2005).

Mettinger, Arthur. 1994. *Aspects of Semantic Opposition in English.* Oxford: Oxford University Press.

Miall, David. 1996. 'Empowering the Reader: Literary Response and Classroom Learning' in Kreuz, Roger, and Sue MacNealy (eds). *Empirical Approaches to Literature and Aesthetics.* Norwood, NJ: Ablex: 463-78.

Miall, David. S. (ed.) 1982. *Metaphor: Problems and Perspectives.* Brighton: Harvester Press.

Mielke, T. 1992. *Inanna.* Hamburg.

Montlaur, P. 1990. *Imhotep.* Hamburg.

Moon, Rosamund. 1998. 'Frequencies and Forms of Phrasal Lexemes in English' in Cowie (1998): 79-100.

Munat, Judith. 2004. 'The Caged Bird: The Expression of Sexuality in Twentieth-century Women's Poetry", Paper presented at the Poetry and Sexuality Conference, University of Stirling, Stirling, UK (July 1, 2004).

Munat, Judith. 2005. 'Iconic Functions of Phraseological Units and Metaphor' in Maeder, C., Fischer, O. and Herlofsky, W. (eds.). *Outside-In – Inside-Out.* Amsterdam: John Benjamins: 389-410.

Murphy, M. Lynne. 2003. *Semantic Relations and the Lexicon.* Cambridge: Cambridge University Press.

Nelson, M. W. 1998. 'Women's Ways: Interactive Patterns in Predominantly Female Research Teams' in Coates, Jennifer (ed.) *Language and Gender: A Reader.* Oxford: Blackwell: 354-72

Oakley, Todd, and Anders Hougaard. (eds). *Mental Spaces Approaches to Discourse and Interaction.* Amsterdam: John Benjamins.

Oatley, K. 1994. A taxonomy of the emotions of literary response and a theory of identification in fictional narrative' in *Poetics* 23: 53-74.

Ortony, A. (ed.) 1980. *Metaphor and Thought.* Cambridge: Cambridge University Press.

Patten, K. 1997. 'Teaching 'Discovering Silence'' in Jaworski (1997) 369-78.

Pavlov, I. P. 1927. *Conditioned Reflexes: An Investigation of the Physiological Activity of the Cerebral Cortex* (tr. G.V. Anrep). Oxford: Oxford University Press.

Paz, O. 1973. *Alternating Current.* New York: Viking.

Pilkington, Adrian. 2000. *Poetic Effects: A Relevance Theory Perspective.* Amsterdam: John Benjamins.

Pope, Rob. 1995. *Textual Intervention: Critical and Creative Strategies for Literary Studies.* London: Routledge.

Porto Requejo, M. Dolores. 2003. 'Del Significado de la Palabra a la Interpretación del Texto: ¿Qué es la Magia?' in *Annual Review of Cognitive Linguistics* 1. Amsterdam. John Benjamins: 121-37.

Porto Requejo, M. Dolores. (in press) 'The Construction of the Concept INTERNET through Metaphors' in *Language, Culture and Representation.*

Price, Vincent, and David Tewksbury. 1997. 'News Values and Public Opinion: A Theoretical Account of Media Priming and Framing' in *Progress in Communication Sciences* 13:173–212.

Quirk, Randolph, et al. 1972. *A Grammar of Contemporary English.* London: Longman.

Raum, Richard. D., and James S. Measell. 1974. 'Wallace and His Ways: A Study of the Rhetorical Genre of Polarization' in *Central States Speech Journal* (25): 28-35.

Rennell, Tony. 2003. 'Listen to Us; The People's March: A Tide of Protest – Britain Says No to War' in *Sunday Mirror* (16 Feb. 2003).

Renouf, Antoinette, and John Sinclair. 1991. 'Collocational Frameworks in English' in Aijmer, Karin, and Bengt Altenberg (eds). *English Corpus Linguistics.* London: Longman: 128-43.

Reynolds, Jack, and Jonathan Roffe. 2004. 'An Invitation to Philosophy' in Reynolds, Jack, and Jonathan Roffe (eds.) *Understanding Derrida.* London: Continuum: 1-4.

Richards, I. A. 1924. *Principles of Literary Criticism* in *I. A. Richards' Selected Works 1919-1938*, Vol. III (ed. John Constable). London: Routledge, 2001.

Richards, I. A. 1929. *Practical Criticism: A Study of Literary Judgement* in *I. A. Richards' Selected Works 1919-1938*, Vol. IV (ed. John Constable). London: Routledge, 2001.

Richards, I. A. 1934. *Coleridge on Imagination* in *I. A. Richards' Selected Works 1919-1938*, Vol. VI (ed. John Constable). London: Routledge, 2001.

Richards, I. A. 1936. *The Philosophy of Rhetoric* in *I. A. Richards' Selected Works 1919-1938*, Vol. VII (ed. John Constable). London: Routledge, 2001.

Richards, I. A. 1938. *Interpretation in Teaching* in *I. A. Richards' Selected Works 1919-1938*, Vol. VIII (ed. John Constable). London: Routledge, 2001.

Richards, I. A., and C. K. Ogden. 1923. *The Meaning of Meaning: A Study of the Influence of Language upon Thought and of the Science of Symbolism* in *I. A. Richards' Selected Works 1919-1938*, Vol. II (ed. John Constable). London: Routledge, 2001.

Richardson, Samuel. 2001. *Pamela; or, Virtue Rewarded* (eds.) Thomas Keymer and Alice Wakely. Oxford: Oxford University Press.

Rimmon-Kenan, Shlomith. 1983. *Narrative Fiction: Contemporary Poetics*. London: Methuen.

Roulston, Chrisine. 1998. *Virtue, Gender, and the Authentic Self in Eighteenth-Century Fiction*. Gainesville, FL: University of Florida Press.

Rumelhart, David E. 1980. 'Schemata: The building blocks of cognition' in Spiro, Rand J., Bertram C. Bruce and William F. Brewer (eds). *Theoretical Issues in Reading Comprehension: Perspectives from Cognitive Psychology, Linguistics, Artificial Intelligence and Education*. Hillsdale, NJ: Lawrence Erlbaum Associates: 33-85.

Ryan, Marie-Laure. 1991. *Possible Worlds, Artificial Intelligence and Narrative Theory*. Bloomington: Indiana University Press.

Sacks, Harvey., Schegloff, Emanuel. A. and Jefferson, Gail. 1974. 'A Simplest Systematics for the Organization of Turn-taking in Conversation' in *Language* 50: 696-735.

Sampson, Geoffrey. 2003. 'The Structure of Children's Writing: Moving From Spoken to Adult Written Norms' in Granger, Sylviane, and Stephanie Petch-Tyson (eds). *Extending the Scope of Corpus-Based Research*. Amsterdam: Rodopi: 177-93.

Saussure, Ferdinand de. [1916] 1983. *Course in General Linguistics* (tr. Roy Harris). London: Duckworth.

Saville-Troike, Muriel. 1985. 'The Place of Silence in an Integrated Theory of Communication' in Tannen, D. and Muriel Saville-Troike. (1985): 3-18.

Schank Roger C. and Robert P. Abelson. 1977. *Scripts, Plans, Goals and Understanding*. Hillsdale, NJ.: Lawrence Erlbaum Associates.

Scott, Clive. 1990. *Vers libre. The Emergence of Free Verse in France.1886-1914.* Oxford: Clarendon Press.

Scott, Mike. 1999. *WordSmith Tools*. Oxford: Oxford University Press.

Sebeok, T. 2001. 'Nonverbal Communication' in Cobley, P. (ed.) *The Routledge Companion to Semiotics and Linguistics*. London: Routledge: 14-27.

Self, Will. 1994. 'Chest' in *Grey Area*. London: Penguin Books:125-64.

Semino, Elena, and Jonathan Culpeper. 2002. *Cognitive Stylistics. Language and Cognition in Text Analysis*. Amsterdam: John Benjamins.

Semino, Elena. 1997. *Language and World Creation in Poems and Other Texts*. London: Longman.

Shaw, J. B. 1958. *Selected Works*. Moscow: Foreign Languages.

Short, Mick. (ed.) 1989. *Reading, Analysing and Teaching Literature*. Essex: Longman.

Short, Mick. 1996. *Exploring the Language of Poems, Plays and Prose*. London: Longman.

Short, Mick. 2001. 'Epilogue' in Van Peer, Willie, and Seymour Chatman (eds.) *New Perspectives on Narrative Perspective*. Albany: State University of New York Press, 2001: 339-355.

Short, Mick, and Dawn Archer. 2003 'Designing a worldwide web based stylistics course and investigating its effectiveness'. In *Style 37* (1): 27-64.

Short, Mick and Willie van Peer. 1989. 'Accident! Stylisticians Evaluate: Aims and Methods of Stylistic Analysis', in Short, M. (ed.) *Reading, Analysing and Teaching Literature*. London: Longman: 22-71.

Simms, Karl. 2003. *Paul Ricoeur*. London: Routledge.

Simpson, Paul. 2004. *Stylistics. A resource book for students.* London & New York: Routledge.

Sinclair, John. 1991. *Corpus, Concordance, Collocation.* Oxford: Oxford University Press.

Sinclair, John. 2004. 'Preface' in Lewandowska-Tomaszczyk (2004): 7-11.

Snow, Charles Percy. 1998. *The Two Cultures* (ed. Stephen Collini). Cambridge: Cambridge University Press.

Sobkowiak. W. 1997. "Silence and Markedness Theory" in Jaworski (1997): 39-61.

Sperber, Dan, and Deirdre Wilson. 1986. *Relevance: Communication and Cognition.* Oxford: Blackwell.

Sperber, Dan, and Deirdre Wilson. 1995. *Relevance: Communication and Cognition* (2nd ed.). Oxford: Blackwell.

Steinbeck, John. 1985. *The Winter of Our Discontent.* Moscow: Vyssaja Skola.

Stewart, Larry. 2003. 'Charles Brockden Brown: Quantitative Analysis and Literary Interpretation' in *Literary and Linguistic Computing* 18(2): 129-38.

Stewart, Larry. 2005. 'Empirical Analysis, Gender Assumptions, and the Language of Narration in Eighteenth-Century British Fiction' in *Empirical Studies of the Arts* 23: 65-77.

Stockwell, Peter. 2000. *The Poetics of Science Fiction.* London: Longman.

Stockwell, Peter. 2002. *Cognitive Poetics. An Introduction.* London: Routledge.

Storey, D. 1980. *Early Days. Sisters. Life Class.* Harmondsworth: Penguin Books.

Stubbs, Michael. 2001. *Words and Phrases.* Oxford: Blackwell.

Sweetser, Eve. 1990. *From Etymology to Pragmatics.* Cambridge: Cambridge University Press.

Tan, E. 1994. 'Film induced affect as a witness emotion' in *Poetics* 23: 7-32.

Tannen, D. 1985. 'Silence: Anything But' in Tannen, D. and Muriel Saville-Troike, (1985): 93-111.

Tannen, D. and Muriel Saville-Troike. (eds). 1985. *Perspectives on Silence*. Norwood, NJ: Ablex.

Taylor, Lisa. 2002. 'From Ways of Life to Lifestyle: The 'Ordinarization' of British Gardening Lifestyle Television' in *European Journal of Communication* 17 (4): 479-93.

Teliya, Veronika, et al. 1998. 'Phraseology as a Language of Culture: Its Role in the Representation of a Collective Mentality' in Cowie (1998): 55-75.

Thellefsen, Torkild, and Bent Sörensen. 2007. *Livstegn. Encyklopaedi.dk*. Copenhagen: Haase and Söns Forlag.

Thorne, James P. 1970. 'Stylistics and Generative Grammars' in Freeman, Donald C. (ed.) *Linguistics and Literary Style*. New York: Holt, Rinehart and Winston: 182-96.

Toolan, Michael. 2001. *Narrative: A Critical Linguistic Introduction.* (2$^{nd}$ ed.) London: Routledge.

Turner, Mark. 1991. *Reading Minds. The Study of English in the Age of Cognitive Science*. New Jersey: Princeton University Press.

Turner; Mark, and Gilles Fauconnier. 2003. 'Metaphor, metonymy, and binding' in Barcelona (2003): 133-45.

Vainiomäki, T. 2004. 'Silence as a Cultural Sign' *Semiotica* 150-1/4: 347-61.

Van Dijk, Teun A. 1988. *News as Discourse*. Lawrence Erlbaum Associates.

Van Dijk, Teun A. 2006. 'Discourse and Manipulation' in *Discourse & Society* 17(3): 359-83.

Van Peer, Willie. 1987. 'Top-Down and Bottom-Up: Interpretative Strategies in Reading E. E. Cummings' in *New Literary History* 18: 597-609.

Van Peer, Willie, and Seymour Chatman (eds). 2001. *New Perspectives on Narrative Perspective*. Albany, NY: SUNY Press.

Van Peer, Willie; Frank Hakemulder, and Sonia Zyngier. 2007. *Muses and Measures.Empirical Research Methods for the Humanities*. Cambridge: Cambridge Scholars Publishing.

Verdonk, Peter. 2002. *Stylistics*. Oxford: Oxford University Press.

Verschueren, Jef. 1985. 'What People Say They Do with Words: Prolegomena to an Empirical-Conceptual Approach to Linguistic Action.' Norwood, NJ: Ablex.

Volosinov, V. N. 1973. *Marxism and the Philosophy of Language*. New-York : Seminar Press.

Vyncke, P. 2002. 'Lifestyle Segmentation: From Attitudes, Interests and Opinions, to Values, Aesthetic Styles, Life Visions and Media Preferences' in *European Journal of Communication* 17(4): 445-63.

Wåhlin, Kristian. 1999. *Studier i äldre svensk metrik. Valda problem 1300-1650. Efterlämnade skrifter*. Eva Lilja & Mats Malm (eds). Göteborg: Centre of Metrical Studies.

Watson, Greg, and Sonia Zyngier. 2006. *Literature and Stylistics for Language Learners*. London: Palgrave/Macmillan.

Weis Margaret, and Tracey Hickman. 1988. *Forging the Darksword*. New York: Bantam Books.

Werth, Paul. 1994. 'Extended Metaphor. A Text World Account' in *Language and Literature* 3(2): 79-103.

Werth, Paul. 1995. 'How to Build a Text World (In a Lot Less than Six Days, and Using Only What Is in Your Head)' in Green, K (ed.). *New Essays on Deixis: Discourse, Narrative, Literature*. Amsterdam: Rodopi: 49-80.

Werth, Paul. 1999. *Text Worlds: Representing Conceptual Space in Discourse*. London: Longman.

West, C., and D. Zimmerman. 1987. 'Doing Gender' in *Gender and Society* 1: 125-51.

Widdowson, Henry G. 1975. *Stylistics and the Teaching of Literature*. London: Longman.

Wilson, Deirdre, and Dan Sperber. 2003. 'Relevance Theory' in Horn, Laurence, and Gregory Ward (eds). *Handbook of Pragmatics*. Oxford: Basil Blackwell: 607-32.

Wodehouse, P. G. 1983. *Life with Jeeves*. Harmondsworth: Penguin Books.

Wolf, W. 2005. 'Non-supplemented Blanks in Works of Literature as Forms of Iconicity of Absence' in Maeder, C., O. Fischer, and J. Herlofsky (eds). *Outside-In – Inside-Out*. Amsterdam: John Benjamins: 113-32.

Wray, Alison. 2002. *Formulaic Language and the Lexicon*. Cambridge: Cambridge University Press.

Zillman, D., and J. Cantor. 1977. 'Affective Responses to the Emotions of a Protagonist' in *Journal of Experimental Social Psychology* 13: 155-65.

Zyngier, Sonia, and Tania Maria Granja Shepherd. 2003. 'What is Literature Really? a Corpus-driven Study of Students' Texts' in *Style* 37(1): 15-26.

Zyngier, Sonia, and Tania Shepherd. 2002. 'Hidden Concepts of Literature in a Pedagogical Setting: A Corpus-based Approach' in Csábi, Szilvia, and Judit Zerkowitz (ed.). *Textual Secrets: The Message of the Medium*. Budapest: Eötvös Loránd University: 220-235.

Zyngier, Sonia, and Tania Shepherd. 2003. 'What is Literature Really?: A Corpus-driven Study of Students' Texts' in *Style* 37(1): 15-26.

Zyngier, Sonia, Olivia Fialho and Danielle Menezes. 2004. 'Invisible Wars: violence in daily papers' Paper presented at the 9th conference of the International Society for the Empirical Study of Literature and Media (IGEL) (Aug. 3-7, 2004). Online at: http://www.arts.ualberta.ca/igel/igel2004/Proceedings/Zyngier.pdf (consulted 14.03.2005).

Zyngier, Sonia. 2006. 'Stylistics: Pedagogical Applications'. In: Keith Brown, (Editor-in-Chief) *Encyclopedia of Language & Linguistics, Second Edition, 12*, pp. 226- 232. Oxford: Elsevier: 226-232.

Ефимов, А. И. 1961. Стилистика художественной речи. Москва: Изд. МГУ.

Оликова, М. А. 1979. Обращение в современном английском языке. – Львов: Вища школа.

Телия, В. Н. 1988. Метафора как модель смыслопроизводства и ее экспрессивно-оценочная функция // Метафора в языке и тексте. – Москва Наука

# Index